Praise for
THE MISSIONARY KIDS

"The American church has been reevaluating long-held practices as pertaining to sex abuse, women, and race. It's long past time for the church to grapple with how we do 'mission work' across the globe, and *The Missionary Kids* is a good wake-up call. Author Holly Berkley Fletcher, herself a missionary kid, exposes a relatively unpublicized underbelly of mission work—the children taken to unfamiliar locations, disconnected from their parents, and left to fend for themselves all in the name of God."

—**Nancy French**, author of *Ghosted: An American Story*

"Dr. Berkley Fletcher's very personal look into the experiences of white evangelical missionary kids (MKs) will leave few readers unprovoked. Many will be provoked to shock and further disillusionment with the white evangelical subculture. Many others will be provoked to defensiveness, protesting about all the people missionaries serve or the many MKs who've cherished their experiences. (I found myself provoked in both directions as I read.) Most importantly, however, this book will provoke serious discussion about the blind spots of American Christians and what it really means to love God and love people, within our homes and abroad."

—**Samuel L. Perry**, professor of sociology, University of Oklahoma, and author of *Religion for Realists: Why We All Need the Scientific Study of Religion* and coauthor of *Taking America Back for God: Christian Nationalism in the United States*

"*The Missionary Kids* mixes sensitive retellings of what happens to children when parents place spiritual calling above the obligation to protect and care for their own kids, within a system of white evangelicalism that holds itself above and often apart from those abroad whom they say they are called to serve. This sensitive, thoughtful interrogation of the missionary lifestyle reveals sharp truths as witnessed by those raised within, flagging sexual abuse abroad that often gets covered over but leaves another dark mark on church institutions that tally metrics for baptisms and churches planted as missionary wins, while failing to account for the practice's harms."

—**Sarah Stankorb**, author of *Disobedient Women*

"This sad, aching, beautifully written book is part memoir, part investigative report, part exposé—not just about what it is like to be a missionary kid, but about the distorted, misguided white US evangelical imagination that has produced the missionary enterprise as it now exists. The discussion of sexual predation in overseas missionary contexts is stunning and horrifying. This book is a must-read, and a crucial addition to the post-evangelical literature that is rapidly growing these days."

—**David P. Gushee**, professor of Christian ethics, Mercer University, and author of *After Evangelicalism: The Path to a New Christianity* and *Defending Democracy from Its Christian Enemies*

"Through the keyhole of missionary kids around the globe, Holly Berkley Fletcher provides keen insights not just into evangelical Christianity, but also into America's political morass in the twenty-first century. Blending first-person accounts with deep research, Fletcher has produced a highly readable and enlightening analysis of the intersection of church and politics."

—**Mona Charen**, syndicated columnist, policy editor of *The Bulwark*, and host of *The Mona Charen Podcast*

"This book is a must-read wake-up call for the evangelical church! Yes, it details the heart-wrenching realities that missionary kids all too often experience. But more than that, *The Missionary Kids* is a thorough, insightful critique of evangelicalism as a whole. As Holly Berkley Fletcher explains in detail how and why missionary kids were made to feel expendable, she helps us see how evangelicalism has gone off track too. And she invites those of us who want to cling to Jesus to a faith that doesn't demand child sacrifice, but instead focuses on flourishing and wholeness. We simply must do better, and this book leads the way."

—**Sheila Wray Gregoire**, author of *The Great Sex Rescue: The Lies You've Been Taught and How to Recover What God Intended* and host of the *Bare Marriage* podcast

"Given recent political and cultural events in our country, readers cannot do enough to understand the complicated and powerful world of white evangelicalism. *The Missionary Kids* is no exception. As author Holly Berkley Fletcher writes, the book exposes the good and the bad, the beautiful and the brutal, and the wondrous and the woeful, from the forgotten perspective of those who often saw it all. America's former missionary children tell a story of paradox the rest of us best pay attention to and learn from if we want to see real change."

—**Cara Meredith**, author of *Church Camp*

THE MISSIONARY KIDS

The Missionary Kids

Unmasking the Myths of

WHITE EVANGELICALISM

HOLLY BERKLEY FLETCHER

Broadleaf Books
Minneapolis

THE MISSIONARY KIDS
Unmasking the Myths of White Evangelicalism

30 29 28 27 26 25 1 2 3 4 5 6 7 8 9

Unless both first and last names are used, all names have been changed, and some details have been obscured to protect identities.

Library of Congress Control Number: 2024951874 (print)

Cover design: Amanda Kain

Print ISBN: 979-8-8898-3203-4
eBook ISBN: 979-8-8898-3204-1

Printed in China.

For my fellow missionary kids

CONTENTS

Introduction

I've only known one probable murderer in my life, and he was an evangelical missionary. I grew up calling him "uncle." Children of missionaries—missionary kids or MKs, as we are commonly known in the evangelical world—are usually told to refer to the adult missionaries in their orbits as uncles and aunts.

This particular uncle wasn't just any old missionary, either. He was a highly celebrated one, a charismatic speaker with the numbers of converts to prove it. He supposedly led big revivals and baptized hundreds, although since then, I've heard multiple people question his self-reported spiritual exploits. Many more in the missionary community questioned his claim that it was thieves who killed his wife on an isolated road late one night. They knew he was having an affair with another married missionary, giving him a possible motive, and his story had some discrepancies, starting with the couple's inexplicable nighttime drive, something most people there tried to avoid due to poor road conditions.

His case never faced any legal process or scrutiny—Americans who commit crimes overseas often benefit from jurisdictional gaps—so I can't say he was guilty and thus won't identify him here. What I can say is he left the country where he served to avoid possible prosecution, with the help of his mission organization, which apparently kept the information related to his departure to itself. He went on to further ministry, at least for a time. According to an MK-turned-missionary I interviewed for this book, he showed back up on the mission field, in another country, with a short-term missionary team, and once again made highly exaggerated claims of leading large numbers of people to Christ.

Most American evangelicals would be shocked to hear that a missionary could be a murderer or even a charlatan. American Christians have celebrated missionaries ever since they first started going out to places like China, India, and Nigeria in the nineteenth century. Lottie Moon, one of the original Southern Baptist missionary celebrities, has a Christmas offering named after her, to which all the churches in America's largest Protestant denomination contribute every year. Growing up Southern Baptist, I probably learned the name Lottie Moon simultaneously with that of Jesus Christ—although to be honest, I didn't realize she was a person for a long time. I thought she was a satellite, or maybe a snack cake.

Individual missionaries these days are rarely as famous as Lottie Moon was. But as a collective, they are still lionized in white evangelical America, and the missionary endeavor continues to be seen as the highest form of Christian calling in that culture. If you want to grow up to be a saint, you surrender to a call to missions. Do a quick poll of white evangelicals, and most of them will be able to tell you of a time when the missionaries came to speak at their church and how formative that was. The stories of persecuted Christians in distant lands. The photos of poverty-stricken villagers receiving blankets and Bibles. The miraculous accounts of Muslims dreaming of Jesus during Ramadan (that's a newer missionary story, one that has become familiar post-9/11).

Your white evangelical friends will probably tell you how much they looked up to these most lauded of Christians. Maybe they were challenged to do more for God with their own lives and in their own communities. Maybe they went on a short-term mission trip with their church. Maybe they put part of their allowance in the offering plate to help or had a prayer calendar of missionary birthdays. Or maybe they quickly dismissed the idea that they could ever belong to this spiritual league and moved on with their morally inferior American lives, happy to be represented by and associated with Christians of such stellar devotion.

In the minds of many, missionaries were—and remain—on a whole other level. I've heard my parents literally introduced as "Super Christians" and regularly saw people in two hemispheres fawn over them as if they were Bono. In Kenya, where I grew up, the missionaries were always the special guests, always revered, always celebrated, always sought out and deferred to. In America, congregations ate up their photographs and stories and hung on their every word.

These days, even as scandals in white evangelicalism pile up like logs on a bonfire, even as many believers become disillusioned and despondent over the sorry state of the evangelical church in America, missionaries continue to be admired. Missionaries have even earned the respect of secular journalists, such as the *New York Times*'s Nicholas Kristof, who has written extensively and glowingly about the missionaries he has encountered in his travels abroad.[1]

In 2022, Russell Moore, who resigned his position as the head of the Southern Baptist Convention (SBC)'s Ethics and Religious Liberty Commission in disgust over the Executive Committee's mishandling of hundreds of cases of sexual abuse, excoriated his now former denomination over its dereliction of duty to its members and the cause of Christ, calling the situation "an apocalypse." In that same article, he bemoaned the "weaponization" of Southern Baptist missions by those who claimed that bringing abuse allegations to light would harm fundraising for missions and that therefore the SBC had to be defended at all costs.[2]

At the same time, however, Moore called the missions themselves, and the SBC's Cooperative Program, "the greatest missions-funding strategy in church history." He added that "Southern Baptist missionaries are some of the most selfless and humble and gifted people I know."[3] And Russell Moore, for whom I have a lot of respect, is not alone in keeping missionaries on pedestals. Even as we watch so many other pillars of evangelical life come tumbling down, many American Christians see missionaries as something close to saints.

Before we continue, it's important to briefly define evangelicalism. Hereafter, when I say "evangelical," I'm referring to the white American sort unless otherwise noted. There are many evangelicals of color, in the United States and around the world, and increasing numbers of them, particularly from Korea, Brazil, and various African countries, are missionaries themselves. While the United States is still by far the leading missionary-sending country, missionaries from other countries now make up around half of the world's roughly half a million evangelical missionaries.

But my focus is on the white American variety of evangelicalism and white American evangelical missionaries because that culture has so dominated and shaped the modern missionary movement as a whole—and, as we'll see, missions are central to white American evangelicals' self-concept in a way they aren't for other evangelical or broadly Christian communities. Theologically, for our purposes, evangelicalism is defined by a proclaimed literalist (in reality, it's pretty selective) interpretation of scripture; an emphasis on personal, experiential conversion and faith; the belief that Jesus's death and resurrection atones for human sin and offers believers, and only believers, eternal life; and the goal of converting as many people as possible to faith in Christ in order to rescue them from hell.[4] Over the last several decades, *evangelical* has also become a cultural and political designation in an American context.

In white evangelicalism in the United States, particularly in the last several years, things are shaking loose and tiles are falling off the walls. The walls themselves are crumbling. The old songs sound off-key, and the platitudes no longer provide comfort. The triumphalist narratives are wearing thin, or never rang true—particularly the narrative of Evangelicals vs. The World, in which scrappy, uncompromising, born-again Christians battle for the soul of a morally imperiled nation and humanity writ large. In which the Christian side is always righteous, always superior, always wise, always certain. In which American Christians are called by God himself to fight for cultural and political dominance as a means to save the world from itself.

For many disillusioned evangelicals—especially after witnessing so many of their brothers and sisters in Christ dismiss abuse, ignore racism, abandon democracy, and condone a dangerous, narcissistic president—a lot of what they grew up believing just doesn't hold much water anymore. Or rather, it just doesn't hold much Jesus anymore.

But they still have their missionary heroes. The mission field has long been the rugged frontier in a grand evangelical narrative, the ultimate proof of the American church's virtue, rightness, and importance. So perhaps it's not surprising that missions may also be the "final frontier" in that narrative's dismantling, as journalist Rebecca Hopkins put it to me.[5] Yet while my (probably) murderous missionary "uncle" is far more rare than Russell Moore's missionary paragons, all missionaries are very human and unavoidably flawed, as is the system in which they operate.

Even in this internet age, geographical distance can still conceal that fact from American Christians. Few missionary newsletters reveal the uninspiring side of things. Few mission boards even privately report when and why missionaries are sent home, even if it's for abuse. Few indigenous partners, who often depend on American missionaries financially and are in many cases culturally conditioned to defer to them, have the desire or opportunity to criticize the system.

But mission boards, church leaders, indigenous partners, and missionaries themselves can't hide from missionary kids. MKs live the complex reality of missions: the good and the bad, the beautiful and the brutal, the wondrous and the woeful, the bullish and the bullshit. We are the beneficiaries of its rewards and the victims of its pain.

If missionaries are the evangelical rock stars, we are the roadies, of sorts—although we're along for the ride involuntarily, and perhaps not performing much actual labor. Then again, we're definitely carrying the baggage. Many of us grew up feeling it was on us to help make the stars look good: show up, do your job, don't complain, don't screw up.

And thus American evangelicals, while they probably have all heard a missionary sermon or two, have not often heard the voices of MKs, any more than the average rock fan has heard the roadies sing. They probably saw us, though, as our parents often brought us on stage to participate in Sunday evening services or weekend missions conferences or at least had us stand and wave to the congregation, sometimes wearing clothing inspired by the local cultures where our parents served. Sometimes we spoke to children's Sunday School classes or stood around after the service to field questions, such as whether we rode an elephant to school or had access to a toilet (my friend's renegade brother reportedly responded to the latter question with "No, we just hold it until we return to America"). We were intriguing points of interest, exotic and enigmatic characters, but not the main draw.

But like the roadies of rock, MKs are an essential source if you want to understand the business. MKs are both close and distant enough to see the truth. We have a unique view of not just the mission field but the culture that undergirds it.

And that is what this book is ultimately about. American evangelical missions are the product of the American church and have served its cultural needs in addition to serving the spiritual and physical ones of people around the world. White American evangelicals have elevated foreign missions to heights rarely, if ever, seen elsewhere in Christian history or Christian life and inspired our parents to serve the broader evangelical cause in ways most other American Christians only preach. We grew up in far-flung, international settings, but most often within carefully transplanted evangelical enclaves. By virtue of our parents' exceptional commitment, we lived in the hardest core of a hardcore religious culture.

And these days, many of us can clearly see that its dysfunctions don't stop at the water's edge. These days, after lifetimes of watching and waiting behind the scenes, many of us are ready to talk.

* * *

For many years, few people sought out MKs' views or gave their experience much consideration. God had called our parents to do great things; what impact that had on us, pro or con, was beside the point. In evangelical life, you don't question God—or rather, you don't question someone's interpretation of him or his will. If he tells your friend to haul their children off to a war zone or a remote rain forest or an urban slum, you don't ask questions. You just pray for them.

During what many consider to be the dimmest decades of MK life, it was common—even required, by some mission boards—for our parents to send us to boarding school, usually mission-run schools, at very young ages and to subsequently go months at a time without seeing us. Some of us went to school in another country than the one in which our parents were serving, sometimes to keep us safe from dangerous situations at home, but not from the worry for our families still there. No one thought to ask if we were being abused; we were in the care of other missionaries, and, well, you might as well accuse Jesus himself. And no one considered the less dramatic difficulties of navigating all the challenges and changes of adolescence without an emotional home base to which we could retreat. I have a distinct memory of being with my parents at a church, back in the States, where they were speaking, and hearing a group of women consoling and praising my mother for the hardship of sending her children to boarding school. I wanted to scream, "I'M STANDING RIGHT HERE. Don't you ladies care what it's been like for ME?"

This first began to change in the 1980s with the publication of *Third Culture Kids: Growing Up Among Worlds* by David Pollock.[6] Pollock built on the work of sociologist Ruth Hill Useem, who coined the term "Third Culture Kid" (TCK) in the late 1950s. She and her husband studied how Americans who lived and worked in India in various capacities interacted with locals in a postcolonial context.[7] TCKs, of which MKs are a subset, include anyone who has spent significant amounts of time as a child outside their "passport country."

Pollock put MKs and their unique challenges and gifts on the map and began to create a village of support for them. Researchers of various types began studying TCKs and MKs and discovering their patterns of behavior and needs, which mostly arise from the constant pressure to adapt to new settings and cultures and their resultant jumbled sense of identity. Much of the attention focused on the difficult transitions from childhood to adulthood and from the mission field to the "passport" country, and the deep grief and dislocation most MKs felt. Soon mission organizations themselves caught the vision and created or commissioned "re-entry" seminars and other resources to try to help MKs adjust to their new lives.

Honestly—and I hate to say this, because these efforts are so well-meaning and certainly better than nothing, but—in my experience, none of it even begins to offset the tsunami of pain that many of us experience. Between the sudden death of our homes, our fabricated cultures, our makeshift families, and our improvised identities, when it comes time for us to return to America, debriefing workshops just don't cut it.

More recently, attention has turned to the MK experience while on the mission field. Within the broader context of an expanding cultural conversation on mental health and abuse, more light has been shed on the trauma many MKs experience. According to the most recent and thorough survey done by TCK Training, the industry leader in preventive care for TCKs and training for those who parent or work with them, such trauma occurs at a higher rate among TCKs than any other general population surveyed.[8] In my own research, too, I found that most MKs have experienced some kind of potentially traumatic event. Unfortunately, the ones who experienced any trauma often experienced a lot of it based on their particular settings. Witnessing or experiencing violence, abuse, parental neglect and separation, severe illness, political turmoil, economic insecurity, being repeatedly uprooted—all of these things come up frequently in my conversations with my fellow MKs.

Equally damaging, perhaps, is the fact that this pain is often laundered in a spiritual detergent that, over time, proves to be as poor a wash job as the low-grade soap of many mission field settings. The American church isn't entirely honest about MK trauma in part because it threatens the mythology surrounding missions and their place in evangelical culture. MKs often don't process their trauma until much later, or they process it alone, sometimes in secret, without much parental or community support. In my conversations with MKs, I could see it start to dawn on some of them, in real time, that what they experienced as "normal" or even God-ordained was actually harmful, reckless, and at times abusive.

As awareness has grown, so have improved accountability mechanisms and mental health resources for MKs and missionary families generally. But as we will see, even the best of intentions cannot fully compensate for the structural challenges and theological underpinnings of the mission field.

Of course, many of the MKs I talk to—including some who endured hardship—express great wonder about and attachment to their experience. Many discuss the magic and whimsy of their childhoods, of running barefoot through lush, tropical gardens, or chasing monkeys out of their kitchens, or climbing fruit trees to get a snack, or attending church in a thousand-year-old cathedral, or just having deep friendships with other MKs, people who know what it's like to belong in a painfully specific context that is neither here nor there. Both the good stories and the bad are often tinged with longing, an almost palpable grasping for something they can't truly have.

In fact, the struggle for belonging is one of the closest companions of any MK over the course of their lives. I spent the bulk of my childhood in Kenya (a.k.a. the Most Beautiful Country in the World, and yes, I will die on that hill). The sublime splendor of sunsets over the Rift Valley remains in my heart and mind as a lovely memory, a horrible yearning, and an eternal wish to be enveloped by something that feels like home.

* * *

The missionary story has always contained a healthy dose of myth, perhaps by design. (And by "missionary story," I mean the cultural narrative surrounding the missionary endeavor, not the actual work done by the real people; I want to clearly make that distinction.) The purpose of missionary work has been to save souls and serve people. But the purpose of missionary myths for the American church has been one of inspiration, in terms of personal faith and collective action, and—if we're being honest—distraction from American Christians' discomfort with their insecurities and failures.

I don't think it's any coincidence that the largest, most successful missionary enterprise in the history of the world—the Southern Baptist Convention's missions arm, the International Mission Board (IMB)—was built by a church founded to defend slavery. And Southern Baptists began this endeavor not many repentant years later but WHILE IT WAS STILL DOING THAT. I mean, those folks must have been unparalleled moral acrobats, the Mary Lou Rettons of the Hypocrisy Olympics. If you were a nineteenth-century white Southern Baptist, or even a twenty-first-century one, it was—and still is—a whole lot more satisfying to go to Africa to preach the gospel to Black people than to live out the gospel among Black people at home—people who, with good cause, are not terribly impressed with white American Christianity. White American Christians might humbly consider how foreign missions, in addition to being a sincere manifestation of faith, can serve as a pretty effective exercise of self-gratification and avoidance for the church.[9]

Regardless of our religious leanings, we humans all love mythology for its clean lines, simple characters, and clear dichotomies. Myth is a cognitive shortcut, a way of organizing disparate and contrasting information. It's also solace in the midst of the moral failures that are part and parcel of every life, every society, and every human endeavor but that are nonetheless so difficult to face. Myths can involve more or less truth—they usually include at least a kernel—but they never harness the whole truth, which is always less organized, more nuanced, more troublesome and vexing.

It's true that American missionaries are mostly well-intentioned, decent people of strong faith who try to do good things and often succeed. They have built schools and hospitals and churches and paid school fees and fed the hungry and brought Christianity to many places and millions of people around the world. Many hold a cherished place in my own heart: from the dorm parents who spoke love and grace into my young life, to the doctors who administered compassion and healing to my body and soul, to surrogate aunts and uncles who felt like real family. In confronting the evangelical myths about missions, I do not wish to diminish the good they have done or disrespect any of them personally. I am not talking about any one of them; rather, I am looking at the system in which they have found themselves, and the narratives that surround them and hurt them as well.

I also do not wish to feed a counter-myth of evil, colonially minded missionaries who run around the globe wrecking everyone's cultures. The popular narrative of missions as colonialism—in which missionaries were always and everywhere agents of governments—is an exaggeration. The historical record shows a more complicated story, in which missionaries occasionally worked in tandem with military or political forces while in other cases, obstructing those agendas.[10] The truth is more complicated than that story, too.

The myths about missionaries and missions with which this book will grapple include the myth of calling, the myth of multiculturalism, the myth of saints, and the myth of indispensability. First, missionaries' calling isn't without ego, its pursuit can be dangerous and hurtful to themselves and their children, and it could stand some scrutiny. Second, MKs are particularly attuned to problematic cultural assumptions that underlie the system of American missions. The MK experience is a living, breathing testament to the shortcomings of missions' proclaimed multiculturalism. Third, as MKs will tell you—sometimes through tears—missionaries aren't saints. Some of them are not even good parents, and a handful of them are honestly awful people. Their behavior and work require as much accountability as anyone else's, yet they operate in a context in which that's hard to institute, even with the best of intentions. Fourth, MKs see American missions' questionable utility in some cases and can both appreciate the value of getting out of the way and the draw of keeping everything as it is.

The MK experience speaks to how missions embody the broader American evangelical paradox: insistence on control and certainty in their rightness while proclaiming faith in an omnipotent God who has always moved in mysterious ways. For the myths of American missions are ultimately those of white evangelicalism writ large. They are chapters in a story about specially called, essential people of superior faith on a quest to convert people everywhere to their highly specific, culturally rooted vision.

But why can't we have our myths? you might be asking by now. Maybe you know some really good missionaries, or your church supports some. Maybe you *are* one. Why must I be a skunk at the evangelical party?

Well, for one thing, because I'm a historian by training. You should never invite a historian to your myth celebrations; we will ruin them every single time. But also because myths aren't true, or at least not the whole truth. And the truth, while not being a great time in the short term, is the only thing that will set us free in the end. This guy named Jesus—many of whose followers ironically seem to be some of the biggest fans of myth out there—said something to this effect.

Myths are also used to exercise and perpetuate human power and control, something else of which Jesus was not terribly fond. Myths exclude and deny the truths of those who challenge them. The myth of America denies the experiences of Black Americans and other Americans of color whose very existence, as a living reminder of the nation's moral failures and hypocrisy, seems threatening to the keepers of the myth. Religious myths distract from the shortcomings of churches and religious cultures, which are almost by definition built on being right. And those invested in missions have too often wanted to avoid the experiences of MKs.

One thing I've heard over and over from MKs is the jarring discontinuity between how their families were idolized by American churches and what they actually experienced. In reality, many of them lived in families that were under enormous strain, had parents who were neglectful or simply too overwhelmed to parent well, or were abused by other missionaries. And then there were just their ordinary personal struggles, those we all have as children, but ones they didn't feel they could express because they threatened to disrupt the missions narrative in some way. One MK, discussing a conflict she had as an adult with her parents, expressed it so well. After forcing her to be independent as a child, her parents now wanted more frequent contact with her than she wanted with them. She asked them why they were upset with her when "I've just done what you've asked me to do."

This young woman had done her MK job effectively. She had upheld the missions myth by taking care of herself and not troubling her parents. At the end of the day, however, it was a shoddy substitute for a more honest family relationship that acknowledged and prioritized her childhood needs. And most myths, however satisfying they feel at the time, however easy they are to perpetuate, are cheap alternatives for wading into uncomfortable truths and emerging with more authentic community.

The bottom line is this: dismantling the myths surrounding and undergirding American evangelical missions will help the American church see itself more clearly, tend to its own wounds, and invite it into more equal partnership and fellowship with Christians around the world. Understanding the MK experience is vital to this process.

Also, MKs will be less annoyed all the time, which I realize is a bit of a pet project.

* * *

Now here's the part where I save all the people who won't like this book the trouble of finding fault with it by laying out all its weaknesses. (You're welcome!) First of all, I will not even try to pass any theological or doctrinal tests out there. My Christian faith is a work in progress, and I have a lot of doubts that admittedly influence my view of missions. In my defense, I have tried to put my own particular experience with faith aside and take evangelical missionaries and their supporters at their word—they do really, truly, sincerely believe most of humanity is going to hell; they desperately want to prevent that from happening; and they honestly think missions are essential to that end. So, for our purposes here, hell is real. And there's a pretty solid chance I'm headed there.

Second, this book is not the definitive account of the MK experience; such a thing does not exist. I have been led by my own story and those of many dozens of others whom I interviewed, but I recognize the great variety of MK experience—you'll see it in the stories I present here—and the need to distinguish between the typical and the rare. In that vein, I have balanced individual narrative with other research, including two large surveys of MKs done by other experts and my own smaller one, as well as the work of historians, journalists, sociologists, psychologists, missiologists, theologians, and child protection experts.[11]

But ultimately, my major goal here is not to fully detail the entirety of the MK experience but rather to use it as a lens through which to examine the missions enterprise as an expression of white American evangelical Christianity. Whatever your view of missions is (and there is ample evidence to undergird a wide variety of opinions), my hope is that you will listen to these stories and think about what they have to say about the enterprise itself—and, more importantly, about the American church that so cherishes it.

This book will raise some questions I think the American church needs to ask about the missionary endeavor, and ultimately about itself. But I can't promise too much in the way of answers, partly because I am afraid of them myself. I, like many of my fellow MKs, am deeply conflicted about missions. Certainly there is a lot of comfort for many us in everything continuing mostly as it is, regardless of our beliefs. I have friends and family whom I love with all my heart and who are or were missionaries. I deeply hope that my beloved boarding school in Kenya will still be perched on the edge of the Great Rift Valley, hosting spectacular sunsets and wind-borne lullabies, for many decades to come. I still financially support friends who teach there, as well as other missionary friends.

But ambivalence itself is part of being an MK. There's ambivalence about our homes—both of them, all of them, to the extent we have them—and ambivalence about our families.

There's ambivalence about our faith and about ourselves. We want to belong, but not at the high cost of our full, complex identities and the truth of our experiences.

You don't have to be an MK to relate to this feeling of angst and alienation. You don't have to have an exotic upbringing with Super Christian parents. The MK experience is a distilled version of what many people have experienced in evangelical Christianity. And the myths surrounding missions derive from the wider white evangelical story and manifest in other ways within American borders.

For those who don't find themselves in that story, who can't quite buy in, who struggle to leave their doubts at the door, who can't quit asking the tough questions, who challenge the myths, who bring in life experiences that are awkward for the dominant culture to hear: you may be left feeling like an alien in those communities. Like the only zebra without stripes, to play upon a traditional African metaphor. And if or when you leave those spaces, as increasing numbers of people are doing, you may not find immediate relief. There's no easy sense of belonging to be had except with other wandering, wondering people who are unafraid to show their hands.

For the uprooted and off-balanced, for those who stay uncomfortably and those who leave equally so, for the strangers in strange lands, for those who hate being asked where they come from or where they belong: welcome to our MK herd. Though this book is not explicitly about you, I hope you see yourselves in these pages as well and find belonging here.

Because if there's one thing MKs know is important, it's that.

Part I

The Myth of Calling

1

Accessories to Martyrs

George was six when his parents put him on a ship, alone, bound for the United States from Burma.

He was the stepson of one of the most famous missionaries of all time, the first white American missionary to go overseas: Adoniram Judson.[1] George's parents were colleagues of the Judsons in Burma, and George's mother, Sarah, married Adoniram after both of their spouses died of disease.

With Sarah and his other two wives, Adoniram had thirteen children of his own. Six died before their third birthdays.[2] The surviving seven Judson children were barely raised by their parents at all. Once they reached age six or seven, they, like their stepbrother George, were sent back to the United States, some of them unaccompanied on a months-long sea voyage, to be raised by extended family or members of the mission board. They had no guarantee of ever again seeing their parents, who had committed to stay in Burma for life.

Edward Judson, who published a memoir of his father in 1883, explained that this was hardly a choice for American missionary parents, as the children who stayed in such unforgiving climates would be "in danger of death . . . or . . . feebleness of mind and body."[3] Another missionary from the time gave another, less sympathetic reason, explaining the need to keep their children away from the local "heathen" children. "With such vile companions, no Christian parents can permit their children to associate," she wrote.[4] Edward concluded that separation from their children was "peculiarly distressing to the missionary." It was, "perhaps, the keenest suffering that falls to his lot."[5]

There is scant mention of the Judson children in the numerous hagiographic books written about their parents, particularly in the nineteenth century, when the Judsons were national celebrities in religious circles and wider popular culture. The children's main appearances are accounts of their deaths and departures, events portrayed in the maudlin language typical of nineteenth-century mass-market literature. The inclusion of these scenes seems designed to underscore the missionaries' martyrdom, which scholar Melani McAlister identifies as a long-standing feature of American Christians' interest in missions.[6] In one account of Ann Judson, Adoniram's first wife, she is sick with smallpox and nursing her similarly afflicted baby daughter, Maria. She is also taking care of sick household staff while shuttling food to her husband, locked in a Burmese prison on suspicion of spying for the British, and visiting multiple officials to plead for his release. Her breastmilk dries up, and she resorts to taking "the emaciated creature" house to house in a nearby village to prevail upon the mercy of nursing mothers there. Ann eventually collapses in her bed, unable to move for two months, and the entire household is left to the care of their Burmese cook. Maria died before her second birthday; Ann preceded her by a few months.[7]

George shows up in the Judson story in a heart-rending account of his departure from Burma to return to the United States, where he had never been before. His mother, Sarah, wrote that "his eyes were filling with tears, and his little face red with suppressed emotion," as she said goodbye, as it turned out for the last time.[8] "It was not till he had turned away and was going down the steps that he burst into a flood of tears." In this moment, she reflected not on the pain and fear her son must have felt, but her own sacrifice, which she considered a "*delightful privilege*" made possible by her love for "poor perishing souls . . . these wretched heathens to Christ."

George's sea voyage—alone, at age six, for several months—was apparently quite harrowing. According to his half brother, Edward, he was nearly kidnapped by pirates, in addition to "the tortures of terror to which the shrinking child was subjected on board the ship." One can only imagine what those were, as Edward provides no further detail.[9]

The Judsons' primary concern for their children, when they were away from their influence, seemed to be their spiritual salvation. Sarah was overjoyed when she heard that fifteen-year-old George had been saved, but she was apparently not satisfied with his spiritual condition (it's not clear how she might have assessed that from a different hemisphere). She pressed him in her reply to ensure he had given Christ his whole heart, that he might "never . . . do nor say nor think anything contrary to his will."[10] Adoniram similarly harped on George's spiritual condition via letter, at one point sending him a small Burmese idol "that you may not forget what sort of gods they worship in this country," and warning him that any moral failure on his part would send his mother "down to the grave in sorrow." (His mother was actually sent to the grave by disease in Burma a few years later.) "Perhaps we shall live to see you come out a minister of the Gospel," Adoniram wrote to him.[11] George did indeed comply with the wishes of his saintly, celebrated parents, who had abandoned him at age six so they could spread the gospel to "heathens."

Edward also became a pastor, and a social gospel reformer of some renown, in New York City. Sarah, who was also Edward's mother, had died in Burma shortly after his birth, in 1845. Adoniram left baby Edward and the youngest of his siblings in Burma with another family and returned to the United States, where he farmed out the rest of his children to guardians and married his third wife, Emily. In 1846, Adoniram and Emily Judson returned to Burma when Edward, who had no idea who they were, was two years old. After Adoniram died in 1850, Emily stayed on another two years, then returned to the United States, where she died in 1854, weakened by her missionary sojourn. Edward, age ten, and his four minor siblings went to live with four different guardians.[12]

Edward dedicated his 1883 memoir of his father in this way: "To the children of missionaries, the involuntary inheritors of their parents' sufferings and rewards."[13]

* * *

By the time the Judsons left for Burma in 1812, several historical and religious streams were converging to create what became the modern, American-dominated missionary movement, centered around a sense of calling—at once personal, spiritual, and national—and the family unit as the vehicle for carrying it out. The children in those families were inconvenient from the start, pitting missionaries' calling against their responsibilities and affections as parents. (Spoiler alert: the calling usually wins.)

To understand how a family-based missionary calling became so elevated in American evangelicalism, we need to take a brief tour through the history of missions. Missionary activity reaches back to the very beginning of Christianity, to Jesus himself, followed by the apostle Paul and others in the early church who established it as an enduring, global faith. Evangelicals today point to Matthew 28:16–20, in which Jesus exhorts his followers to "go and make disciples of all nations," as the foundation of missions and a universal, timeless mandate for international evangelism. More liberal theologians dispute this designation, arguing that Jesus was speaking in a specific context and focusing in particular on the verb "go." They maintain that the word Matthew used is better translated as "as you go," making it less of a specific commandment and more of an ethic.[14] Regardless of its interpretation, the elevation of this passage and its labeling as the "Great Commission" didn't take place until much later, perhaps during the seventeenth century, and that term was not in wide usage until the nineteenth century, when the modern missionary movement was well underway.[15] But then, Christianity mostly hasn't been spread by vocational evangelists who traveled specifically to win converts. Rather, the gospel has more often accompanied migrations of people, who took their faith along with them as they moved, or at times via military conquest and state mandate.[16]

For our purposes in this chapter—understanding the origin of the modern idea of missionary calling and the place of MKs in that—the European Age of Exploration, beginning in the fifteenth century, marks a less distant starting point than the early church. Navigation technology, competition between European states, economic interests, and male adventurism—particularly by younger sons who inherited nothing and needed something to do—fueled an explosion in global travel, trade, conquest, and colonization. Catholic priests joined these voyages, seeking to convert Indigenous people, forcibly if need be. This held a triple benefit for both secular and religious European powers: saving souls for eternity, making them more easily controlled here on earth, and bolstering the power of the church at a time when the Protestant Reformation was beginning to threaten its authority.[17]

For their part, early Protestants weren't initially that interested in missions; many believed Jesus's exhortation in Matthew had already been fulfilled and was not a binding commandment.[18] (That distant roar is millions of their missions-addled evangelical descendants screaming in horror and confusion.) But what all European Christians, Catholic and Protestant, inherited from this period, as they came into contact with non-white, non-Christian peoples, was a comingling of bigotry and religious calling, in which a sense of racial and cultural superiority was imbued with religious belief, intertwined for centuries to come. In 1493, Pope Alexander VI made it official via a set of edicts that came to be known as The Doctrine of Discovery, which essentially put a divine seal of approval on European conquest and colonization.[19] The Doctrine stated that any land inhabited by non-Christian people was free for the taking by Christian powers; it became the basis for all European claims in the Americas, as well as for westward expansion by the United States, as cited in an 1823 Supreme Court case.[20]

The assumptions that not only is Christianity a superior faith that must be propagated all over the world but that the white Western variety is its purest expression and continues in missions culture to this day. Although it is more subtle than the explicitly racist notions pervading missionary accounts well into the twentieth century, many MK accounts suggest it's still there.

American Christians added yet another ingredient to this racialized calling, one that has ultimately made the United States the preeminent force in evangelical missions up to the present: American exceptionalism. The sense that the United States is a divinely ordained nation has penetrated and guided our national life in both secular and sacred expression. The Puritans aimed to build a "city on a hill," nineteenth-century pioneers and explorers claimed "manifest destiny" for westward expansion and Indian removal, and the United States has engaged in repeated foreign military interventions, of mixed success and moral justification, all motivated by a sense of American mission.

By the end of the nineteenth century, when the United States, having expanded across its own continent, set its sights on global influence, American missionaries were inseparable from and morally essential to America's larger ambitions, painting over a more worldly pursuit of national interest with a holy veneer. At a large missionary conference in New York in 1900, two American presidents and one future one all took to the dais to extol missions as the ultimate expression of American superiority and responsibility to spread democracy, human betterment, and Christianity around the world. President William McKinley called missionaries "pioneers of civilization" and asked, "Who can estimate their value to the progress of the nation?" The whole gathering joined together to sing "My Country 'Tis of Thee."[21]

The theology of nineteenth-century American Protestantism translated this grandiose national errand into a personal calling. Building on the Protestant Reformation, which asserted the religious authority of the individual, and the Enlightenment, which elevated the individual in the secular political realm, waves of Anglo-American revivals—starting in the mid-eighteenth century and continuing into the middle of the next—redefined Christian faith in emotional, experiential, and personal terms.[22] Faith and salvation manifested primarily through individual conversion, piety, devotion, and experience. This had a few implications for missions.

First, at scale, the spread of Christian belief and its definition according to personal conversion and piety gave American culture a much more Christian cast, transforming a largely secular nation at the time of the Revolution into an overwhelmingly Christian one by the end of the nineteenth century and altering Americans' self-conception and view of their history. Nineteenth-century Americans read Christianity back into the Revolution, imbuing a secular event with a sacred hope that human society, led by the United States, was reaching its zenith, that progress was on the march, and that God's kingdom was indeed coming. In religious terms, this translated into post-millennial eschatology: the idea that Christ would return only after Christians had established his reign on earth by perfecting society through reform and the conversion of souls (the implication being that this was possible and that Americans would lead the way). Second, this period saw an explosion of religious institutions, including new denominational and nondenominational voluntary societies, as American Christians pooled their efforts and resources to carry out this grand vision. And third, the emphasis on personal conversion and piety gave missions a concrete, achievable goal: winning individual converts, who could be counted by mission boards. This made missionary work a defined vocation to which one might receive a special calling as a lay person. The "democratization" of American Christianity and the weakening of religious authority during this period meant there were fewer institutional restraints on and more opportunities for pursuing a vocational missionary calling or supporting that of others.

One small wrinkle complicated conditions that were otherwise conducive to the missionary adventure: the missionary family. Jesus, Paul, and generations of Catholic clergy did not have spouses and children, but Protestants did. Migrating to "uncivilized" lands overseas posed physical and perceived spiritual dangers to women and children who, in the nineteenth-century mind, were increasingly viewed in sentimental terms—as precious beings needing protection from physical hardship and especially from moral peril.

American Christians had to ask, "How do we save the world with wives and children in tow?"

* * *

Churches and mission boards considered wives necessary both for the care and moral protection of male missionaries and for securing the female converts deemed essential for the successful propagation of the gospel. Historian Carol Ann Vaughn Cross told me the Southern Baptists' mission board even ran a matchmaking service for prospective missionaries in the nineteenth century so that young men wanting to become missionaries could first acquire a helpmeet.[23]

But the difficult and sometimes dangerous conditions on the mission field also challenged emerging notions of the middle-class family, which romanticized the home and femininity and made children more cherished than in earlier generations that had viewed them through the lens of economic value. The industrial revolution and the rise of a middle class created the idealized notion of "separate spheres" for men and women. While men ventured out into the grubby, greedy world of market capitalism, women guarded the values of the home—beauty, virtue, purity, emotion, self-sacrifice—and passed them on to their children through affectionate parenting. The Puritans had seen children, literally, as fresh hell that should be beaten into submission, but by the nineteenth century, Americans were rethinking the definition and purpose of childhood as a time of innocence, protection, and nurturing.[24] The mission field challenged new ideals of domesticity as it thrust women into arduous, perilous partnership with men and pushed children away from their parents' protection.[25]

Initially, women's presence on the mission field was the more controversial piece of this arrangement. Not only would idealized gendered spheres be difficult to maintain in such a setting, white women would venture into what Americans assumed to be the sordid world of "heathenism," with its immorality and lack of domesticity. It's interesting to observe in nineteenth-century accounts the pains taken to describe missionary women as feminine, maternal, and genteel. Even the abandonment of their children—the Judsons' experience was the norm for nineteenth-century missionaries—is set in the context of self-sacrifice and heartbreak for mothers. Missionary women—who traversed jungles alone, built houses out of bamboo, mastered languages and aided biblical translation, and did any number of badass, atypical things, often with babies clinging to them—were described as having "unusual feminine delicacy" and being "well-bred and very intelligent," "fragile," "graceful," and "ethereal."[26] Having known many missionary women myself, including those from denominations that extol and insist on their female submission, I can tell you these ladies were in fact tough as nails, fiercely independent, and probably more than a little bit terrifying. Women, including single women and many extremely insubordinate wives, have in fact comprised the majority of American missionaries and continue to be the backbone of American missionary endeavors.[27]

The challenges to domestic life and the hardships of missionary children, it seemed, were simply part of the sacrifice missionaries had to make in order to fulfill their calling. Even in cases where MKs did remain on the mission field with their parents, the rigors of missionary life and their parents' all-consuming dedication to their ministry could leave them feeling abandoned. MKs in late nineteenth-century Hawaii sometimes referred to themselves as "orphans" even with both parents present.[28] In the missions-boosting literature of the time, MKs' suffering was never presented as any indictment of their parents or the missionary enterprise, and the MKs themselves almost always went along with the program, indicative of norms that mandated children's utmost respect for and obedience to their parents. Historian David Hollinger includes a heartbreaking, "religiously correct" account of a young MK being dropped off at an America-bound ship, in which the child "tearlessly assured her mother, 'We'll get along alright.'"[29]

That American children were increasingly seen primarily as cherished innocents needing nurturing and protection rather than as free household labor makes the lack of concern for MKs in nineteenth-century missionary narratives more notable.[30] Missionaries' inability to offer their children a stable domestic life was alternately glossed over or played up in the context of their sacrifice and martyrdom. The failure of missionaries as parents was particularly ironic, since they often commented on the inferior family values of other cultures and aimed at inculcating American domesticity along with the gospel. Historian Joy Schulz, writing about missionaries in Hawaii, wryly observed that missionary parents, who abandoned and neglected their own children, lecturing Hawaiians on family values "demonstrated an amazing ability to compartmentalize their lives."[31]

In American Christians' estimation, the sacrifice of children was worth it because the calling—to save souls from eternal damnation through faith in Christ—and America's particular obligation to that calling were so strong and vital. As we will see, the particular forms and structures of American missions have changed over time, driven by medical and other technological advances that have made the mission field less deadly and also by the needs of the missionary family and greater concern for missionary children. Beginning around the turn of the twentieth century, for example, American missionaries pushed for regional mission-run schools to allow families to stay together (well, sort of).

But the myth of calling—the idea that God so needs the American church to spread the gospel that any hardship or danger, even the sacrifice of one's children, is justifiable—has endured. Consider a 2017 article by megachurch pastor John Piper, in which he asks and answers his own question. "Should a Christian couple take their children into danger as part of their mission to take the gospel to the unreached peoples of the world?" he writes. "Short answer: *Yes*."

Piper goes on to claim that "there are worse risks for our children than death. This is simple Bible-reality. Not easy. Just simple. It is not complex or hard to grasp. There are things vastly worse than death. Wasting your life is worse than losing it." He goes on: "A life not given to great things is not worth living . . . risk your life—and the life of your children—to be part of greatness."[32]

A missionary who was inspired by Piper's words to take her kids to a war zone assuaged her guilt in a 2017 *Christianity Today* article by claiming that *all* children face risk. While hers faced "guns, limited government, lack of health care, and low-quality education"—and possible physical harm—life in America presented all that *plus* spiritual harm, including "pressures of secularism, campus rape, cell phone addiction, pornography, consumerism, disordered eating, greed, loneliness, loss of faith, underage drinking, drugs, campus shooters, and the allure of Western wealth."[33] (I hate to break it to her, but pretty much everything on that list of horrible American things is also found on the mission field. Keep reading.)

Piper's use of "greatness" is telling. From the beginning, the American missions movement was caught up in its own greatness. And it has been, by many measures, "great." Certainly, in the history of Christianity, no one nation has so relentlessly and doggedly pursued the religious conversion of the whole world. This achievement has fed the conclusion that our way of doing missions—which is different from previous ways—is superior.

More generally, missions have been a key part of American Christians' sense of greatness, as if Jesus didn't really reign until we came on the scene, as if our way of being Christian is the long-delayed ultimate version. This belief has created a culture so convinced of its own rightness that it has left little space for self-reflection, even when proven to be catastrophically wrong.

One is left wondering, "Whatever did the Lord do before there were American Christians?"

2

A Very Special Calling

Helen is tired.

She has a world-weariness far beyond her twenty-something years. As we speak, her young child crawls all over her and fusses. Her husband eventually arrives to take the child off her hands, puts him to bed ,and then returns to listen in on our conversation, occasionally chiming in with words of support and empathy. As I listen to her story, I find myself thankful she has him.

Helen's early childhood was happy. She was born in Uzbekistan and lived there until she was eleven, with the exception of a few years in the United States when her mother and brother needed treatment for severe hepatitis. In Uzbekistan, she had plenty of friends, both other MKs and locals, and plenty of freedom. She played outside, ran around town with other kids, and picked up the language easily.

But then the Uzbek government cracked down on missionaries. The country is a secular but overwhelmingly Muslim state, and proselytizing is illegal. Helen's family had ten days to leave, a sudden parting with a place to which she still feels a strong connection. Such short-circuited goodbyes, as a result of political forces or family turmoil, are some of the most dreaded of MK experiences and often result in profound heartbreak. Helen did grieve, but what came next was the bigger challenge. "That was a big turning point in my life," she says. "Life got very serious."

Her dad had long had "a passion for Afghanistan"—a calling, he believed—and decided that was the family's next move. It was 2005, and security in the country was slipping again after a brief *pax Americana* following the US military invasion. Helen overheard family friends telling her parents it wasn't safe to take children there. "I was scared but wanted to be agreeable," Helen recalls. "I was aware of 9/11 and the war, but I didn't really connect it to where we were going." Their family's security or their daughter's fears did not ultimately discourage them. After all, they had been called by God. He would take care of them.

The family moved to a village a ten-hour drive north of Kabul. Although not as violent as some other parts of the country, there Helen's life became one of anxiety and loneliness. As a girl, she didn't have the freedom and companionship she'd had in Uzbekistan. The Afghan girls around her were strictly controlled or married off very young. She didn't have local playmates and didn't learn the language as easily. As she approached puberty, she also became acutely self-conscious and aware of the terrible realities of Afghan women's lives. She overhead a conversation about old men marrying girls her age. She recalls being "disgusted" and subsequently "terrified" of men. She watched with foreboding as her own body changed, and she became afraid of being seen at all. Being a foreign girl made her even more conspicuous.

Wearing a full burka started as a requirement for attending school, but she came to experience it as a safe haven. "I enjoyed people not seeing my face," she says. "I was able to make it fun." This "fun" was, of course, highly relative. Helen didn't believe she could express how she felt without making things more difficult for her parents. "It wasn't safe for me to just feel sad," she says.

As a young adult back in the United States, she felt lost and disconnected from her emotions. "I was startled by anger, grief. I had resentment, but it scared me to think about it," Helen recounts.

She returned to Afghanistan, where her parents still lived, a few years after high school as a missionary of sorts—even though she didn't like it there—because she didn't know what else to do. She worked as a homeschool teacher for other MKs. She ended up in an abusive, sexual relationship with another missionary, someone from whom she was receiving counseling. This compounded her depression and shame, particularly because the therapist was a woman. She told her parents, who seemed paralyzed about what to do. She felt they blamed her and expected her to find her own way out.

A few years later, Helen is still trying to find her way. She's married to a good man now, and she has a baby and a life she is creating for herself. She tells me her story in a blunt, detached manner, occasionally making light of things with a smile and easy but exhausted laughter. Maybe it's just from being the mother of a young child; I remember those days. But she admits she remains more distant from her emotions and those of others than she would wish, and she has trouble expressing compassion and empathy.

Helen is particularly annoyed by American evangelicals' attitude toward missions, though she is still an evangelical Christian herself. "They think it [missions] is this holy thing," she says dismissively. "I think people do it for themselves. What's good for them. It's like, 'I have my own problems, maybe I need to work on that in another country?'" She shrugs. "I think missions is just the Christian life. Friendship, opening our lives to people. Doing life together."

Then she corrects herself. "But I'm not going to judge others' calling unless asked."

* * *

Calling remains a pervasive yet ambiguous concept in present-day American evangelicalism. It is often claimed, rarely explained, and almost never scrutinized. The myth of calling is that a person can receive clear, unequivocal guidance from God—divorced from ego needs and not subject to critical analysis or communal discernment—to take a specific action and that the rest of one's life and everyone in it must be subsumed beneath it. The culture and messaging surrounding American evangelical missions, as well as many other areas of evangelical life, is shot through with this myth. And maintaining this myth can result in devastating consequences, particularly for the children involved.

My own run-ins with calling go from the humorous to the disastrous. I figured out at a young age the power of "calling," as a concept, for getting buy-in for massive, possibly crazy decisions. When my dad declared he was retiring from the army and moving us all to Kenya to be Southern Baptist missionaries, my parents became instant rock stars in our Christian circles. The only people who seemed to question them were my heathen grandparents, and my parents probably saw their disapproval as a good sign they were doing the right thing. Well, at first my mother wasn't too keen on my dad's calling, either. But she quickly submitted (at least in technical terms) like a good Southern Baptist wife. In my admittedly hazy memory, everyone at our church fell all over themselves with excitement, like they were at the Oprah show when she gives out cars.

So when I wanted to make a massive, possibly crazy decision at age ten and needed some parental buy-in, I knew the language in which to couch my desire. In this case, I wanted to follow my older sister to boarding school. Our family lived in a mid-sized Kenyan town, and I attended a local primary school that was absolutely fine. I wasn't unhappy, I learned things, and I had fun. But my older sister was too old to go there and had no other appealing options. So she went to Rift Valley Academy (RVA), a boarding school a few hours away, run by an American evangelical mission. And I missed her. She was my best friend, and I missed her.

Now, I could have just gone to my parents and said that God had called me to go. But it's better if you have some connective tissue in there: a vision, a strange coincidence, a Bible verse. On the latter front, there was a school of thought that the Bible could be used as a kind of Magic 8 ball. You asked God to give you guidance, and then you propped the Bible up on its spine and let it fall open. With eyes shut tightly, you plopped your finger on the page, and wherever it landed was the word God had for you.

My dad had used this very method as one of several ways to verify his calling to missions. It was as good an exposition of calling as I had found at the time, so I decided this was the way to go. I got out my Bible and let the Christian magic happen.

I closed my eyes and put my finger on the page. The first few attempts were confusing: "The rock badger is unclean to you because it chews the cud even though its hoof is not divided" (Leviticus 11:5 NET). Weird. What is a rock badger? They have hooves? What? I tried again.

"Because of the suffering your enemy will inflict on you during the siege, you will eat the fruit of the womb, the flesh of the sons and daughters the Lord your God has given you" (Deuteronomy 28:53). Well, that's just disturbing. Next.

"The Lord had said to Abram, 'Go from your country, your people and your father's household to the land I will show you'" (Genesis 12:1). BINGO. My name's not Abram, but other than that, this is the definitive word: leave your father's house and go to the land. Doesn't get any clearer than that.

Armed with the Word of the Lord, I went to my parents to pitch the idea. "Mom and Dad, I know we planned for me to go to Mt. Kenya Academy for another few years," I began. "But I have received a Word from the Lord. God has told me he wants me to go to RVA."

"Is that right," said my mom skeptically.

"Yes, that is right. I prayed and asked God for guidance, and he gave me this verse." I handed my open Bible over to my dad and pointed to the verse. (I did not mention that this was actually the third Word from the Lord I had gotten and that I had opted against eating rock badgers or my own children.)

"Well, how about that," Dad said. "It does say that pretty clearly."

And that was that. God said it, we believed it, and that settled it. I went to boarding school at age ten, which was absolutely not the right decision, I think my parents would now agree.

So perhaps I am not the best one to speak about calling. But who is, because what even is it? How is it different from just living a life of love and virtue wherever the road may take you?

You can fulfill that Christian calling anywhere. You can do that as a fast-food worker. Personally, and I mean this sincerely, I have been deeply blessed by many fast-food workers. Anyone who offers a harried parent a break from meal prep has a very high calling from the Lord indeed.

In many ways, our concept of calling is a pretty modern, Western idea—one of many at the heart of American evangelicalism—and the result of an overabundance of choice that simply doesn't exist for most of the world's or history's people. I imagine even the most devout nomadic herder in a remote part of Kenya spends no more time trying to discern God's exact, "special" plan for their lives than they do on what to cook for dinner. Americans are awash in choice, and making the decisions that define our lives gives us a sense of agency and destiny. But also anxiety. What if we go down a less-than-ideal path? What if we miss a better option? What if we waste our lives? Or worse, what if we are disobedient to God?

For those blessed with such an extensive menu of life options, how do you know when God is calling you to do something versus when you want to do something for your own reasons? And if it's the latter, is that a bad thing?

I believe all of us, whether we are religious or not, are gifted with certain talents and traits, guided by passions and joys, prompted by misery and frustration to change course, and nudged along by the unexpected twists and turns of our lives and the people we meet along the way. And what we *want*—as long as it is an expression of love of self and others, not of unfounded fear or loathing—is instructive. Desire is not necessarily a bad thing. Ego is not necessarily a bad thing. Certainly it's unavoidable; it just needs to be kept on a leash. In secular contexts, we are honest about our motivations: I want that job because it's interesting to me, I am qualified for it, or it pays well and I enjoy buying new shoes. I want that job because I want it, I need it, to fuel my body and fund my life.

But what if that job lies in a war zone to which I'd have to take my kids? If I were going to that area just to make some money, you'd probably have a problem with that. But what if I tell you God has called me there, because people are going to hell and so it's worth the risk? It's far less likely that any American evangelical would bat an eye and more likely that they would hold a big farewell party for me. John Piper would be so proud. In practical terms, however, there's no difference. I'm taking my children to a dangerous place where they probably will experience trauma. But one version is celebrated.

Few Christians question a missionary's calling, because it's hard to imagine there could be any ego in missions. If someone wasn't called by God, many think, why on earth would they go? Historian João Chaves offers this devastating assessment by a Southern Baptist missionary to Brazil in the early twentieth century regarding some of his colleagues' calling: "I firmly believe there are missionaries here who came because they were not capable of commanding a decent job at home."[1] I'm not going to endorse that harsh take. I will say that, in my experience, missionary life can have real appeal. Certainly for adult MKs, many of whom become missionaries, it's familiar and all they've ever known. Several of the MKs I interviewed, including two who became missionaries, echoed this theme of missions as an escape or, for MKs, a default career option. "I didn't understand work-wise what I could do to make a living," one said. "Sometimes it feels like people are chasing an experience," said another.

MK, pastor's wife, and therapist Jennifer Christian told me that for too many people in ministry, including missionaries, their sense of calling can arise from a lack of awareness and healing from past trauma. A calling to ministry can become a Band-Aid or an avoidance tactic that can create further harm as the person plunges into a pursuit of sainthood. "I see in ministry families a culture of martyrdom," she explains. "It's pursuing God's will, full steam ahead, out of a sense of 'God needs me to save these people.' People rarely, if ever, pause to consider the possible harm to self or others in their wake."[2] She says that with conscious awareness, our sense of calling is a healthy, thoughtful, constructive outgrowth of who God has made us to be, but without it, the result is too often an unhealthy, destructive manifestation of unmet needs, unhealed hurts, and unloved hearts.

Another Christian psychologist's work suggests a link between calling and what he identifies as a culture of "collective narcissism" in American evangelicalism.[3] In his recent book, Dave Verhaagen shares research indicating that the white American evangelical subculture as it currently exists attracts a higher-than-average number of people with narcissistic personality disorder (NPD). Narcissists have an inflated sense of self that overcompensates for and masks a fear of introspection and an unconscious shame over weakness and failure. He finds that American culture in general is highly narcissistic, but that white evangelicals supercharge it with a sense of spiritual importance, goodness, and, via a theology of certainty, rightness. American evangelicals are heavily, cosmically, existentially invested in being right, being special, and following a divine plan to save the world. Most evangelicals, of course, don't see things that way. They wholeheartedly believe they *are* right, and that if they don't assert their rightness, if they don't "share the love of Christ" with others, those folks will burn in hell for eternity.

This is a sincere belief, and I think many secular people don't fully grasp that. If they did, they might give missionaries more credit for the extraordinary commitment to an authentic conviction that is indeed one dimension of the missionary enterprise. But a hallmark of a narcissistic culture is the inability to clearly see itself and a lack of critical thought about beliefs and behavior, and we can't ignore the less inspiring drivers of missionary activity. Like all human enterprises, missions represent a complicated set of motivations, both expressed and sublimated.

Few devoted believers within evangelical circles question calling, even if they can't quite pin down what it is. If you've been "called," you must go and do, if you love God. And thus everything one does becomes spiritualized—ego, service, ambition, decision-making, tactics, relationships, consequences. Calling is king. The ends justify the means. I'm just out here trying to serve the Lord, goshdarnit.

Such "special" callings as mission work aren't simply unquestioned in American evangelicalism, they are idolized (see John Piper in chapter 1). Many American Christians seem uninspired by the sacred ordinary of a universal Christian calling. They want over-the-top, epic Hollywood action, and a great missionary story is the church version of that. As scholar Melani McAlister put it, referring to young, short-term missionaries, "Young evangelicals wanted to go where God sent them, but they expected God to choose someplace extraordinary."[4] All the missionary epics that are passed around the church and all the missionaries who have become heroes are those who go to great lengths, face any hardship, sacrifice all, stare danger in the eye, and even die in pursuit of the lost. Jim Elliot, who was killed by

Indigenous people in the Amazon in the 1950s, is a classic. His widow, Elisabeth, went on to massive evangelical celebrity, as did some members of the tribe who later converted to Christianity.[5] More recently, there were breathless articles in Christian publications, and even in secular ones, about the missionaries who were kidnapped in Haiti in 2021, five children among them, and their supposedly miraculous escape.[6]

American evangelicals love their heroes and martyrs because they vividly act out how evangelicals want to see themselves, and their choices reinforce confident, unquestioning belief. Evangelicals want to identify with those persecuted and even killed for the faith, whether they be missionaries or believers elsewhere in the world, because they love to portray themselves as persecuted.[7] And how strong and real must a faith be that inspires followers to give their lives? I remember as a child hearing stories of Christian martyrs and imagining myself being killed for my belief. It was at once terrifying and comforting, because, I thought, surely martyrdom would prove my faith as genuine, and then I would know for certain I was going to heaven. The greater the sacrifice, the worse the place, the more faith-affirming the stories. Several MKs I spoke to said their parents exaggerated hardship, peril, or spiritual triumph when speaking to American churches. One MK from South America who responded to my survey claimed her parents concocted wholesale an elaborate story of persecution by terrorists because it helped them raise more support.[8]

Among missionaries, too, there is what one MK called "a worship of toughness." She experienced that when the staff at her boarding school accidentally gave her a regular, massive overdose of a needed medication, which made her extremely sick for a time. When the cause was discovered, the staff didn't apologize; they only complained that her outraged parents were being "overly dramatic."

I remember how I and other MKs bought into the culture of toughness. Whose lifestyle was most "hardcore," difficult, or risky was a bit of a status symbol. When I was a junior in high school, the war that would overturn the Derg regime in next-door Ethiopia broke out. I was at boarding school with MKs from Ethiopia whose fathers refused to evacuate (their mothers came to Kenya). My friends would get periodic word from their dads to assure them of their safety, but they also included details like having to stay on the floor of their homes to avoid flying bullets. An explosion at a massive munitions depot came perilously close to destroying one of their houses.

Looking back, I imagine my friends must have been extremely fearful. If they were, they never let on. Mainly what I remember is their pride that their parents stayed and their disdain for the missionaries who evacuated—missionaries who happened to be from my mission organization.[9] I remember feeling ashamed that my mission was so wimpy. The *real* superhero missionaries did not leave during conflict; they went to the roughest places and put themselves in the most peril, sometimes with children in tow.[10]

I also remember feeling enormous pride that I was an African MK. At missionary or MK gatherings with those from different regions of the world, we would poke fun at others—the European MKs in particular—for how easy their lives were. *Please, tell us again about that nightmarish time you burned your lips on an Italian coffee.* We tried to out-compete each other with the most harrowing stories (I got a parasite dug out of my big toe by a safety-pin-wielding teenager, but that was nothing compared to my friend's years-long battle with bilharzia). Africa was where it was at, a missions obsession, an MK from Southeast Asia I interviewed called "Africa porn."

When kids growing up in American churches aspire to be missionaries, they invariably imagine going to "deepest, darkest" Africa, where the people are the poorest, the most different (let's be clear: they are Black), and presumably the most "heathen."[11] The number of short-term mission trips to the continent is astounding, and on any given flight into Nairobi or Lilongwe or Lusaka, there's a decent chance you'll see a group of Americans wearing matching T-shirts proclaiming their service to Jesus.[12] Never mind that most of sub-Saharan Africa has been more evangelically Christian than the United States for decades, and light years more so than secular Europe. No matter that proselytizing in Europe is a road paved with ridicule and rejection, while in Africa, American missionaries are often met with smiles, waves, and at times downright celebrity treatment. Set aside that the cost of living in Europe is such that missionaries there often live in poverty, whereas most missionaries in Africa I've known live in lovely (if somewhat basic) homes with lush gardens and household help. Nope, Europe is too familiar, too nice, too safe (and too white). If you want to be a church hero, it just won't do. You probably won't see many planes full of matching-Jesus-T-shirt-wearing Americans en route to Paris.

* * *

Because there's a demand in American churches for heroism, there continues to be a supply of missionaries who put themselves and their children in not just hard places but dangerous ones, based on a claimed calling from the Lord. Although MK life writ large has probably gotten safer over the years by virtue of the world as a whole becoming richer and more stable, I still know of families who live with their children in incredibly precarious situations. I still know of families who have fled civil war and those who have lived in places under such a high threat of terrorism or violent crime that they could not go anywhere without armed guards. In my interviews with MKs of all ages, I heard stories of severe illness and a lack of medical care, kidnappings and sexual assaults, violent crime and political unrest, war and communal violence, harassment by security forces, shortages of food and other severe deprivation, emergency evacuations, and the complete loss of home and possessions. "There was gunfire many nights," one MK who grew up in then war-torn Angola remembers. "One night it was so intense, we got out of our beds and laid on the floor."

One MK who spent his early years in Haiti said his first sentence was "bad man go bang bang." His family later moved to Rwanda, where he witnessed a bombing, his family's car was attacked by a mob, and his nanny was murdered in the genocide after the family fled. Another MK from the unstable southern Philippines—which he describes as so beautiful that it was "like a dream world"—recalls the "constant terror our parents would die" while at boarding school in Manila. One time, his parents decided to surprise him and his siblings by showing up unannounced. When their teachers summoned the children to the principal's office, they all assumed it was to inform them of their parents' deaths. "Our parents always told us, 'God will take care of us,'" he remembers. "But then people we knew died. So what did *that* say?"

An MK from Pakistan, several of whose friends were kidnapped while she was growing up, says she doesn't blame her parents for putting her in that situation. "They just had so much faith," she says. "They believed with all their hearts we were as safe as we could be." I asked her if she would do the same thing as a parent, and she didn't hesitate to say no. "An angel would have to appear," she laughs.

Such risky settings, and even safe but remote ones, can also result in the additional pain of extreme isolation. As mission strategy has shifted aggressively in the last twenty years or so toward using data-based methodology to identify and target the dwindling number of "unreached people groups," this isolation may be becoming a more prominent feature of missionary life.

The Joshua Project, a research group that collects data on Christian adherence around the world, defines an "unreached" or "least reached" people group as a community with less than or equal to 5 percent Christian adherents and less than or equal to 2 percent evangelicals (that distinction is important; most evangelicals do not consider non-evangelical Christians, such as Catholics and mainline Protestants, "real" believers).[13] Many of these groups live in what missiologists call the 10/40 Window, an area of Africa, the Middle East, and Asia that falls mostly between 10° and 40° latitude.[14] But even heavily Christianized countries might have pockets of the unreached, regions densely populated with a non-Christian minority or the remote homes of ethnic communities who live disconnected from modern life. Thus, missionaries serving an "unreached people group" often live in far-flung, isolated locations. Or they might be "undercover" missionaries, outwardly assuming a different profession in a country that bans Christian evangelism. The secrecy involved in such a life—including withholding missionaries' identities or assignments in mission board literature, missionaries using coded language in email correspondence, and pretending to perform or actually performing other work as a cover for proselytizing—can breed a form of isolation, too.

Multiple MKs in a variety of settings told me loneliness and a lack of community were a pernicious and pervasive feature of their childhoods. Their families had moved them across the globe, yet, ironically, their worlds were terribly small. They generally were confined to their homes and, apart from boarding schools, had few, if any, friends. With the increasing prevalence of homeschooling over boarding schools (more on that later), many of these MKs spent their entire childhood this way.[15] "I don't think people realize that MKs in rural settings have no access to friendship," said an MK who grew up in far northern Kenya among the Turkana, a remote, "partially reached" people group.[16] One "covert" MK was not allowed to tell her schoolmates at her missionary boarding school that she was an MK, nor she could she attend mission-sponsored MK gatherings, which she felt compromised her feeling of community (the necessity of this strains common sense; I'm sure her schoolmates figured out what the real story was, especially since there are few non-MKs at the school). She developed severe mental health issues, including suicidal ideation.[17]

MK advocates say extreme isolation is their biggest concern these days, particularly for girls, whose activities tend to be more curtailed. I spoke to an MK from Europe who is now a clinical psychologist working with missionary families in Africa. She told me that the challenge of MK isolation is only growing given the rise of homeschooling. She considers the lack of socialization that homeschooled MKs experience as more detrimental to development than the boarding school experience (I'll discuss this later). Tanya Crossman, director of research at TCK Training—which provides curriculum and support for Third Culture Kids and the adults in their lives—agrees, citing their research showing that not having peer group support raised rates of all trauma risk factors and had a major impact on adult outcomes.[18] Therapist Caleb Adams, who is also an MK, told me he has known multiple MKs who grew up in "covert" missions and exhibit anxiety and OCD-like behaviors. "The impact of having to be in a constant state of vigilance during your most formative years is massive," he says, noting that missionary support and training for such a lifestyle is usually substandard.[19]

I have heard many stories of MK trauma, whether from exposure to violence or other physical risks or isolation, over the course of my life, and at times I found it easy to write them off as unrepresentative because that mostly wasn't my experience. Thanks to new research by TCK Training, however, we now have hard data that supports such anecdotal evidence. Their survey of almost 2,000 TCKs (with MKs accounting for over half that number) found that TCKs experience a higher number of adverse childhood experiences (ACEs) than the general American population or any other population studied worldwide. Whereas 25 percent of adults from twenty-three US states reported three or more ACEs and 12.5 percent reported four or more, 35 percent of respondents in the TCK Training sample reported three or more ACEs, and 21 percent had four or more. More than four ACEs has been found to put an individual at high risk for emotional and physical health challenges.[20] My less rigorous survey of more than three hundred MKs found that 53 percent of respondents reported experiencing trauma (I did not ask about the number of traumatic experiences).

Unfortunately, neither survey suggests that these experiences are a vestige of the past, although TCK Training did find a decline in reported ACEs among MKs born after 1970 compared to those born before. But both datasets include a broad age distribution, and over half the respondents to TCK Training's survey were born between 1980 and 1999.

My survey also queried those MK respondents who had subsequently served as missionaries themselves about their attitudes toward putting their own children in danger. I was dismayed to find that only a third of respondents disagreed with the statement, "I am willing to put my family in a potentially dangerous situation or setting if that is what I believe God is calling me to do." Such results suggest we need to continue asking hard questions about the idea of calling.

There are multiple ways we might pose such questions, and theologians and psychologists, of which I am neither, can help us ask them. But if I may be so bold, I offer one here: what impact will the course to which you feel called have on the children involved, children who have no agency of their own? If the answer is that your decision endangers or otherwise hurts them, then in my book, that calling is not of God. Full stop. Save the world by serving in your own community instead. Or wait until your children are grown and then go be a martyr-hero on your own time. Jesus and Paul both understood that family and ministry aren't always compatible, and both chose lives without family.

It's one thing if you happen to be a native-born South Sudanese mother trying to raise your kids amid war, famine, disease, and extreme poverty. Trauma, violence, and severe deprivation will, tragically, be your children's companion. But most American Christians do not find themselves in this situation. Most of us have choices that a South Sudanese mother cannot fathom, and it's incumbent upon us to factor in the kids when we make those choices.

I get that it's not our job as parents to remove all hardship from our children's lives. That is not possible, nor is it advisable. All lives have pain, and our children do need to be taught resilience. If we're in a position to do so, all parents have to decide what balance of comfort and risk to create for our kids.

But I'm not talking about forcing your kid to walk to school in the snow uphill both ways (honestly, for my son, separation from his video games is a fiery crucible of unbearable cruelty). I'm talking about deliberately putting children in physically or emotionally dangerous circumstances that can inhibit their healthy maturation. And even more, I'm talking about spiritualizing that abuse to the point where they can't even name it properly—they aren't allowed to—because it's bathed in the blood of Jesus.

Because it's one thing to have flawed parents who sometimes make choices that hurt you; we all have those. It's another thing to be told by everyone around you—the entire culture in which you are raised—that those flawed parents aren't flawed at all. To be told that they are in fact saints, carrying out the will of God, and that any pain or suffering you feel as a result either doesn't exist or is too upsetting for others to acknowledge.

Let's be clear: missionaries who put their kids in traumatizing or dangerous situations are not "heroes of the faith." They are bad parents. And a culture that encourages them to do this is toxic.

There's a story in the Bible in which God commands Abraham to sacrifice his long-awaited son, Isaac, only to call it off moments before Abraham obeys. I grew up being told this story illustrated that the God of the Bible, unlike some other gods of the time, did not demand child sacrifice. That by extension, in Christianity, God loves us unconditionally by his grace, regardless of our performance. You don't get bonus points in heaven for martyring yourself or your family.

As one MK expressed to me, "I'm angry at [my parents] for going. I'm angry at the mission board for letting them go. I'm angry at the whole culture for celebrating them for doing it. They were revered for child abuse."

3

Jesus Is Their Favorite

Julia is a Badass Woman.

That's an official designation, by the way. There's a group of them, friends for decades now. As MK graduates of Faith Academy, a mission-run boarding school in Manila, Philippines, they've seen each other through a lot—childhood abuse, abusive marriages, loneliness, grief, divorce. They helped raise each other. And then they helped each other remember who they are. They still do.

Julia learned to rely on her friends from the age of seven, when her parents, who were missionaries in Borneo, Indonesia, sent her to boarding school. It was 1971, a time when most missionaries sent their kids to boarding school almost by default. Her mother felt God telling her she would have to send her children to boarding school from the time they were babies, and she tried to get her kids emotionally ready well ahead of time.

"She emphasized the positive," Julia says, "She prepared me so well. By the time I went, I was excited. Mom was crying, but I was fine."

And I believe her. Despite ample research that shows it is not healthy for children of that age to be separated from their parents, Julia clearly has a "special sauce" of resilience that bowls me over as I talk to her. She is feisty and spunky and sharp, and I think she must in fact be the President of all Badass Women.

Her eyes flash with mischief and joy as she recounts what she and her schoolmates got up to at the small missionary-run boarding school she attended in Indonesia before she went to Faith. There were a couple dozen children there, in second through eighth grades, living in largely unsupervised dorms across the yard from the dorm parents' house. The dorm parents changed frequently and were mostly bit players. The best ones, in her estimation, were those she barely remembers at all. They left the kids alone. The ones she does recall clearly bordered on abusive, like the former military officer who was the dorm dad one year and tried to run the place like a boot camp. He beat the kids as punishment, leaving one boy with giant welts on the back of his legs.

"We grew up semi-feral," she laughs. "When new dorm parents arrived, the first question we asked was, 'Where are the boundaries?' Like, literally, how far can we roam?"

They swam in a dammed-up creek and carved matchbox car tracks into ant hills and collected nearby farmers' discarded scythe blades. On Friday nights, they played "Go home, Stay home," a more mobile version of hide-and-seek, moving through the shadows to evade capture from the designated seekers, pausing to stare up at brilliant shooting stars that raced across the night sky like fireworks.

It all suited her fine. She was independent and steely by nature. But she could see that not everyone thrived and not every experience was happy. Some kids perennially struggled, particularly those who had special needs or sensitivities.

"You didn't get any personal care," Julia chuckles. She tells of one year's dorm parents forcing everyone to drink milk every day, not cognizant or caring that she was allergic. It made her chronically ill. "My mother was livid over that one when she found out."

Julia once overheard a girl who was visiting from another missionary boarding school tell her older friend about a teacher who tried to assault her. He had trapped her in a classroom and chased her around the desks until she was able to escape. "I was only ten, but I understood what he was trying to do," Julia recalls.

But it never occurred to her to tell her parents or any other adults. "We took care of each other. The older kids helped the younger ones. We looked out for each other," she says.

Once at Faith Academy in Manila for high school, she continued to enjoy life in a tribe of other MKs. There she had teachers who genuinely nurtured her. "Everything they touched was filled with grace," she says. But generally, she and her friends relied on each other. She felt there were things she couldn't say and help she couldn't obtain from the adults around her. There, too, she had a friend who was abused by a missionary teacher. "When you can't trust the adults, you take care of each other," she says.

And that is what she and her friends still do, many years later. I interviewed another Badass Woman who told me the same. She, Julia, and several others of their cohort ended up in abusive marriages that they eventually left. They think this is no coincidence, citing both conservative evangelical theology that demands women's submission and a life of self-negation and forced accommodation in the absence of parents. Julia recalled scoping out the new dorm parents every year, "always watching, always adapting, always trying to figure out the power structure." This pattern continued when she returned to the United States for college and confronted a massive cultural change, and then again when she got married and conformed to the needs of a narcissistic husband.

She thinks for a moment before summarizing how things had gone wrong.

"I adapted right out of myself."

* * *

A more common, quieter source of MK trauma than their physical environment is parental neglect. Sometimes it manifests as actual abandonment or lack of care, forcing children into extreme self-reliance. But more often it's a kind of emotional neglect that prevents children from expressing their deeper needs and getting them met. And if you dig down to the roots of why generally loving, well-intentioned parents end up failing their kids in this way, you'll once again find the evangelical notion of calling.

One of the sentiments I have heard repeatedly from MKs—from the majority of the hundreds with whom I've interacted and from my own experience—is that our parents' calling is so sacred, so important, so necessary, so definitive, we feel we must necessarily fall underneath it in importance. We feel that even when it's not true, and even when our parents try to tell us it's not true. And most of our parents do try. It's pretty rare that a missionary parent would explicitly admit to deprioritizing their children. True, one of my subject's mothers did: "It was God first, my marriage second, the Africans third, and you children last," she told her daughter apologetically years later. Yet most of us are still inundated with reverent messages surrounding our parents' calling, and we feel we can't possibly matter by comparison.

In TCK Training's survey, an astounding 40 percent of MKs experienced emotional abuse from an adult member of their household, and 37 percent reported emotional neglect. That's compared to 11 percent in the general American population. Crossman feels this widespread reporting of "neglect" by survey respondents—though that word appears nowhere in the text of the survey—is especially striking. She explained that "this does not mean a third of missionary kids are unloved, but that a third of missionary kids . . . do not feel loved, do not feel special, do not feel important, do not feel that their family is close and supportive."[1] In my survey, of those who experienced trauma, parental neglect or abandonment was the most common source. In a conversation I had with Crossman, we agreed that such a pervasive feeling of being unloved, even when MKs say rationally they understand their parents love them, speaks to an unhealthy culture surrounding missions, particularly when it elevates a sense of calling over the well-being of people.

The MKs I interviewed almost all have stories of navigating serious situations by themselves at clearly inappropriate ages, including medical emergencies, treacherous or complicated travel, abuse and assault, harassment by security services, natural disasters, escape from mobs and riots . . . the list goes on. One of the more tragic cases I heard was an MK who became pregnant after being raped by a local man and then was forced at age seventeen to marry and live with him and her newborn baby in a remote location. I also know of a missionary family who allowed their daughter to be circumcised by the community they served, a truly extreme case of a child's welfare being subsumed by calling.[2]

Often MKs tell the less horrific stories with a disbelieving humor at how our crazy parents thought it was OK to let us fly solo across several African countries, or make our way home from school during a typhoon, or stay in a hospital for surgery by ourselves. Some of my peers insist they were not traumatized in the least and loved the independence they had and the self-reliance it fostered. Most of us, however, will then admit "it probably wasn't OK" and say we would never put our own children in such situations. For me, the traumatic experiences of my childhood didn't hit with full force until I had my own kids. Imagining them in situations I had been in as a child felt like a gut-punch, resurrecting long-buried memories of feeling afraid, overwhelmed, and inadequate.

When it comes to feelings of neglect or abandonment, the boarding school experience probably features most prominently among MKs. As I previously mentioned, MK boarding schools, which mission boards began to erect in the late nineteenth and early twentieth centuries, were an improvement over giving permanent custody of children to friends, family, or supporters in the United States. But among mission agencies and in evangelical culture, more generally in recent years, there's been an evolution of thought on sending MKs to boarding school, particularly at young ages. Doing so is increasingly seen as unacceptable.

For example, in a post on its website, Focus on the Family wrote in 2017 that sending little kids to boarding school was "out of the question," that the parent-child relationship could be harmed by sending even older kids, and that family considerations should come before ministry.[3] Over time, and particularly over the past twenty years, fewer missionaries have sent their kids to boarding schools, and fewer still have sent elementary-aged children. This is due both to increased concern for the impact on families and children (and more evidence of its detrimental impact) and because there are many more homeschooling resources available, including online ones. However, homeschooling in a remote mission-field location swaps the problem of family separation for the problem of isolation, as we have already discussed. Despite the trends, almost 80 percent of respondents of all ages to my survey attended boarding school at some point. Only 12 percent of TCK respondents in the TCK Training survey attended boarding school, but almost all of them were MKs.

For those kids who do go to boarding school, cell phones and the internet have improved communications with parents and greatly enhanced parents' ability to nurture kids from afar. My only communication with my parents at boarding school was snail mail (like, I think it was actually loaded onto the backs of snails for transport) and a phone staffed by a highly uncooperative operator armed with unreliable phone lines. These days, I have missionary friends whose vigilance over their teenagers at school in another country makes my own in-home parenting look positively checked-out by comparison. But there's no question that, even in the best of cases, the day-to-day, mundane stuff of life that makes up the parent-child bond is winnowed by the boarding school experience. And those small interactions, and especially small conflicts, may have a cumulative effect that forms the foundation of trust. Living far away from each other, many parents and children avoid the conflicts that test and prove the bonds of unconditional love.

In my generation and earlier, sending young kids to boarding school was an accepted part of missionary life. Some mission boards required it, so that missionary parents would not be "distracted" from their ministry, according to several MKs I interviewed. A number of my boarding school classmates started in first grade. I don't recall any of those friends discussing the impact of that experience while we were in school together, but the MKs I have interviewed formally almost all consider the experience traumatic to a degree. Some MKs from multigenerational missionary families discussed the compounding effects of early boarding school, creating severe family dysfunction. "I still carry anger toward my grandparents for sending my mom off to boarding school when she was in second grade," one second-generation MK told me. "I see the anxiety that stuck with my relatives who went to boarding school because they had to essentially raise themselves."

"The pain hit at night," one MK told me, of the creeping, smothering homesickness that enveloped them in the quiet darkness at school, unleashed as the busyness of the day receded. It's a feeling I myself remember all too well, as a ten-year-old boarding school student. Although I had wanted to go, as my parents have reminded me repeatedly, I had no way of assessing the consequences of my choice. I couldn't foresee feeling permanently on the edge of tears that first year, my stomach always slightly twisted, my guard up. I lived in a kind of emotional survivalist state. "The term homesickness does not do justice to the immensity of the grief suffered by the child in this moment of loss," writes British psychologist Joy Schaverien, an expert on the impact of boarding schools on child development. "The profound anguish of this separation is actually bereavement, but it is not treated as such. Therefore the appropriate reaction, which would be acknowledgment and mourning, cannot take place."[4]

The trauma that many children experience at boarding school is especially acute if the environment is abusive (we'll look at this further later on). But even in non-abusive environments, and even when the staff try their hardest to nurture the children in their care, it is simply not humanly possible to parent at scale. It is inevitable that children will feel neglected and will find themselves inadequately parenting themselves and their peers.

An MK who boarded at a mission-run school in Malaysia described helping younger girls through puberty: "Several of them got their periods for the first time in the dorm and thought they were dying. They were too embarrassed and afraid to tell the dorm parents." She continued, "To this day, I carry deep resentment and sadness toward their mothers, who were not there and did not prepare them for this important part of coming of age. . . . these responsibilities left me carrying weight and guilt that I was too young to handle."[5] I, too, had peers help me navigate the rituals of growing up, but I didn't trust even them with my deepest fear: that something was horribly wrong with me when I still hadn't gotten my period years after it seemed everyone else had. There was no one in whom I felt I could confide.

Nonetheless, many, and perhaps even most of us, ended up emotionally attaching to our schools and creating a type of replacement family there. Given how dysfunctional her home life was, one of my friends believes boarding school saved her. And many of us had a lot of fun, too. I regale my generally unimpressed children with rollicking tales of pranks played on our dorm parents, impromptu costume parties and water fights and dance parties, sliding around soapy floors during dorm cleanup, hikes in the forests surrounding the school, and campus-wide rounds of Capture the Flag. We had no real entertainment, no real parents, no real culture or home beyond ourselves. Sometimes we let each other down, sometimes we were cruel—inexcusably cruel—to each other, and sometimes we were not equipped for the emotional tasks at hand. We were always children and not qualified to parent. As a family and a society, we were not a sufficient or permanent source of stability. At graduation, we were ripped apart and scattered. A lot of us suffered significant grief.

And that, ultimately, was my problem with boarding school. For me, it disrupted the parent-child relationship and offered no lasting, adequate substitute. I launched into adulthood completely unmoored and feeling I had no safe harbor. It's no wonder I got married to a man I didn't love at age nineteen.

Whether they went to boarding school or not, however, MKs widely report feelings of emotional neglect by and detachment from their parents, manifested as a belief that they can't express their hurts and fears, that they must handle their own emotional needs or subsume them underneath those of their parents. When MKs get into trouble, feel afraid, or are harmed in some way—or if they simply struggle with the more mundane concerns of growing up—many of them choose to keep their troubles to themselves. I certainly did. When I was molested at age twelve by an older teen and then spent years wrestling with disordered eating, I never even considered telling my parents or anyone else. I still tell them only what I absolutely have to, out of habit, out of pattern, out of a distrust I can't quite shake or fully explain. As one MK succinctly put it, "My parents were not a safe place to express my emotions."

There are various reasons, specific to each family, why this is the case, but one foundational driver is a concern for calling. Many MKs have a sincere desire to honor and protect their parents' calling, to help them fulfill it, to not distract them from it, and certainly to not destroy it by necessitating a return to the United States. MKs often witness their parents' own struggles. They see them overwhelmed and distressed, and they simply don't want to add to the load. Tanya Crossman found a strong correlation between MKs' reports of neglect and their parents' mental illness. In my interviews and survey, multiple MKs reported that one or both of their parents clearly dealt with serious mental health crises on the mission field. One MK told me she realized as an adult that her mother was simply "absent" from all her memories, which she surmised was the result of a long-term struggle with untreated depression. MKs often express a need to protect their parents' emotions and serve their emotional needs. One MK raised in Southeast Asia told me she didn't want to tell her parents she was being abused by a dorm mother because she knew there were no other educational options and she didn't want her parents to feel badly about sending her to the school.

In the more distant past, boarding schools actively discouraged MKs from sharing their negative feelings with their parents, even going so far as to censor their letters home. An MK who attended Faith Academy in the Philippines as late as the 1990s told me a dorm parent instructed him, "When you cry, it's harder for your parents." MKs often express the sense that their parents' work—which is presented as divinely ordained, with eternal consequences—is contingent upon their ability to handle their own emotional needs, to behave well, and to be low-maintenance.

MKs have also related numerous cases in which their parents or missions culture appropriated or "repackaged" their negative feelings and experiences for inspirational use, much like the MK death and departure scenes in those nineteenth-century narratives. For example, one MK from Angola said her father used what was for her a traumatic event, in which she and her siblings were surrounded by men when their parents left them alone in a parked car, as a compassionate plea for the lives of the Angolans in one of his newsletters addressed to churches and supporters in the United States. "That was your nine-year-old daughter in that car!" she raged, so many years later, in our conversation. An MK from the Congo told me a chilling story of being confronted by armed soldiers with evident bad intentions while playing with her teen sister, who had Down Syndrome, in the forest. Though she was only ten, she was able to talk her way out of the situation and get them both home safely. She seethes as she describes to me how her mother recast the story into a heroic tale to tell in fundraising pitches to American churches. "That's *my* story," she says. "I wasn't a hero; I was a frightened child."

I was probably more intimidated by than concerned for my own parents' calling. It fed into my belief in their moral unassailability. I saw them as overly powerful and morally authoritative based on their calling and the reverence others had for it. They were the ultimate arbiter of mine and others' faith and behavior. I feared I could never measure up and that, from their high missionary perch, they would judge my weakness and fallibility more harshly than I could bear. So I gave them no chance to assess anything but my outward success.

Michèle Phoenix, an MK from France who has taught, mentored, and studied MKs for over thirty years, calls the pressure MKs feel to neglect or hide their own emotions in order to protect their parents "the tyranny of shoulds." In her research and other work with MKs, she has identified five "shoulds" that MKs feel implicitly: I should behave well at all times; I should be exemplary in every way; I should not cause my parents more stress; I should have a mature faith; and I should serve others until I have nothing left to give.[6] Another MK advocate, Dr. Grant Jones, an MK from West Africa who now works with MKs as a therapist, told me he believes this sort of emotional negation, among other factors, can cause disproportionately high levels of anger in MKs as assessed by the Taylor Johnson Temperament Analysis.[7]

The ultimate MK fear (for most of us) is that our inability to thrive or our resultant bad behavior will be a career-ender—a calling-destroyer—for our parents; that if the family can't manage on the field, they will have to return "home." Growing up, I perceived a condescending pity for missionaries who "went home," who resigned and returned to civilian life. "They couldn't cut it," I often heard. Or worse, in my mind, "Their kids were having problems; they had to get them help." When I heard that, it translated to, "Their kids wrecked everything." The sympathy was laced with criticism and disappointment. No MK wants to be a cause of their parents' failure.

In addition, for most MKs, the United States often isn't home at all. It is a place where no one understands them, where they know few people or even no one, where they don't feel comfortable at all. So not only do MKs have the pressure of believing that the eternal salvation of untold numbers of people rests on their ability to manage their own issues, but they have to face the prospect of losing their entire world in one sudden move if they can't. It's no wonder that MKs become experts at hiding—emotional stealth ninjas, if you will.

I think all this boils down to the fact that the concern for calling can produce a fundamental, unspoken lack of trust in missionary parents' unconditional love. When you don't trust someone, you don't force reality onto the relationship, and you don't set up a choice in which you will lose out. You don't want to know the truth, because you fear it will be too painful. MKs don't want an overt competition with their parents' calling, because they can't stand the thought of losing out to it explicitly. Better to avoid the contest altogether and remain comforted by the open possibility that you might win, that your parents might choose you. In most cases, this distrust is irrational and not at all based on missionary parents' actual feelings for and devotion to their children. This is why the American church bears at least some of the blame for perpetuating a system and a culture in which children would ever feel they are at odds with a calling from God.

As an MK from eastern Europe put it, she felt "sacrificed on the altar of ministry. It made me feel very insecure, unworthy, and like I was never good enough." Another young MK, who hopes to go into missions herself, told me adamantly, "My kids will be *first* over anything."

Despite missionary parents' efforts and intentions, I wonder if the culture of missions, built on evangelicals' unquestioning celebration of calling, will always blur the message of unconditional love.

But then, MKs' perception that they are less important than belief, and their practice of self-denial for the needs and narratives of their faith community, is just a more extreme example of what many people experience in American evangelicalism writ large. In my life in and around evangelicalism, I've repeatedly seen rigid doctrine trump the experiences and well-being of flesh-and-blood people. From disowned gay children to women constrained in the use of their talents to abuse victims' "inconvenient" pain to non-white people's run-ins with discrimination—not to mention the quiet doubts and questions of those who look on the outside like they fit in beautifully—there is a library of stories that add up to one unavoidable conclusion: white evangelicalism is more interested in protecting inflexible beliefs and its own self-conception than in following an ethic of love and humility.

This dynamic has also hampered American evangelicals' ostensible aim of building a multicultural, multiracial global church through missions. Missionary kids' experiences and perspectives demonstrate the limits of that narrative, too. With the MK story as a starting point, we now delve into the broader history and context of missions' engagement with race and culture. And we'll see the ways American Christians have used missions less to learn and grow than to burnish their own image, to lay claim to "true" Christianity, and to engage in difference while mostly remaining the same.

Part II

The Myth of Multiculturalism

4

Bubble Boys and Girls

Dan may be the only Alabaman alive who is a "football agnostic."

It might be because he isn't really from Alabama. He was raised in Europe, where his father—from the "backwoods of Alabama" and without any theological training—decided God was calling him to be a missionary. He had previously tried to plant his own church in the United States and had been rejected by the Southern Baptists' IMB because he lacked the requisite educational qualifications.

But as often happens in the missions world, Dan's dad found a way. When it comes to calling, there is much reading into open doors and explaining away of closed ones. And there is always another mission agency with which to go, or one can go independently. Many, if not most, missionaries who are affiliated with a mission board raise their own support anyway, from personal connections with American churches and Christians who don't scrutinize anyone's plans and intentions much after they are labeled "missions." In the case of Dan's father, he got tangled up in the ultra-conservative Independent Fundamentalist Baptist (IFB) church, which some (now including Dan) consider a cult. But the beliefs are only slightly more extreme versions of mainstream evangelical ones, including strictly delineated gender roles, a literalist reading of the Bible, and hostility to secular American culture. Dan's father decided he wanted to go to western Europe because it had the fewest IFB churches and was highly secular, a rational choice that many missionaries don't seem to make in preference for more "exotic" locales and people.

I said Dan was raised in Europe, but that's not entirely true. He was actually raised in an American evangelical enclave that happened to be in Europe. Like the increasingly isolated evangelical subcultures in the United States, Dan's world was small and sheltered. Most of the family's friends were other American IFB adherents or missionaries. His access to both American and European popular culture was controlled. He was exclusively homeschooled and had few friends, which he found especially difficult, and he struggled with depression. His curriculum was mostly Bill Gothard's Advanced Training Institute (ATI) fare, which taught a highly propagandized version of American history in which white Christians were the founders and heroes and sought to prepare American Christian youth to be soldiers in the culture war.

Dan was a true believer. As a teen, he worked in the small congregations in which his family served, even leading the music at one point. He found the militant rhetoric about spiritual conflict "exciting." But he didn't really have a choice other than to believe. The IFB taught that strict adherence to authority was essential to salvation.

Meanwhile, Dan's father struggled to establish a ministry, as is the case with many missionaries in western Europe (most successful missions there primarily involve immigrants). But the IFB's theology seemed particularly untenable to cosmopolitan Europeans, and the idea that an Alabaman with little education was going to win converts there was "foolhardy," in Dan's estimation. The family had to move a few times, once across a border to evade the Netherlands' ban on homeschooling. Their meager financial support from American churches didn't go very far in Europe. Dan's father ended up getting work as a chaplain on an American military base, where he pastored an established IFB church. Ironically, his father's most effective ministry in Europe was with American transplants.

Dan's transition to ultra-conservative Patrick Henry College in Virginia was not a huge leap, despite the fact that it was a transnational one. It was essentially the same culture in which he had grown up. He missed aspects of life in Europe—biking everywhere, good public transportation, good food—but he realizes now he didn't have an "authentic" cultural experience there. He had managed to learn Dutch, more through schoolwork than social interactions. "I have a lot of regret," he says, as if he had much choice in the matter. "When you view the dominant culture as 'the enemy,' it's hard to have a rich cultural experience."

The IFB world was all Dan knew, so as an adult he kept working for the IFB's mission board on the financial side of things, which he soon discovered was a disaster. The mission was basically insolvent, and Dan was determined to get things in order. Then he discovered some leaders were stealing money outright, and as he dove deeper and deeper, he found a culture of widespread corruption. At one point he went on a tsunami relief mission to Sri Lanka, where he saw little evidence of actual work being done. "Is all of this legit?" he recalls thinking. He consulted his father, who admitted that during his time with the IFB, he saw many things "that should have landed people in jail." This included two missionaries whose "calling" to go overseas happened to coincide with pending sex crime charges in the United States. Both of them were able to raise the money to go, and both were celebrated, Dan says.

Dan was horrified by it all. But his father's attitude was one of resignation, as in, "Well, whatcha gonna do?"

* * *

In the pre–civil rights era of American missions, multiculturalism was not a goal for white Christians at all. Indeed, most missionaries and mission boards explicitly aimed to change, and in some cases eradicate, culture (more on this later). But in the postcolonial era, missions has been reframed as a way to build a harmonious, global, "color-blind" church, comprising "every tribe, every tongue, every nation," in the words of a popular praise song that draws from Revelation 7:9.[1] The goal of a multicultural church is a worthy and beautiful one, but the progress toward that end has been exaggerated by American evangelicals, who have used their power within global evangelicalism to shape it in their own image while insulating themselves from challenge or change. Most MKs' partitioned experience growing up in other cultures reveals this point.

In almost any conversation with almost any MK, the word "bubble" comes up. We MKs like to think we are from a real place, that we belong to the countries of our childhoods, of which most of us are so fond. Our identification with these places and cultures is often the only thing we get to bring with us into adulthood, so we lay as much claim as we can.

But whether we recognize it or not, whether we can bear to admit it or not, MKs are in fact *not* from Burundi or Thailand or Hungary or Peru. We are from "the bubble": a temporary, imported, usually highly privileged world that lives inside those places. Like a real country, the bubble has its own linguistic practices and customs and foods and traditions and shared experiences. Unlike a real country or culture, it has no durability. It bursts, and everyone scatters. And its residents are left dazed and confused on the ground of whatever real country over which they once floated. Many of them hop immediately into another mission field bubble, where they feel they belong and where things make sense.

The historical record suggests the missionary bubble was created in the first place specifically for MKs. Early American missionaries, despite their inexorable assumptions of racial superiority and separation, didn't often have the luxury of a protected, bubble life. They expected their calling to result in a permanent move, and many did die on the mission field. As previously detailed, many left their children in the United States in the care of others once they reached school age. These nineteenth-century missionaries also depended on local communities for survival and success and lived in closer proximity and standard of living to them compared to their modern successors. As Christians responding to a calling, they were willing to make extreme sacrifices.

But as time passed and mission infrastructure grew, it became more feasible to raise children on the mission field, children for whom missionary parents wanted a more comfortable, American lifestyle. And in the mindset of the time, missionary parents were hypervigilant about their children's association with local "heathen" or non-white populations for fear their children would be "corrupted" or form interracial relationships. (I recall some missionary parents' concern for this even in my day.) Historian Joy Schulz demonstrates how American missionaries to the Hawaiian Islands in the late nineteenth century transformed their *modus operandi* in order to provide more American-style lives for their children. They came to reject the mission board's original communally based compensation and demanded individual salaries and permission to buy land in order to provide financial security and inheritance for their children. They also established a boarding school so their children could receive an American education without leaving Hawaii. In Hawaii and elsewhere, the desire to provide an American standard of living and identity for their children and to blunt the influence of local culture was a major impetus for creating mission field bubbles. In the case of Hawaii, many of the MKs stayed and became a permanent political and economic ruling class, not wholly unaffected by Hawaiian culture but not identifying with it either.[2]

Some bubbles are more permeable than others. Dan's experience in Europe was an extreme version; most European MKs experience a bubble with much thinner walls, sometimes barely there, depending on mission board beliefs and practices and parents' preferences. These are majority white, developed countries, well connected to the United States, and MKs there often go to local schools, live at roughly the average socioeconomic level (if not below), have mainly local friends, and learn the language. Missionary culture in Latin America, with its proximity to the United States and heavy Christian influence—Catholic, but increasingly evangelical, too—seems to similarly encourage more cross-cultural experience for MKs. Linguistically, too, Latin America is more accessible for an American than most other regions. Not only is Spanish a more familiar language to an English-speaker from the United States, but its linguistic dominance over a large swath of geography makes it unavoidable and therefore easier to attain. Every Latin American MK I've met speaks fluent Spanish (or Portuguese if they grew up in Brazil). Globally, urbanization is eroding cultural bubbles. Americans can more easily relate to the world's growing urban, educated middle classes, many of whom study and travel abroad, and in the internet era, culture moves at lightning speed.

Another example of a more permeable MK bubble is the experience of the children of Bible translators, who attempt to live deeply immersed in local communities in places starkly different from the United States in order to acquire the cultural expertise that is so intertwined with language. Jenny Hoffman, whose parents were Wycliffe Bible translators in the Philippines, told me her family mimicked the Agta community's grass housing construction so that they could migrate along with them according to environmental dictates. They lived as close to the Agta as possible, although Jenny said, "We had our white privilege things," among them canned tuna and medical evacuation when necessary. But even they couldn't escape some kind of cultural bubble imposed by the Agta themselves, who looked to them for help and as a curiosity. "I spent a lifetime being stared at," Jenny laughed.[3] Another MK whose parents were Bible translators said that although they lived in close proximity to the community, he still felt ambivalent about their higher standard of living. He enjoyed the comforts of their "basic" house—it was "pretty tricked out for the jungle," he said—but also "recognized our possessions as a barrier to friendship." One MK who was raised enmeshed in a local community pushed back strongly at the notion of a bubble. "I didn't have a bubble life," he said. "It [living among local neighbors] was meaningful to me. It's who I am."

The African mission field perhaps represents the ultimate bubble, rooted in the history of missions there and the racial and economic disparities at the heart of that endeavor. For one thing, in the early days of American missions, the African context was objectively the most perilous; missionaries died of disease at an alarming rate until the advent of more modern medicine in the mid-twentieth century. In the racial-religious hierarchy of the white American Christian mind, too, Africa was the most extreme environment, the most racially different, the most foreign and exotic, the most "heathen," according to scholar Kathryn Gin Lum.[4] White missionaries often established segregated "beachheads" of sorts: insular mission stations from which they interacted with surrounding communities and which sometimes took in converts rejected by their communities. In more recent times, economic hardship and political instability continue to drive stark separation between most missionaries and local communities in Africa. Even in remote locations, missionaries almost always have far nicer homes, far more security, and a far better standard of living than their indigenous neighbors. One childhood friend who went on to become a missionary in a dangerous location in Africa, with his young children, told me they did not leave their home without a full contingent of bodyguards. (This made me wonder what exactly he was doing there—other than probably traumatizing his children—as I can't imagine the presence of armed men is terribly conducive to ministry of any kind. Certainly, it's not conducive to relationship.)

Most MKs with whom I spoke and whom I surveyed reported a wide chasm between their families and local communities. Some initially painted a picture of mutual relationship, true friendship, and authentic community. But over time, as I listened, their responses to questions about where they lived and with whom they ate meals, played, and socialized—as opposed to ministry—generally told a different story. When they think of missionaries, American Christians probably imagine sacrifice, scarcity, and life in the mud huts I've been so frequently asked about as an MK. And, as we've seen, that is one form of missionary life. But the reality is that, despite inconveniences and dangers in some cases, most missionary families enjoy what is in some respects a higher standard of living than they would attain in the United States. (I, for one, certainly miss having a household staff.) Several MKs who responded to my survey and with whom I spoke were contemptuous about this feature of missions, regardless of how they themselves may have benefited from it as children. One respondent, who had also worked as an adult in ministry overseas, wrote, "There are missionaries here who live in houses that are excessively high rent . . . and spend most of their days going to yoga, working out, having coffee, and calling it 'building relationships with locals.' Thousands of dollars are going to support a no-work lifestyle overseas."

* * *

My own childhood was as utterly bubble-wrapped as the china my parents inexplicably hauled over to Kenya. True, we were more privileged than most missionaries. My dad had retired after twenty years in the military, and, in addition to his pension, we got a US-government-funded move to anywhere in the world. So my parents, perhaps foolishly, decided to bring every last thing they owned to the mission field (as well as cream-colored sofas that didn't stay that shade for long). Our house was decorated with carpets and fine furniture and a piano and silver tea sets.

Now, the structure of the house itself was not up to American building codes. My sister's room had a massive, 360-degree, ceiling-to-wall-to-floor crack through which you could see daylight. We sometimes didn't have electricity or enough water pressure for a good shower. And we had no television, movies, extended family, roller rinks, shopping malls, or junk food. We somehow eked out an existence with only two or three kinds of breakfast cereal. My social circle was small, and my activities were extremely limited. But most of the time, I lived comfortably and stayed put in my own little, slightly shoddy reproduction of America. Most of my interactions were with other Americans, or Westerners at least, usually other missionaries and their kids, or middle and upper-class Kenyans, who largely took on a Western lifestyle and spoke perfect English.

My experience appears to be typical. In my survey, 80 percent of respondents said they lived at a much higher (45 percent) or slightly higher (35 percent) standard of living than the local community. As it does here in the United States or anywhere, socioeconomic distance, which often overlays with race, education, and culture, creates barriers in forming truly equal, mutual relationships. A plurality (42 percent) reported that their families primarily socialized with other missionaries or expatriates, and only 26 precent of MKs said their own friends were primarily locals. The vast majority (70 percent) of the respondents, who did not socialize much with local children at all, said they had no opportunity to do so.

My conversations about many missionaries' separation from local communities varied somewhat, and it seemed to dawn on some of my interlocutors for the very first time that they indeed knew very little about the people and culture of what they likely claim as their home country. Upon hearing where they were raised, I'd mention something about the history, current events, or political trends there, and they'd often have no clue as to what I was talking about. One MK I interviewed admitted he knew nothing about the country's politics, despite having attended school with one of the president's children.

Most of my subjects, however, claimed a keen awareness even as children of, if not the bubble per se, the wide separation between their lives and those of most everyone around them. Multiple MKs told me they witnessed or overheard outright bigotry within the missionary community toward local people and cultures. Most talked about the economic disparities, of feeling guilty or uncomfortable about their higher standard of living, while also feeling grateful and relieved.[5] The word "awkward" came up frequently in my conversations about the relationships between missionary families and locals. "Sometimes I wished I could give all my possessions away," one MK said. For some, the level of poverty and hardship around them shook their faith at a young age. "I read in the Bible about Jesus cleansing the lepers," one MK told me, "but I actually saw lepers; what about them?" The more bubble-aware MKs all voiced deep regret about the missed opportunities to learn, to form cross-cultural friendships, and to broaden their horizons, and they expressed contrition for their own childhood choices and proclivities that reinforced contextual factors—factors over which they had had little control.

One of the epiphanies I had in interviewing MKs was realizing that the bubble was far more extreme for MK girls than it was for boys.[6] I always had a sense of this as a child; the MK boys just seemed more "African"—more "authentic," somehow, than the girls did. They were more likely to speak local languages and have local friends. I was jealous of them—not really of the act of leaving the bubble, where I was quite content to stay, but of the results of doing so. I wanted the "street cred" without the discomfort of the streets. But regardless of our own desires, we girls were kept cloistered away in our towers, safe from the local men, who, it was assumed—correctly, in some contexts—had less respect for women and girls and more entitlement over women's bodies. (Of course, this "protection" is sadly ironic, given the abuse of some MK girls by missionaries themselves.) As a high schooler, I spent a day wandering around Nairobi with a friend while being stalked and then chased, at breakneck speed, by two men. In addition, we girls had fewer opportunities to make friends with local girls, who in many cultures have no time for play amid a heavy load of household chores from a young age. In highly traditional societies, many of the girls would already be married off by age sixteen. So, while MK boys told me stories of exploring the woods or helping herd cattle with local cohorts, picking up language as easily as if it were wildflowers in open fields, we girls played inside, alone, in English, with our sisters or other MK friends. One female MK from Africa remembered how her brother would go roaming around town with other boys while she "sat in the house and tried to pass the time."

* * *

Regardless of how segregated, or not, missionary families are from the local context, MKs are almost always at some point herded into their own corral, especially for school. The vast majority of respondents in my survey (75 percent) reported attending a mission-run boarding or day school at some point in their schooling; another 46 percent spent at least some of their education at international schools (which, in my experience, are usually dominated by American culture). Some 38 percent were homeschooled for at least some schooling; and only 24 percent reported ever attending a local school, even for a short time (and this included the western European contingent). For MKs, school is almost always an American cultural enclave, and usually a highly evangelical one, and the major source of the bubble experience. As in the case of nineteenth-century Hawaiian missionaries, this is by design. While overtly racist concerns are (hopefully) not factors for missionary parents anymore, the need to acculturate, educate, and socialize—and, it must be said, spiritually inoculate—MKs for a future life in America is a conscious aim. Many MKs described having "two lives": a highly segregated one at school and one at home where they had slightly more contact with locals.

Mission-run boarding schools are a next-level bubble, like one of those Zorbing things in which you roll down hills. You could roll through fire and over a cliff in one of those things, and you wouldn't even know it, so impervious is it to the outside world. One MK from Latin America I interviewed told me they literally greeted new students to their mission-run school by saying, "Welcome to the Bubble!" Although the student body at such schools is somewhat diverse, including citizens of the host country, most of the students and staff are usually American evangelicals. Because students live there full time, the bubble is institutionalized both culturally and religiously. You eat, breathe, sleep, learn, and play in it. You get white American evangelical Christianity dished up to you more often than actual food and in various forms—as history, as sex ed, as science, as literature, as Bible class, as entertainment, in daily chapels, in dorm devotions, in school. Some of these schools, like Faith Academy in the Philippines, are in urban areas and include a mix of day students and boarders. Students come and go from campus more freely and have more opportunities for diverse experiences. Nonetheless, the Faith alumni with whom I spoke strongly related to a bubble experience in which they learned little about the country or region, didn't necessarily learn the language, and were exposed to few ideas beyond a narrow slice of white American evangelicalism.

My own school, RVA, is probably the world's most extreme missionary bubble. It was founded as such, complete with a former American president (Teddy Roosevelt) laying the cornerstone in 1909. From that foundation grew an American-style enclave in the middle of East Africa. All these years later, it remains. Although it's only about an hour's drive from Nairobi, it feels like another planet, complete with a breathtaking, almost ethereal setting overlooking the Rift Valley. You take a tiny, once-dirt road off the main highway along the top of the escarpment and wind your way down through forests to reach it. The entire small town there, Kijabe, is in fact one big Africa Inland Mission (AIM) station, including a hospital, a seminary and high school for Kenyans, and the headquarters of the Africa Inland Church (AIC), which has been wholly independent from AIM since 1971. Kijabe is still so controlled by the church and mission that you can't buy alcohol there.[7]

And then there is RVA, which is largely segregated from the rest of Kijabe Town, apart from monthly joint church services at AIC and occasional runs by RVA students and staff to a small row of shops. Since the US embassy bombing in 1998, RVA has a high security fence all the way around it, staffed by guards in guard stations, making physical what has always been metaphorical. Kids come from all over the continent and even the Middle East to attend. Although they represent over twenty nationalities—including members of the Kenyan elite—most are American, as are most faculty, and its culture is definitely white, evangelical, and American. Its curriculum is American too, rigorously preparing students for college in the United States, where most graduates end up. This was not something I thought much about while there. I just took for granted that RVA culture was mainly mine and assumed everyone else found a place in it as well.

But as I entered adulthood and studied history, and then began researching this book and participating in alumni discussions on social media, I realized just how much of a white American evangelical bubble RVA was, and still is, despite some attempts at change. As an adult, I finally studied African history, which made me realize I knew practically nothing about Kenyan history. There was no African history course of any kind offered at RVA when I was there. There was no African literature or in-depth look at culture. Swahili was offered (I took French instead), but like all classes at RVA, it was taught by missionaries, albeit quite fluent ones. Kenyan staff did all the menial labor, and I cringe to remember how little I registered their presence or service, as if they were part of the scenery rather than real people worth knowing and from whom I might learn. During my senior year, Kenya had its first multiparty election, but other than concerns about violence, I scarcely understood the political context or its background. These days, RVA has integrated some Kenyan history, politics, and culture into other classes and has made some attempt to hire African teachers (as of this writing, there is one). But it is precious little for a school that owes its existence to Africa.

The experience of non-American alumni is telling, and while the majority with whom I've spoken had an overall positive experience, many say they felt like outsiders. A few of the non-white alumni say they endured overt racism, either while a student there or within alumni circles since then. But mostly they have described obliviousness, thoughtlessness, ignorance, and the manifestation of a dominant cultural claim, which I imagine must have been particularly unsettling for Kenyan students to experience in their own country. A 2019 culture audit commissioned by RVA concluded that "RVA's culture is defined, in part, by passive conflict and division between the majority and minority students on campus, although many members of the dominant majority population, adult and student, seem unaware and lack understanding of the ethnic and racial issues. Substantial discomfort and hurt is evident among minority students, coupled with perceived discrimination against them and favoritism among the adults for their American classmates."[8]

The non-Americans I interviewed reflected various facets of this discomfort. A Malagasy alumnus, whose parents were missionaries in Cameroon, noted that he didn't feel the divide between his missionary family and the local population in Cameroon, but that changed at RVA. "I felt poor," he said, compared to other students, and he felt uncomfortable about the chasm between the RVA students and faculty and the Kenyan staff. A Korean alumnus, one of an increasing number as Korea has become a major missionary-sending country, said he felt denigrated and sometimes mocked because he didn't conform to white American evangelical notions of masculinity that emphasized athletics and a love of the outdoors. One missionary teacher told him he wasn't "MK enough," because

MK boys played sports and did adventurous things. A Dutch alumnus and a Mexican alumnus, both of whose parents served with mainline Protestant missions, felt their faith did not meet the RVA definition of Christianity and resented implications or even explicit declarations that their parents or extended families were not saved. One of them told me she still "code switches" when at RVA gatherings, using certain words and phrases to signal she is actually a Christian.

The religious nature of the mission field bubble means that MKs (and their parents) are also strangely and more generally sheltered, certainly from secular American culture, and myopic for people with such global experience. Some MKs who went on to attend non-evangelical colleges said the transition to a secular environment was more jarring than any other aspect of their reentry to American life. Particularly as American-style evangelicalism has spread around the world, the mission field has become an extension—and perhaps a more extreme version, as it's easier to control contact with American culture—of an isolated white evangelical subculture within the United States. MK schools and homeschools use much of the same curriculum as American homeschoolers and Christian schools in the United States, and many MKs go to evangelical colleges after leaving the mission field (I attended a Southern Baptist college). Particularly if they then return to the mission field in short order, MKs may never encounter or get an accurate understanding of American culture as a whole.

The mission field can reinforce the religious bubble of white evangelicalism rather than expose it to the wider aperture such an experience might otherwise offer.

* * *

One of the questions I always ask MKs—one that has been asked of me many times in my life—is: "Do you speak the language?"[9]

My own answer used to be no, and that's the answer I get from many MKs, particularly women, and particularly those raised in Africa and South and Southeast Asia. In these regions the bubble is perhaps most impenetrable, and the multiplicity of languages, colonial pasts, and present-day economic opportunities mean English is widely spoken.

When I ask the question of those who didn't acquire a language, I see a painfully familiar feeling flash across their faces. It's more than casual regret about a missed opportunity or wistfulness over a path not taken. Some of them go on to name it explicitly, but they don't need to. I know it all too well.

It's shame.

In questions of identity, language is a tell. You can't be a member of a tribe if you don't speak its language. When I told people I was from Kenya but then admitted I never learned Swahili, I was caught in a humiliating lie. I was exposed as a fraud.

I said I was from Kenya because I wanted to be, because that is where I left my heart and that is where I knew who I was. I certainly didn't want to be a "regular" American. The more I identified as such, the more of my past and sense of self I felt slipping away.

But the fact remains: I am not from Kenya, and I never was.

My home is a bubble that burst long ago. My tribe is a diaspora of ghosts. I'm from a moment in time, a land of make-believe. I was raised in a slap-dash culture, a made-up country.

There is grief in being from a bubble. There is disconnection. I believe the bubble life is a big part of the enormous challenge that almost all MKs experience when they return to the United

States. Like an immigrant, they miss home. Unlike an immigrant, it's not obvious where that is. Nor does it become obvious once you get to know an MK. There is grief. But there is indeed shame, too. I mean, who do you think you are? An MK from Spain, whose nickname at his Spanish school was "Hamburger," told me he wanted to be Spanish so badly growing up. But he eventually decided that was a "childhood fantasy. . . . Becoming an adult is becoming American."

Mekdes Haddis, an Ethiopian American author and advocate for more equitable missions, recalls meeting an MK from Ethiopia in college at Liberty University. She started speaking to the young man in Amharic. He had no idea what she was saying. She tried to connect with him in other ways but felt confused. "How is that possible?" she thought to herself, assuming anyone who grew up in Ethiopia would speak its most widely used language.[10]

As an adult in the Washington, DC, area, where I still live, I had the opportunity over a decade ago to begin Swahili lessons. I jumped at the chance. Long story short, I am now pretty fluent, at least in speaking. I'm not that great at listening in any language, as I far prefer to hear myself talk, and I continue to work on that in both English and Swahili. I have used Swahili sometimes in my professional life, but I expend far more effort on it than any professional use would warrant. Mostly, I do it for the love. For the joy. For the connection to a time and a place and a part of myself I can't let go. And for the more authentic connections it offers when I travel back to East Africa or encounter Swahili speakers here in the States—the types of connections I didn't make much as a child.

I still know that I am not Kenyan. I no longer say I am "from" Kenya; I say I was raised there. It's up to real Kenyans whether or not they want to claim me. But at least I have made an effort. At least it's something.

* * *

My point here is not to argue for or against the mission field bubble or to say there is an ideal way of living overseas as missionaries. As a child, I loved my bubble-girl life and hated leaving it for any length of time. It kept me mostly safe and warm, even while it may have robbed me of a more authentic identity and rooted my sense of self in an entirely too specific context. But honestly, I was never going to truly belong in Kenya, and the grief and alienation of leaving was inevitable.

Some MKs who grew up in less bubble-wrapped environments cherished closer cross-cultural relationships, although they still experienced the frustration of being an object of curiosity and deference. But others had more traumatic experiences, as we have already seen. MKs who grew up in such contexts have told me about seeing domestic abuse, child rape, and violence of other kinds that can coexist with poverty and social instability. They have told me about contracting disease and being robbed and bullied by other children. And the transitions in and out of those contexts are difficult in other ways. MKs like these may have less regret and shame and more cultural knowledge, but they still experience the loss, and often trauma, too.

The bubble is probably unavoidable. It results from and perpetuates the power and privilege structures that are inherent in American missions. It also challenges claims of—and constrains—progress toward a multicultural vision for the global church.

And the bubble replicates what exists in modern human society writ large. The mission field is often a pretty extreme bubble experience. But in fact we all live in our bubbles. Haddis points out that modern life, with its acute economic stratification and urban planning, has created separation that did not exist in earlier times and discourages forming community across these boundaries.[11] We who struggle to form mutual, equal relationships over the noxious hierarchies of race, class, education, politics, nationality, religion, gender, and many more categories can feel as if we are trying to embrace each other while wearing sumo wrestler costumes.

I don't know how to overcome these differences, either here or there. But I do know that it starts with awareness of their existence. It starts with honest introspection and conversation. It starts by seeing the costumes. And then it continues with deliberate confrontation of the underlying structures themselves, which is at least as painstaking and arduous as learning a whole new language.

Last, I will say that the broader cultural-religious bubble American evangelicals have created for themselves both at home and abroad is less the result of stubborn economic and educational disparities than a deliberate choice, made in fear for theirs or their children's "corruption." (I have sometimes wondered if evangelical missionaries have purposefully fled the United States to escape a perceived threat from American culture.) More and more evangelical families send their kids to Christian schools or homeschool them, in addition to exclusively consuming an array of evangelical products, including movies, television, books, music, and even insurance and banking services. I know many evangelicals who have no close non-evangelical friends. (I didn't have any before I went to graduate school at a secular institution.) And in my view, this fear-based self-segregation is as anti-gospel a phenomenon as I can imagine. Jesus clearly engaged in culture and with all kinds of people, risking his own "purity" and comfort and bending rules here and there to do so.

But his modern-day American followers have bubble-wrapped themselves so tightly, it strangles their relationships with those outside their world and chokes off their access to external oxygen. And they lose their ability to think critically about themselves or access information that challenges their worldview. Instead, they rely on their own air supply, recycling it over and over, inhaling only what others of their insular communities exhale.

5

The Great (Race) Escape

Marcus describes himself as "a Black kid from Philly."

Who grew up in a mostly white world.

In Africa.

His physician father felt called to medical missions. So, they moved to Kenya to work in a mission-run hospital in 1990, when Marcus was seven. At their first large mission gathering, they were the only Black family. They were the only Black American family in most every context.

As a kid, he recalls how his family straddled the lines between Black Kenyans and white missionaries. Marcus noticed things that nobody else seemed to notice and experienced things as strange that others in the missionary community apparently considered normal. There was the time a jewelry store security guard stopped and questioned him, something that would never happen to a white American. Many of the other missionaries rarely had Kenyans in their homes except to clean. Many of the MKs didn't play with local children. Their parents would voice concerns about Kenyans stealing from them or not performing work correctly. A missionary apologized to Marcus's family for their dog barking at them because the dog "always barks at Black people." One missionary wouldn't let his daughter date a Kenyan boy. Then there was the white missionary teacher who made the assertion that all American Christians were Republicans. "*My* parents aren't," Marcus informed the teacher.

Marcus attended RVA, and he thought it was odd that there were no Kenyan teachers. He didn't know how to respond when one of his teachers told the class about once performing in a minstrel show. He learned nothing about Black history or experience on either side of the Atlantic. He got in trouble for using the "n-word" while quoting banned rap lyrics, but other students and even some teachers commonly used the word "wog," which is basically the British version of it.[1]

He didn't hang out much with the handful of Kenyan students, however. "They treated me like an American," he says. Unlike the vast majority of MKs, Marcus enjoyed going on furlough, back to Philadelphia. "I got to be with other Black Americans," he recalled. But sometimes they told him he "sounded white."

Marcus made a lot of friends and generally had a good experience in Kenya. He doesn't think the people acting in racially insensitive ways in his missionary community were malicious; they were just clueless, the product of living so disconnected from and unaware of broader cultural and historical patterns. Missionary culture didn't seem to think it needed to be connected to or informed by much outside of itself. Many missionaries, like many white evangelicals, believe they are "color-blind" and think that's a good thing. Many of the ones on the mission field have scarcely lived outside that airtight world.

"Missionaries are like second and third generation now," Marcus observes. "There just needs to be more diversity."

Then he says with a sly grin, "Missionaries are like cow manure. Spread them out, they can do some good. But pile them up, and they stink up the place."

* * *

In my understanding of race in either an American or African context, I was the typical MK by whom Marcus was surrounded: completely oblivious. I had a vague sense of the past—colonialism, slavery, Jim Crow—but I had little appreciation for how it shapes present realities, including the inherent biases and subtle prejudices of good white people like myself. Certainly, I would have dismissed out of hand the suggestion that there might be any connection between the racial past and the current forms and mindsets behind American missions. It never dawned on me how bizarre it was that, although I went to school in Africa, I didn't have a single lesson involving African history, literature, or deeper-than-surface-level culture. I never considered why almost all the American missionaries I knew were white. I had no real sense of what the Black experience was back in America, or why it might be easier for white Americans to engage with race far away from home, well beyond their cultural context and inheritance.

When I returned to the United States, the latter point began to sink in, but not in a convicting way at first. I went to a predominantly white evangelical college, so I didn't know many Black Americans, but what I saw of them on TV and in pop culture mystified and frustrated me. For one thing, it was the early 1990s, and there was a resurgence of interest in all things

Africa among Black Americans. There were movies and T-shirts and Kwanzaa celebrations. And I am not proud to admit that this grated on me. From what I could tell, few Black Americans seemed to know anything about Africa. They couldn't name individual countries. They didn't realize Kwanzaa wasn't celebrated there at all. I didn't like their claim to Africa (MY Africa!), where I had grown up and where I left my heart. Of course, never mind that my own claim, even on my own terms, was pretty shallow, especially given the bubble version of it that I had made little effort to escape.

I also resented their "complaints" about racism. In contrast to the deprivation and lack of opportunities Africans faced, I felt Black Americans had an embarrassment of riches and choice. I couldn't understand why more couldn't seize them, why they preferred to "whine" about the past. And why they preferred to point fingers at white people like me—me! The child of missionaries in Africa! How dare they! These Black people weren't deferential like the Kenyans I had known. They didn't reflect back to me the image I wanted to have of myself—a good-hearted white person with superior skills, knowledge, and resources I could share with them if only they would accept my help.

At this point, I had very little concept of Black American history. I had studied American history, of course. But the version I came away with—and I'm not sure if I got it primarily from the white evangelical missionary school I attended, from my family, or from random bits of American popular culture that happened to make their way across the Atlantic—portrayed slavery and segregation as an unfortunate "chapter" in American history that had been fully and successfully cleaned up, leaving behind no residue. The version of slavery I got was pretty sanitized, a *Gone with the Wind* story, in which Mammies were part of the family and enslaved people loved and dutifully served their white enslavers.

It wasn't until I went to graduate school in American history that I finally understood the long shadow slavery and racism has cast and the devastating cultural, political, economic, religious, psychological, and generational trauma it has left behind. I began to learn the truth of the Black experience in America, how inequalities have seeped deeply into laws and norms and mindsets, Black and white. More broadly, I learned just how slow and hard change can be. I also studied African history and learned about the damage that colonialism left, similar in character to American forms of racial oppressions and exploitation. I could see a direct line from that history to all the red carpets rolled out for my family and for myself. I began to be grieved by what lived in my own heart—the bigotry, the condescension, the sense of superiority. I saw the lack of compassion, education, empathy, and understanding that fueled it. And I regretted that, as a child, I had made so little room in my heart and mind for the Africans I had encountered as people of equal talent, worth, and complexity.

I now know better, and I try to do better. This book is part of my repentance.

* * *

To understand both why a Black American MK could be so rare in Africa and how a white MK raised there could end up with such an obtuse, myopic mindset, we need to take a deeper look at the racial history of American missions. How and why missions became such an overwhelmingly white enterprise speaks to the centrality of racial identity in white evangelicalism more broadly and how it has shaped so many of that culture's beliefs and practices.

There were some Black American missionaries from the beginning. The digital archives of the Southern Baptists' IMB includes an entire "African American Heritage" section, documenting the history of its Black missionaries to Liberia and Sierra Leone in the nineteenth century.[2] An IMB-published history of the organization devotes a chapter to these early missionaries, including George Liele, whom the IMB hails as the first Baptist missionary from the United States to go overseas.

It's ironic—to put it mildly—that a mission board that began specifically to defend slavery well after Liele's work as a missionary ended now lays claim to his legacy. After securing his freedom from slavery, Liele went to Jamaica in 1783 to spread the gospel among people who were enslaved there. British authorities in Jamaica later jailed him because of fears he would foment a slave rebellion.[3]

What the Southern Baptist rendering of Liele and other Black missionaries does not detail are the discrimination and institutional barriers Black Christians have long confronted in the missions world. In the antebellum period, mission boards were keen to send Blacks to Africa in particular, as white people erroneously presumed them to be better suited to surviving the harsh environment and African diseases (in fact, they died at rates similar to white missionaries).[4]

In addition—the IMB literature I've read omits this part—sending Black Americans to Africa as missionaries was part of a larger antebellum movement to solve the "race problem" and preserve slavery and the racial order through the colonization of free Blacks—that is, to remove them from the United States altogether. In *The Color of Compromise,* historian Jemar Tisby quotes American Colonization Society founder Robert Finley, a white Presbyterian minister, explaining his organization's rationale: "Could [free Blacks] be sent to Africa . . . we should be cleared of them; we should send to Africa a population partially civilized and christianized for its benefits; our blacks themselves would be put in better condition."[5]

In the post–Civil War context, when missions gained prestige and professionalism, Black Christians found it difficult to access missionary opportunities and meet the higher educational and other requirements white-run mission boards mandated.[6] Mission boards, for example, questioned the quality of degrees from Black colleges.[7] Black churches and institutions, which grew rapidly after the Civil War as a result of exclusion and discrimination, lacked the resources of their white counterparts and were overwhelmed by the needs of their communities at home in the aftermath of slavery.

When they did go out as missionaries, Black Americans faced discrimination from white missionaries, mission boards, and colonial governments. They were shut out of leadership roles and given more menial positions, their accomplishments were overlooked or diminished, and their theological views were scrutinized.[8] Black missionaries, like Black Christians in general at the time, connected Christian faith to Black uplift and liberation in the United States and around the world, but they often had to curtail or quiet their activities and connections to civil rights or nationalist movements for fear white mission boards or colonial governments would shut down their work.[9]

Marcus was the only child of Black American missionaries I interviewed. I've personally known very few. Only 1 percent of American evangelical missionaries are Black.[10] It's not for lack of Black religious devotion; Christian belief and church attendance among Black Americans is significantly higher than that of white Americans, according to Pew survey data.[11] The structural barriers to Black participation in missions remain, with Black Christians having access to fewer resources. And their theology is still questioned by white power structures. Historian Jesse Curtis details how white evangelicals continue to use the "ownership of the gospel" to maintain their control. "No matter how many failures, somehow evangelicals (in their own self-conception) are the ones who 'get the gospel right,'" he told me.[12] Certainly I grew up hearing in evangelical settings that many Black American Christians weren't "real" Christians, as demonstrated by their voting for Democrats and, as I was told anyway, their lesser concern for sexual morality.

"The Black church in America has been forced to stay," writes Ethiopian American author Mekdes Haddis, "[Yet] many in missiology culture . . . shift the blame to Black pastors and leaders, and their inability to inspire their congregation to go."[13] She calls white evangelical churches and mission boards' near frantic attempts these days to correct the racial disparities in their ranks "a romanticizing of the Black missionary" that seeks to maintain relevance while avoiding deeper change.[14]

The history and current state of Black missions can't be understood without a broader awareness of how missions have served white American Christians' racial identity and avoidance of their complicity with slavery and racism. Consider the beginning of the IMB, which is now the largest mission board in history, in 1845. Northern and Southern Baptists had been coexisting somewhat uncomfortably within a coalition called the Triennial Convention that was formed in 1814 in support of a shared, grand goal of foreign missions. They managed to mostly avoid the issue of slavery until 1833, when Britain outlawed it. British Baptists, with whom Americans coordinated on missions, lobbied the Convention to do the same. The Convention, wanting to circumvent the issue of slavery altogether, responded with what was essentially nervous laughter and eventually a "neutrality" resolution in 1841.

But over the next several years, tensions mounted over slavery, and eventually southerners selected two slaveholders as prospective missionaries specifically to test the Convention's tolerance. Their applications were designed to force the Convention to take a definitive stance that would declare enslavers fit for the high calling of missionary work.

When the Convention, recognizing the effort for what it was—a trap—refused their applications, the southerners walked out, not because the Convention had called slavery bad per se, but because it wouldn't call it good. Nonetheless, the newly formed Southern Baptist Convention, and its mission board, maintained that the new organization's purpose was *not* to defend slavery but to pursue "the extension of the Messiah's kingdom."[15] And if you believe that, I have an igloo in Miami I would like to unload.

The Southern Baptist origin story is emblematic of the cultural role missions has fulfilled for white evangelicals ever since. Applying psychologist Dave Verhaagen's framing and terminology, missions have functioned as a "spiritual bypass," which is the use of religious belief to head off unpleasant experiences, truths, or emotions—such as the deep shame of slavery and racism—that threaten an individual's or culture's self-image. White American Christians have thrown themselves into evangelism and humanitarianism among non-white people overseas, while trying to avoid the less heroic task of confronting their own responsibility for and complicity in the United States' horrific racial past. Missions have long allowed them "to construct an image of themselves through a particular image of others," in the words of scholar Melani McAlister.[16]

The self-image white American Christians strongly prefer is one of godly ministers to grateful, often compliant people of color at a safe distance. And more broadly, white evangelicals like to think of themselves as the most theologically and doctrinally correct of all Christians. Wading into the costly, arduous work of racial reconciliation and justice with people of color at home, who aren't letting them off the hook, might force them to reckon with the truth that the white evangelical tradition has been repeatedly and grievously wrong at every single turn on issues of race (and possibly on other matters of consequence as well).

Even contemporaneous critics in the early days of the American missions movement pointed out the irony of their positioning. It's hard to imagine now, because missions have become so integral to Southern Baptist identity, but in fact the missionary enterprise was controversial among American Baptists in the early part of their history. While critics most often argued that mission boards violated Baptists' congregationalist and religious liberty principles, anti-missionary Baptist Daniel Parker, who was a virulent racist, nonetheless commented in 1820 on the oddness of men who made their money off of African labor "throw[ing] in liberally to the support of missions."[17]

Not surprisingly, Black Americans also identified this hypocrisy. For example, Frederick Douglass, in the context of slaveholding Christianity more generally, implied that support for missions gave white southern Christians greater moral license for cruelty. "We have men-stealers for ministers, women-whippers for missionaries, and cradle-plunderers for church members. . . .

We have men sold to build churches, women sold to support the gospel, and babes sold to purchase Bibles for the *poor heathen! all for the glory of God and the good of souls!*" Douglass wrote in the appendix of his 1845 autobiography.[18]

During the nineteenth century, missions became rooted in dueling theological and ideological impulses that divided roughly at the Mason Dixon line. In northern evangelicalism, the missionary impulse—along with a flurry of other reform initiatives, including abolition—grew out of an optimistic belief that it was not only possible but imperative to perfect human society in order to lay the groundwork for Christ's return. Southern evangelicals were also influenced by this idea, but its implications were more perilous for a society built on slavery. So southern Christianity evolved toward an emphasis on personal piety, individual conversion, and obedience to (white male) authority, and it assumed a more pessimistic, defensive posture toward a chaotic, constantly changing world. Whereas northerners emphasized saving souls as a way to remake society and hasten Christ's millennium, for southern Christianity—the basis for modern-day white evangelicalism as a whole—making converts through missions, starting with their own slaves, helped safeguard social order.

But after the Civil War, with evangelicals both North and South yearning for reconciliation and confronting new modernist challenges to biblicism, these dividing lines scrambled for a time in American Christianity and in missions. In the latter arena, the eventual modernists evolved toward prioritizing humanitarian work, while traditionalists (eventual fundamentalists) adopted a more southern style of belief and evangelism that focused on individual conversion. In both cases, missions became a replacement for, rather than an expression of, a reform impulse that might have included a push for greater racial equality.[19]

That had implications for America's racial reckoning—or, rather, its lack thereof. Although Southern Baptists never reunified with their northern counterparts, most divided American denominations did, and missions in general took on a new energy and professionalism in the context of expanding American empire, trade, and big business. Missions were a very, very big deal in the late nineteenth and early twentieth centuries, so much so that multiple American presidents addressed missions conferences.[20]

Again, one can't help but notice the glaring, well, *weirdness* of the timing here. This tremendous effort and enthusiasm for foreign missions occurred at the very same time that millions of freed slaves were trying to find family members who had been sold away, secure education and jobs, form community institutions, and build new lives out of nothing. This was also at the same time that Native Americans were being violently divested of the remainder of their land. And, at the same time, anti-immigrant fervor was gaining steam in the context of new, non-Christian, non-European sources of immigration.

In fact, these populations were the target of many missionary efforts by American Protestants at the time, but their concern was rooted in paternalism and social control, not in respect for or identification with them as equals or in a broader movement toward their liberation and inclusion. White American Christians could not even muster the courage to speak out against the horrific racial violence that took place during this period. In a 1904 essay, Black activist Mary Church Terrell lambasted white Christians' tolerance of their own "barbarism" while "thousands of dollars are raised by our churches every year to send missionaries to Christianize the heathen in foreign lands."[21] And consider the absolute absurdity of the General Association of Congregational Churches in California passing a resolution to restrict Chinese immigration, essentially because the Great Commission instructed missionaries to "go" instead of stay, and because "a heathen nation can be . . . transformed only while . . . living in their natural surroundings."[22]

For Southern Baptists, foreign missions were boosted in some cases by an explicit desire to recreate the culture and lifestyle of the slaveholding South. Historian João Chaves documents how former Confederates-turned-Southern Baptist missionaries after the Civil War were drawn to Brazil, where slavery was still legal, and worked to replicate southern culture there, sometimes even owning slaves themselves. One missionary actively recruited other "heartbroken Southerners" to go as missionaries to Brazil after the war by noting the parallel racial structures between it and the old South. Missionary letters and other writings lauded the virtues of the old South and made explicit racial appeals about "join[ing] with the Anglo-Saxon race," which also sat atop the Brazilian racial hierarchy, to "take the world for Christ."[23]

Foreign missions were a far safer and more satisfying way for Americans to engage with race than confronting the fallout from slavery and the growing diversity of American society. For American churchgoers sitting comfortably in the pews, supporting missions didn't cost them much (it cost the missionaries themselves—and their children—dearly, sometimes their lives, during this period). But the mission enterprise contained no such dangerous implications for American life. It happened "over there," far from sight, in a cultural context that seemed to prove white American Christian superiority rather than pointing out its moral failings. And it was something all white Americans, north and south—and even to a degree, Black American

Christians, who also believed that foreign "heathens" needed to be saved—could agree on.

* * *

After World War II, American missions emerged from the devastation of two wars and the Great Depression. In the postwar context, America's new geopolitical power and revolutions in mass communication and international transportation supercharged missionary efforts. Missions had also weathered the climax of the theological battles between fundamentalists and modernists that began in the late nineteenth century, when new scientific theories and more rigorous, scholarly scrutiny of biblical texts challenged evangelicals' literalist interpretation of scripture. The skirmishes between liberals and conservatives all but ended on the mission field after World War II as liberals, conflicted over the mingling of missions with colonialism, began ceding the ground to evangelicals. While in the 1930s, only one of seven American missionaries was a fundamentalist, by the early 1950s, the proportion had doubled. Mainline denominations, which tend to be more liberal, gradually stopped sending missionaries overseas in favor of supporting local, indigenous churches and branches of their organizations or engaging in humanitarian activities and relief and development efforts. I can count on one hand the number of mainline or liberal American missionaries I encountered overseas.[24]

The civil rights movement at home and independence movements around the world made the hypocrisy of American missions more obvious. More progressive evangelicals and many missionaries themselves advocated for civil rights by using such arguments, appealing to white evangelicals' support for foreign missions in hopes of eroding their widespread opposition to greater racial equality at home. African Christians, too, highlighted the outrageousness of American racism. In 1955, the Nigerian Baptist Convention issued a statement to its American counterparts condemning racism and identifying with Black Americans. Some churches on the continent refused to accept missionaries from American churches that practiced segregation, and after independence, some African governments threatened to bar American missionaries.[25]

But white evangelicals retained a striking ability to geographically compartmentalize on the issue of race. Southern Baptist seminary professor Thomas Bufford Matson, who argued that racial discrimination at home harmed overseas missions, articulated white evangelicals' preference for missions over national reform, writing in 1947, "It is comparatively easy to be radical when one does not have to face the real problem or results of his radicalism."[26] In other words, missions allowed white evangelicals to act out a kind of racial enlightenment in a way that didn't impact their own lives. A newly appointed Southern Baptist missionary in the 1950s admitted she had wanted to stay in the South to fight for civil rights, but her parents would have been "disgraced." But her mother was "proud of me now going to Africa as a missionary."[27] Psychologist Dave Verhaagen recalls the strangeness of "missions week," during which students were encouraged to go to Africa to spread the gospel, at his all-white Christian school in the 1970s. His school was one of a wave of such schools founded in the wake of school desegregation that "actively shelter[ed] us from Black people in our own hometown."[28]

It's equally instructive that the color line in some American evangelical institutions was broken by Africans, not African

Americans. In 1962, Ouachita Baptist College in Arkansas formally adopted a policy of admitting African converts from the mission field but not African Americans. Based on that precedent, Harris Mobley, a Southern Baptist missionary in Ghana, and Sam Oni, a Ghanaian Baptist convert, decided to challenge segregation at Mercer University, a Baptist institution in Georgia, by submitting Oni's application. A missionary supporter urged Mercer to accept Oni based on the Ouachita example and said it would "not signify a change in our tradition, but it will mean a slight change in our hearts!"[29] He stated separately that not admitting Oni would prove that "we are in greater need of missionary preaching than Ghana."[30] Finally, in the wake of Oni's application, Mercer dropped all racial barriers to admission.

In the post–civil rights era, white evangelicalism and its missions enterprise confronted its defeat in law and in culture on the issue of race and moved to incorporate, at least on the surface, new standards of racial equality. In the missions world, there was more emphasis on cultural sensitivity and training and greater flexibility on "non-essential" cultural matters so as to adapt the gospel to other cultures. There was more discussion of "partnerships" with indigenous Christians. The reconfiguration of missions to focus on the 10/40 Window and "unreached people groups" was likewise, at least in part, an effort to show greater awareness of colonialism's contrived national borders and curiosity about other cultures, although scholars like Melani McAlister and Kathryn Gin Lum argue this new categorization was equally construed as a successful marketing campaign that played into American Christians' interest in the exotic.[31] In the 1990s, the IMB in particular began redistributing its personnel and resources to focus on the "unreached" and turned many enterprises in heavily evangelized countries over to national churches.

But these efforts and missions writ large continue to serve white evangelicals' redemptive notions of race. J. Russell Hawkins, Anthea Butler, Robert P. Jones, Jesse Curtis, and other scholars have discussed how the concept of "color-blindness" has replaced overt racism as a way for white Christians to sidestep calls for more uncomfortable introspection and systemic change.[32] As it has evolved out of southern Christianity, evangelical theology's emphasis on individual conversion and faith deftly dispenses with issues of race with claims that racism is an expression of personal sin. The aim of color-blindness—"I see people, not color"—shuts down any conversation around race, the Black experience, and white evangelicals' appallingly poor track record by implying that anyone who brings it up is perpetuating the problem and failing to forgive. Black Christians in white evangelical spaces often describe how they are silenced when they try to convey their frustrations with the structures, cultures, and systems that perpetuate racism. Survey data from Public Religion Research Institute (PRRI) shows an abundance of white evangelical self-deception; PRRI found that white evangelicals rate themselves highly in having "warm feelings" toward Black Americans, even while they hold the most objectively racist views of any category of Americans.[33]

Missions are helpful toward this end. Missions offer white evangelicals a safe arena in which to act out a narrative of racial harmony without risking their self-conception, control, comfort, or power. As historian Jesse Curtis pointed out to me, missions can even offer white people an advantageous context in which to support social justice. "If I say that Kenyan police forces are corrupt and brutal, evangelicals won't bat an eye," he says. "But if I say the same of American police forces, well, now we're talking about deeply held emotional/social/cultural commitments. There's a Christian nationalism connection here. Our beloved Christian nation, in its foundation, cannot be wrong."[34]

I have heard American missionaries—and MKs—ask how anyone can say they are racist when they have served decades in African or other countries populated by people of color. And by extension, how can white evangelicals be racist if they support missions by donating money or going on short-term mission trips? From the deference shown to American missionaries in many societies to evangelicals' unshakable belief in the rightness of their particular theology, the mission field helps white evangelicals tell a lovely story about themselves as color-blind, altruistic heroes bringing the truth, often material aid, and sometimes even justice to those who have nothing.

This contrasts to what white American Christians frequently experience from Black Americans, many of whom meet white Christians' own criteria for what defines a Christian (a personal relationship with Christ and a strict interpretation of scripture). American Blacks aren't deferential. Many of them are rather pissed off. They aren't "grateful"; they want more equity and justice. They don't cooperate with the American Christian narrative that is so dear to white evangelicals' self-conception. They remind them—by their very existence—of America's moral failures and the white church's guilt.

The bottom line is this: whatever missions' impact has been around the world—and I will grant that a lot of good has been done—what has *not* been done here at home is equally noteworthy. I can't help but wonder what the United States would be like if white Christians had devoted even a tenth of the money, effort, sacrifice, and prayer toward efforts for racial equality, repair, true justice, and reconciliation as they have chasing dreams of spiritual heroism and cleansing themselves in the warm, inviting waters of other cultural contexts. Other people's problems seem simpler in the light of less familiarity.[35]

I also can't help but wonder how a movement with this kind of largely unexamined racialized background and ongoing function can earnestly pursue its declared goal of building a global, multicultural church. That goal is a challenging one, under any circumstances, for flawed, tribal human beings and the many, perhaps inevitable, power structures we have erected over centuries and millennia. But it surely isn't going to be achieved without every eye open and every truth confronted.

6

A Cultural Trade Imbalance

Lori had to get used to wearing shoes.

When you grow up on the island of Antigua, that's understandable. She has fond memories of PE class on the beach, hiking in emerald hills with friends, warm days and white sands. It was the only home she ever knew, and she felt she belonged.

Most of the time. Until an Antiguan, most of whom are descended from enslaved Africans, called her a "white girl." "It would take me a second to realize they were talking about me," she laughs now, her large, funky earrings bobbing against her neck.

Lori remembers such moments as "unsettling" reminders of the distance between herself and her local friends. Most of them lived without indoor plumbing, which made Lori's cement house seem opulent. Once, a friend stole one of her toys. When the girl was caught, she said, "But you have so much." "I felt so conflicted," Lori recalls. "If she would have just asked, I would have given it to her."

As with many MKs, Lori spent less time with local friends the older she got. She was homeschooled with other MKs, which she hated, and not just because their short-term missionary teachers varied in pedagogical quality but were uniformly strict, if not abusive. One teacher hit Lori's brother, who had special needs, with a shoe across his face. She faced no repercussions.

But the distance between Lori and the local community wasn't just cultural or economic. Lori's parents and their fellow missionaries were fundamentalist Baptists, and their extremely rigid beliefs divided them even from other missionaries. "They thought the Southern Baptists were heretics," Lori says, and we both laugh at the irony. It's hard for me to imagine anyone being more certain and immovable in their beliefs than Southern Baptists.

Almost 80 percent of Antiguans are Christians, and most of those are regular church attenders.[1] But they weren't the *right kind* of Christian, at least not in the estimation of Lori's parents, who constantly bemoaned Antiguans' "false teaching," particularly their charismatic expressions in worship. Making Antiguan Christians "the right kind," even if it meant competition with missionaries from other traditions, was the goal.

To this end, Lori's father ran a radio station that broadcast almost exclusively American content, mainly sermons from American pastors, that met with the mission's theological approval. She recalls one Black pastor from neighboring St. Kitts being allowed on the airwaves occasionally. He had attended an acceptable Bible college in the United States and had "the stamp of approval." The radio station employed Antiguans but never in positions of influence and never with any opportunity for advancement. Lori says the radio station still operates on this basis.

"I felt embarrassed," she says of her father's work. "I wondered why we had all these American pastors on." She was a perceptive, curious child with "a strong sense of justice," who didn't fit into the legalistic evangelical culture of her mission. Her mother would chastise her for being willful and stubborn. "But actually I was a really good kid," she says.

Lori's transition to adult life in America was rocky. "My parents dropped me off at college, and I was set adrift," she remembers. She had no choice but to attend hyper-conservative Bob Jones University, whose strict rules—including against interracial romantic relationships, a ban BJU only dropped in 2000—Lori found galling, coming from her upbringing. "I don't have American cultural assumptions," she explains. "I have different perspectives on faith and politics."

Lori went back overseas as quickly as she could, but not as a missionary. She knew early on she didn't want to go that route. "I just disagreed with so much of what I saw from that world," she says. She currently works at an international Christian school in Asia, which gives her a continuing viewpoint on missionary life. Students who attend the school come from families serving with about thirty different mission organizations, and she sees a mixed bag. Some missionaries are doing good work and live frugally in close community with locals. But she also observes missionaries with "excessive," aimless lifestyles. "There's a lot of people fluffing about," she says. She sees increasing levels of bureaucracy, including "member care," which she says can provide good support for missionaries but also includes more nebulous functions and, in all cases, adds to the overhead of the enterprise. She sees missionaries justifying bigger houses and better cars under the guise of enabling ministry.

The school where Lori works is diversifying, with more locals and business families coming in, families that don't share the same beliefs as American evangelicals. She hears from missionary parents who are upset that their children's protective bubble of belief is being compromised, which exasperates her.

"This is the mission field!" she says. "Why are you here?"

* * *

As they reflect on their experience, particularly their own insulated upbringing, many MKs begin asking questions about the global church. Have American evangelical missionaries exported their brand of Christianity around the globe? Or has the global church adopted and adapted—contextualized, in scholarly parlance—a universal Christian faith and done with it what they will? How much of global Christianity is American-made? How truly multicultural is the church that American missionaries have worked to build?

Further back in history, before World War II, the answers to these questions were surprisingly unclear, despite the narrative, prominent among many educated progressives, of missions as a uniformly colonial exercise that forced not only Christianity but Western culture on other peoples. Certainly, it was the expressed intention of early American (and European) missionaries to propagate not only what they viewed as their superior brand of Christianity but a full spectrum of cultural values and even economic practices. Sometimes they were indeed instruments of governments and militaries. Accounts from the time lament various aspects of "heathen" culture, starting with their spiritual "darkness" but moving on to their lack of affection for their children (pretty rich coming from folks who put their unaccompanied children on ships for months-long voyages), their poor utilization of land and lack of participation in a market economy, the immodest dress of their women, and the licentiousness of their sexual mores.[2] Some of the most vigorous missions work of the nineteenth century took place on US soil and aimed at the complete annihilation of Native American cultures through initiatives such as the Indian boarding school system (and very nearly succeeded).[3]

In other cases, Western missionaries had a clear but positive impact on culture. Missionaries have taken on and helped eradicate many objectively harmful practices, especially toward women and girls, including female genital mutilation, child marriage, foot binding, and the Hindu practice of Sati, in which widows burned themselves alive on their husbands' funeral pyres. Missionaries (not all and definitely not in all cases) have often championed marginalized communities, including the disabled, and combated slavery and caste systems. The modern medicine they have provided and taught has saved lives. The education they have offered has paved roads to greater opportunities; many of the nationalist leaders who overthrew colonialism were educated by missionaries.[4]

But in many contexts, early missionaries' imperialistic ambitions were uneven or flat-out unrealistic, and the historical record shows a dialectical, constantly shifting relationship between missionaries and indigenous cultures. Far from being colonial overlords, many nineteenth- and early twentieth-century American missionaries lived precarious lives that were more dependent on locals for survival and evangelistic success than their supporters at home understood or acknowledged. Some missionary proponents, probably out of sheer pragmatism and particularly in the antebellum era, argued more strongly for local agency and control and respect for indigenous culture than those who came later.[5]

Missionary dependence on local partners in the early period of American missions probably extended into the theological realm, according to the work of the late Lamin Sanneh, a Ghanaian-born and Catholic-bred scholar of religious history. He argued that Western missions' Bible translation efforts (perhaps unwittingly) helped to preserve and empower indigenous culture, became a conduit for the gospel's cultural adaptation, and eventually fed into nationalist movements.[6] Missionaries had to labor with indigenous partners and defer to their expertise in learning and choosing language, which unavoidably shaped interpretation along cultural lines. And indigenous believers' engagement with scripture in the vernacular authenticated and formed their Christian faith. Other scholars have pointed out that the flat, democratic structures of American Protestantism and its elevation of the individual believer further fueled religious adaptation as propagated by American missionaries.[7]

* * *

I don't doubt how cultural adaptation of Christianity may have blunted the influence of American culture in the spread of the gospel through American missionaries, looking at the broad sweep of history. But it's difficult to square with my own observation of American evangelical missions in more recent times and of what seems like the widespread export of American evangelical culture around the world. As the United States has become a global colossus—culturally, economically, geopolitically—since World War II, American missionaries have unavoidably operated from a place of ascendancy, not vulnerability, in contrast to many of their forebears. And that has shaped the resulting cultural and religious exchange. To quote an African proverb, "The hand that receives is always below the hand that gives."[8] Influence usually runs downstream with flows of money, resources, connections, and power.

When I look in particular at large, urban churches in Africa—wholly indigenous churches at this point, with nary a missionary in sight—they aren't easily distinguishable from an American megachurch in either substance or style, even in another language. The pastors have probably been educated at American evangelical seminaries or by American missionaries at African seminaries; some of them seem to be twins of the wealthy, politically connected, celebrity-style pastors prominent in America. The congregation is likely reading popular books written by American authors. Much of the music is either American evangelical praise songs or something in that style, perhaps with lyrics translated and some traditional instruments added.[9]

More importantly, global evangelical theology is largely based on a doctrine of individual salvation and transformation, a message central to the American movement. (To be clear, it's not my purpose or place to doubt the correctness of this doctrine but rather to point out its historical and cultural ties to American Christianity.) There may be an even more stark financial appeal to the prosperity gospel in some evangelical movements outside the United States. But the general promise of faith yielding success pervades American evangelicalism. The critique of wealth and a love of money—a major biblical theme, about which Jesus had much to say—is similarly deprioritized in both American and much of global evangelical Christianity.[10] Instead, a focus on sexual morality is central, as is the tendency for that to bleed into the control and subjugation of women, hypermasculinity, and the targeting of the LGBTQ community, especially in contexts with weaker human rights protections than in the United States.

The more recent, extra-biblical detours of white American evangelicalism have also had an echo overseas. Vaccine skepticism and broad suspicion of science, xenophobia, openness to theocratic government, belief in QAnon conspiracies, and even love of Donald Trump are visible in evangelical cultures around the world. (Outside the United States, Trump is most popular in the Philippines, Nigeria, and Kenya, all countries with large, American-influenced evangelical movements.[11]) The most obvious parallels between American evangelicalism and a global variety have been observed with the Bolsonaro movement in Brazil, right down to a January 6–style storming of the Brazilian legislature.[12] A Ugandan pastor, whose ministry tries to counter American influence on the African church, told me that "aggressive nationalized evangelicalism" and "the shallow theology of convenience, power, and privilege, which is typical of Western evangelicalism, has greatly increased Christian aggression" in Africa, especially against marginalized communities.[13]

The manipulation of evangelical cultures and faith by corrupt, authoritarian political leaders is another resemblance. As it has been in the United States, the evangelical emphasis on personal faith and social order is a convenient device for leaders around the world who seek to duck accountability, shore up their authority, and distract from the roots of social problems.[14] Many of Africa's leaders—not an esteemed club in terms of democratic governance—have cultivated ties to American evangelicals and have been ostentatious in their personal faith. For example, Paul Kagame, the brutal dictator of Rwanda who is responsible for the deaths of many Rwandans, famously declared Rwanda the world's first "purpose-driven country" after reading American megachurch pastor Rick Warren's book *The Purpose Driven Life*. Warren and his church forged a close relationship with the Rwandan government and Rwandan Christians through many mission trips and charitable projects, and Warren hosted Kagame at his Saddleback Church in 2019.[15] Some analysts have linked aggressive claims to power by competing groups of Ethiopian Christians, led by Ethiopia's highly evangelical Prime Minister Abiy Ahmed, to civil war and ethnic cleansing.[16]

* * *

I wondered if my anecdotal, undoubtedly biased observations might be borne out by others' more rigorous study, so I contacted Harvey Kwiyani, a Malawian missiologist and theologian, who currently teaches African theology at Liverpool Hope University in England. "Since the 1970s, American evangelicalism has taken over. 'Christian civilization' is American," he tells me.

As a professor and scholar, he is a leader in an effort to unwrap the layers of Americanism from African Christianity in order to discover and foster a version that honors and incorporates African culture. According to Kwiyani, there is an assumption in many seminaries on the continent that if it's not white American theology, it's suspect. He tells me he has encountered African theology students who have never read any work by an African theologian and, in fact, were discouraged from doing so by their African seminary professors.[17]

"What is African theology?" I ask. It's an earnest question, I tell him, and I wonder aloud whether American evangelicalism has so saturated the global church that it's even possible to unravel what's American and what isn't.

Kwiyani laughs with recognition. He tells me about the rise to prominence of African theologians in the 1970s, such as Nigerian Bolaji Idowu, Ghanaian Kwesi Dickson, and Kenyan John Mbiti. Mbiti, for example, wrote an influential book, *African Religions and Philosophy*, on how traditional African religion can inform Christian faith. "American evangelicals panicked," he says. In response, they championed Nigerian theologian Byang Kato, whose book *Theological Pitfalls in Africa* challenged the work of Mbiti and Idowu specifically and warned of the dangers of syncretism more generally. Billy Graham wrote the foreword for Kato's book, and other Americans sponsored his further education.

The American platforming of and partnering with African Christians who conformed to their image continued, and now, Kwiyani says, "African evangelicals don't know what to do with African religion." The urban, middle-class varieties of even Pentecostalism—a more charismatic form of evangelicalism that is particularly widespread in the Global South—are heavily infused with American culture. But, he says, in the rural hinterland, African traditions have survived. "African villagers process Christianity with the African worldview in mind," he says. That worldview is one in which the spirit world and the physical world are fused, and beliefs and ethics are worked out communally.[18]

* * *

Numerous factors likely account for the greater convergence of American and global Christianity in the last several decades compared to earlier in the history of missions. The simplest one is the inexorable process of globalization, in which so much of particularly the urban world is becoming a monoculture. Mass communication, mass production and consumption, mass migration, the internet, and global trade and commerce—we are all more connected than ever before, making for an energetic cultural exchange with blurry results. Even so, power and money have always weighted influence, and America's cultural reach is undeniably vast. As historian Mark Noll puts it, "American Christianity is important for the world primarily because the world is coming more and more to look like America."[19]

But I wonder, too, how American evangelicalism's strict doctrinal gatekeeping, based on the notion of biblical inerrancy—a view of the Bible, solidified in the late nineteenth century by fundamentalists, as wholly inspired by God and without flaw or contradiction as written on the page—has contributed to that since evangelicals took over the missionary enterprise from more liberal Christians after World War II. Certainly it has prolonged the dominance of American missionaries in the field, as mission boards—which have discussed "local control" and "partnership" since the nineteenth century—fear that turning operations over to locals risks heterodoxy and heresy. Inerrancy continues to be a power-hoarding device within American evangelical culture and institutions writ large.[20] As I previously discussed, white mission boards used concerns over doctrinal purity to limit and police the activities of Black American missionaries, and the culture of inerrancy was the basis for the fundamentalist takeover of the Southern Baptist Convention in the 1980s. As historian Carolyn DuPont put it, in discussing how the doctrine of inerrancy reinforced white supremacy in the South, "In demanding a consensus about the meaning of the Bible, fundamentalism disqualified all other interpretations of Christianity, especially those versions . . . that claimed a Gospel mandate for social change. . . . What often looked like bigotry was actually desperate message control."[21]

Like Lori's father's mission, most evangelical missionaries aren't interested in propagating just any variety of Christianity. They most often work in places where Christianity is already well established, such as Latin America and sub-Saharan Africa. But if a person isn't the *right kind* of Christian—as defined by American evangelicals, certain their version is the true, culturally unadulterated gospel—many missionaries would say they aren't one at all. For example, the Joshua Project, an organization that compiles data on global Christianity, measures not just Christian adherence but *evangelical* Christian adherence, as defined by American evangelicals, to assess which people groups are "unreached." ("Unreached by whom?" Harvey Kwiyani wryly asks. "Who has not reached them?")[22]

The heavy influence of American evangelicalism in global Christianity over the last several decades runs somewhat counter to the deliberate efforts missionaries and mission agencies have made over this same period to promote multiculturalism and local adaptation and control. Most mission boards provide more culturally based training than they used to, including considerations of how best to present the gospel in a relevant way and allowances for some flexibility in Christian practice to accommodate local traditions and even other religions (for example, Muslim converts might continue to pray in the mosque five times a day, especially if their conversion endangers them). MKs, many of whom become missionaries themselves, have probably helped drive these trends. Despite their own biases and limitations, MKs as a collective most likely engage missions with greater cultural knowledge and interest than your average white American evangelical.

But evangelical theology, by definition, can only be so flexible. The doctrine of inerrancy and the American control of its gates, through the continued dominance of evangelical education, organizations, media, publishing, and money, is fixed. At this point, an argument can be made that American evangelicalism *is* global evangelicalism—that it has been so woven into the fabric of so many cultures around the world that it has become self-perpetuating, like pizza in American cuisine or eucalyptus trees in South African landscapes. When and how it all began is becoming almost inscrutable and largely irrelevant.

And you might argue this shared form of faith *is* a triumph of multiculturalism after all. And I might agree with you—if the exchange went both ways, that is, if the American church were being shaped by as much as it has shaped this process.

But that's pretty clearly not the case, as the MK experience in the United States demonstrates.

* * *

Every so often—in my day, every few years—missionaries return to the United States, or wherever they are from, for a few months, or even an entire year. This is called furlough, and missionary children the world over greet it with both foreboding and excitement. But mostly the former.

On the positive side of things, you get to drink in the finer things of American culture that you have been denied for oh-these-many years. It's probably slightly different now, given satellite TV, cell phones, the internet, and freer trade, and I'm sure any minute now Amazon drones are going to start carpet-bombing rural Africa with paper towels and boxes of Kraft mac-n-cheese. But when I was a child, we got few glimpses of America, much less actual tokens. When we returned on furlough, it was like letting a bunch of tween boys lose in a video arcade. Upon landing, we headed to Target or Walmart almost immediately and went on a shopping spree. My sister and I bought new, fashionable clothes that actually fit. We bought cassettes by pop groups of which we had only heard vague rumors, if we could convince our parents they were not too sinful, and lots of parent-approved contemporary Christian pop music groups that we thought were quality music because we were that deprived. We bought M&Ms and Skittles and Pringles, which we started eating even as we cruised the aisles with our shopping carts. I'm sure any witnesses thought we had just been rescued from the outback, where dingoes had adopted us as their own.

Cramming multiple years of American life into the space of a few months, a few suitcases, and the confines of our human bodies was the fun part of furlough. Other than seeing our extended family and getting doted on by grandparents, the rest of it pretty much sucked. First of all, if we stayed more than a month or so, many of us had to go to school: *American public* school, which was big, scary, and filled with heathens who thought we were a freak show and weren't really wrong about that.

But right up there with school was accompanying our parents on their speaking circuits through a bunch of American churches. Compared to many other MKs, I, being a Southern Baptist, had it pretty good. My parents received a salary and so didn't have to pound the pavement asking for money like many of my friends' parents did. Nonetheless, Southern Baptist missionaries do typically make some rounds, urging congregants to give to the Lottie Moon missions offering, putting on slide shows set to the theme from *Chariots of Fire,* and being celebrated like the evangelical superstars they are. Despite my relatively good fortune, the church visits combined all the worst nightmares of tweens and teens everywhere—being the center of attention, having to smile constantly or getting scolded for being rude, and hearing a bunch of strangers gush about how amazing your parents are at a time when you are just discovering their abundant flaws.

I have talked to a few MKs who loved furlough, especially if their mission field homes were traumatic; one MK said a trip back to the States literally prevented her suicide.[23] But most MKs say they resented having to go on furlough and especially despised the performative visits to American churches. Some of the stories I have heard are the very definition of cringe. As a young girl, MK Dianne Darr Couts once rode into a missions conference on an elephant (despite the fact that she lived in West Africa, where there were no elephants, and certainly no Asian elephants, like the one she rode). An MK from Asia said she had to demonstrate how to eat noodles on stage. There was lots of dressing up in traditional clothing and singing songs in other languages in front of congregations. Many conveyed how they felt pressure to make the family look good for fear their parents would lose support. One MK told me her mother pinched her cheeks to make her smile. Another did a stand-up routine, "You know you're an MK when . . . ," that played up the "rough" lifestyle and the strangeness of the people (one of the jokes was "You see people you know in *National Geographic*"). He also said he would "mess with folks and pretend not to know who the US president was."

"We got really good at telling stories," an MK from Latin America told me, confessing that at times they embellished details to play up the drama or exoticism and adjusted the specific message and appeal based on the politics of the congregation. "It was all part of the show."

"We were like organ-grinder monkeys," one MK said, and though she remains a member of a Southern Baptist church, she actively avoids any missions-related events. One MK adopted from the country in which his parents served expressed an even deeper level of disdain for church visits, a feeling that his parents used him to make themselves look even more saintly or interesting or that congregations viewed him through that lens.

Whether on furlough or upon permanent return to the United States, many MKs are none too impressed with American Christians, whose interest in the world seems shallow at best and whose commitment to the missions enterprise doesn't seem to include any real education. Some mentioned Americans' extravagant, entitled materialism that stands in stark contrast to how most of the world lives, while others discussed US Christians' "dead," cheap faith that contrasted with that of believers where they lived. "I grew up with a fervor for God, and they are concerned about whether Dunkin' has their favorite coffee," said one MK from Latin America. Many of the MKs expressed dismay at Americans' lack of interest, beyond the surface, in trying to understand their experiences. One MK told me of her attempts to relate to many in her church: "No one cared. I quit talking about it."

It has to be said that this typical MK reaction—which I shared as a young adult—isn't only about the faults of American Christians. It's also a kind of snobbery to which MKs retreat as a way of holding on to some other identity, clinging to and claiming a fragile connection to the culture in which they grew up by differentiating themselves from other Americans, and working through the grief of leaving. One MK called this disparaging condescension to anything quintessentially "American" as "State-hate."[24] At least at first, many MKs don't want to like America, they don't want to bond with Americans, and they don't want to identify as one of them, because it will minimize some other part of themselves. It will expose that experience and the identity arising from it as flimsy and counterfeit. MKs who have not grappled with their grief, their privilege, and their shallow roots will frequently over-identify with the culture of their upbringing. (I used to call myself an "African American," in a half-deliberate, half-ignorant disregard of why that might be offensive and completely unearned. Lord have mercy on my younger self.)

Despite this inner turmoil at work, MKs' perception of a "consumer" approach to missions among American Christians echoes what other observers have identified. Religious studies scholar Melani McAlister demonstrates how American evangelicals have long looked to missions as a source of identity and confirmation of their faith. In the past, missionary martyrdom was a particular obsession. These days, she finds that evangelicals are especially drawn to stories of Christian persecution around the world that reinforce their own persecution complex here in the United States. So, for instance, American evangelicals were briefly consumed with the plight of South Sudan when the conflict there could be (simplistically) shoved into a Christian persecution narrative. But once South Sudan's chaos and violence defied those categories, American Christians lost interest.

McAlister finds evangelicals have also long fixated on the "exotic" aspect of missions, stories of foreign peoples and cultures, the more foreign the better. In the past, those differences were cast in a negative light, but in the post–civil rights era, this impulse has been refashioned into what McAlister calls "enchanted internationalism," which sees global Christians as more inspirational and pure, and relationships with them as proof of multiethnic harmony (to be honest, I see this depiction in many MK narratives as well). Either way, the interest is a one-dimensional curiosity on the part of Americans.[25] Of course, this same dynamic plays out in secular charity, too—"slum tourism" is one secular version of short-term missions—as well as in leftist, academic circles, where the indigenous culture of "colonized" people is frequently championed in airbrushed form. Evangelical or not, Americans often exhibit an overwhelming lack of knowledge of and disinterest in the real issues, lives, challenges, and joys of people living outside the United States. As with so many things, white evangelicals are not necessarily unique in their biases and shortcomings, only in how they spiritualize them, which makes them that much harder to confront.

American Christians' interest in missions as a gratifying product of which to partake is particularly visible in the experiences of MKs from Europe. Almost all the ones I spoke to and surveyed related their feeling of being "B Team" missionaries in American churches, despite the fact that Europe is far less Christian than many countries that represent other more "fascinating" mission fields. Europe can be a much tougher place for missionaries to work, and in many ways, to live, due to the high cost of living. The IMB has actually designated western Europeans as an "unreached people group."

But Europe is not "exotic," its believers aren't "suffering," and the missionaries there aren't obviously "sacrificing." These MKs heard a lot of questions about why their families were there and a lot of presumptive knowledge of European culture based on family vacations to France or semesters abroad in London. "People don't think I'm a 'real MK,' because I'm not from a 'cool' country," said an MK who grew up in Spain. Her parents struggled to raise support and eventually had to return to the United

States when one of their sending churches decided it would rather fund an orphanage in Zambia. (Zambia, while poor, is one of the most evangelically Christian countries in the world.)

Mission organizations that try to counter American evangelicals' myopic, selective interest in missions find it's an uphill battle. McAlister joined an InterVarsity mission trip to Egypt, and despite the organization's attempts to put missions into historical and geopolitical context in its training—including discussion of racial power dynamics—McAlister couldn't tell that any of it really sank in. The young short-term missionaries she accompanied still seemed to romanticize the people with whom they interacted and display naivete about their warm reception—which happened to be much warmer for the white Americans in the group than for the one Black woman.[26] Author Mekdes Haddis points out that most mission organizations' training materials, while an improvement on past iterations and well-intentioned, are mostly written and taught by white Americans. Across the board, while there are glimmers of change, including large numbers of non-American missionaries, evangelical missiology and theology is still dominated by white Americans, even while their percentage of the world's evangelical Christians continues to decline; 77 percent of evangelical Christians now live in the Global South.[27] "The methods, money, knowledge, books: it's all very Western in context," Harvey Kwiyani says.[28]

It all reinforces many American evangelicals' notion that missions are not only done by them but ultimately *for* them: to inspire and affirm them, to strengthen their faith, to gratify their need for purpose, and to present the world to them through their own lens.

* * *

While earlier generations of American missions supporters may have approached missions with a similar consumer mindset as today's evangelicals, some missionaries—and MKs—of the past tried to use their celebrated platform to challenge and educate them. And in many respects, they succeeded. According to historian David Hollinger, in the late nineteenth and early twentieth centuries, missionaries and their adult children had a major impact on American government, religion, and, at a time when information wasn't so widely available, the American knowledge base about the rest of the world. He persuasively argues that missionaries introduced the concept of international multiculturalism to Americans. Missions at the time may have been intertwined with racial concepts of American imperialism and exceptionalism, and the missionaries themselves may have entered their endeavors with intentions of cultural dominance. But Hollinger shows how their experiences changed many of them and how they, in turn, tried to change America, although it was often "a hard sell to the people in the pews."[29]

Hollinger's particular subjects were the predecessors of what would become American mainline Christians, not the evangelical sort that took over the missions enterprise after World War II. The missionaries Hollinger studied were highly educated social elites, and their theology tended toward the modernist side of the debates of the time. Theologically conservative missionaries, who coexisted, at times uncomfortably, with their more liberal colleagues for decades, tended to be less well-heeled and connected, limiting their influence on American society. Then again, their more rigid theological framework may have constrained the mission field's influence on these missionaries' own views. That no doubt applies to their modern-day evangelical counterparts.

Conservative evangelical missionaries, then and now, seem to have had little influence on their own religious institutions and subculture beyond serving as its icons. During the 1960s, many evangelical missionaries did lobby for civil rights. But this kind of missionary activism, along with more progressive evangelical strains more generally, faded into memory—or was chased there, in many cases—with the rise of the religious right in the 1970s.[30] These days, missionaries' ability to use their experience to enlighten the beliefs and perspectives of American evangelicals appears limited, even while their work and faith remain highly celebrated.

For one thing, the incentive structure of missions discourages missionaries from saying anything that challenges the status quo. The evangelical missions enterprise is wholly dependent on direct donations, and missionaries are its fundraisers. As we've discussed, many missionaries must raise all their own funds, making them beholden to the preferences of American Christians. Even in Southern Baptist–land, where missionaries are paid out of a central fund, that fund is raised separately and directly from Southern Baptist members. If those members think the missionaries are out of step with their own views, if they are challenged or offended in any way, those donations could be affected. The IMB and the Southern Baptist Convention writ large can't afford for their missionaries to step far out of line. To be certain of that, starting in the 1990s, all IMB missionaries had to sign on to the Baptist Faith and Message, which goes beyond the simple gospel story or basic Baptist doctrine and includes the submission of women to husbands and male authorities and constraints on women's role in the church.[31]

So whatever missionaries' private views are—some missionaries are in lockstep with the folks in the pews, while others are privately discouraged by and disgusted with the American church—and whatever wisdom they have gleaned that might challenge and educate their supporters back home, I know of very few who would dare to say anything provocative. Some MKs with whom I spoke remember this being part of their family conversations. One MK told me his parents would say whatever the church believed "if it got [them] funding." Another MK recalled his parents losing support from a church in the 1970s because they saw a photo of him and his siblings "dressed up like hippies."

Of course, expecting missionaries to educate American churches assumes they *themselves* have learned from their experience and are aware of how it fits into larger conversations, contexts, and issues. That's definitely not always the case in modern missions, as my own engagement with race demonstrated. Compared to American missionaries of the distant past, today's missionary families, as we have seen, can more easily live independently and apart, physically and relationally, from local communities. At the same time, in the internet age, a missionary family can remain immersed in the American evangelical information bubble. These days, a mission field experience can reinforce one's views as easily as it tests them, particularly within the American evangelical framework, which prizes conformity and assiduously avoids examination of broader systems, structures, and historical backstories. The strict evangelical compartmentalization of the earthly and the spiritual, the personal and the societal, leads many missionaries into a single-minded focus on evangelism or narrowly framed charity.

In general, most white American evangelicals don't hear directly from global Christians either, except very rarely or within contexts controlled by American evangelical organizations. This is despite the fact that Christians in the Global South comprise three-quarters of evangelical Christians and about half of all the world's evangelical missionaries. With the convergence of American and global evangelicalism, when American evangelicals do interact with their non-American counterparts, the effect is often an echo.

Consider the case of Korean missionaries who have been coming to the United States since the 1970s. Sociologist Rebecca Kim, who is a Korean American Christian, shows how they adapted their message and approach specifically to appeal to white Americans, going so far as to take on English names. Although Korean Christianity was heavily influenced by American missionaries to Korea, Koreans infused it with Confucian ideas that emphasized rigor and discipline. Over time, and with little success among white Americans—their preferred target because the Korean missionaries believed whites had more authority and influence in American society—the missionaries changed tactics, presenting a more comfortable, less countercultural, less self-sacrificial form of Christianity that might have more appeal.

Despite such efforts, Korean and other missionaries to the United States have had little success among white Americans, who have a difficult time understanding why their country would need missionaries from other countries or what they might possibly learn. Most of these missionaries end up working with immigrant populations. "Christians of the Global South may have more passion and religious vigor," Kim writes, "But they will succumb to the worldly systems of power that favor the West. . . . In terms of power and influence, the center of Christianity and missions remains very much in the US."[32]

Cultural bias isn't the only obstacle for such "reverse missionaries," those from the Global South coming to the United States and other Western nations. There are also many structural impediments, including high costs of living, disadvantageous exchange rates, lack of employment and housing, unaffordable health care, convoluted bureaucratic procedures, and, most notably, restrictive immigration policies (that most white evangelicals support).[33] On that front, for example, a sudden green card procedural change in 2023 put the immigration status of thousands of foreign religious workers residing in the United States in jeopardy.[34]

* * *

The limited impact of missions on the beliefs and perspectives of American evangelicals is evident from their engagement in American policy and politics. As it was in the beginning, when Southern Baptists appointed enslavers as missionaries, the narratives of American missions and American evangelical culture often seem to exist on bizarrely parallel tracks. These days, for example, the same people who are funding missionary endeavors around the world are, as a collective, supporting policies that cut America's refugee program and legal immigration to the bone. Evangelicals might support medical missions to vaccinate Pakistani children while indulging in anti-vaccine conspiracy theories here. They may vote for political leaders calling for a Muslim ban while they hail missionaries befriended by Muslims in other countries. Political scientist Miles Williams, analyzing 2014 data collected by Stanford University, found that only about 36 percent of white evangelicals supported US foreign aid or refugee admittance, the lowest number for any US demographic.

And that was before Donald Trump incited white evangelicals' nativist tendencies. More tellingly, respondents' international connections or experiences—perhaps through supporting missions—made no difference in their attitudes.[35]

I don't see a lot of evangelicals openly grappling with these issues. Even many missionaries don't see any incongruity between their work and their supporters' politics. But numerous MKs I interviewed found the disconnect deeply distressing. Multiple people with whom I spoke brought up 9/11 as an experience that made them realize that they held different perspectives from other white evangelicals and Americans in general. An MK who grew up in Afghanistan said, "I prayed for Afghanistan after 9/11. I knew they would be a target. Nobody else prayed for them." While she of course condemned the 9/11 attacks, she was struck by Americans' naive confusion as to why anyone would want to harm the United States. "Where do I start?" she exclaimed. "MKs understand you can love America and be critical of America."

Whatever people around the world learn from missionaries, whatever elements of American Christianity they keep, and whatever the missionaries themselves bring or take away, one thing is clear: the American church has been less affected and less enlightened by those on the receiving end of its missionary endeavor, or even by their own missionaries, than one might hope. Too often missions are less a relationship that challenges and matures the American church and more a pleasing product to consume, a beautiful reflection upon which to gaze.

* * *

As he tried to answer my question as to the nature of African theology, missiologist and theologian Harvey Kwiyani described how issues of belief and morality are worked out in traditional African culture: in community, through conversation, through compromise. Jewish friends have told me similar things about their faith tradition. They wrestle with things together, they learn from each other, and they aren't afraid of some conflict. There is room for disagreement.[36]

And to me, that is a vision of what a truly global church would be and how it would function. Not always in agreement, not at all. But always in conversation, always with an understanding that *all of us*—including and most especially white Americans—contextualize our faith, and none of us have cornered the market on truth.

I include my liberal Methodist church, among the American ones that split with African counterparts over the issue of LGBTQ inclusion. And look: I don't agree with my African brothers and sisters on that issue. But it doesn't mean I can't learn something from their overall perspective. In his study of three multicultural Lutheran congregations in the Twin Cities area, Kwiyani found that the liberal mainline congregation was actually the *least* inclusive and community-oriented. He said its white leaders, who probably have an image of themselves as racially enlightened, weren't happy with his conclusions. I say, tough. Be offended, then listen anyway.[37]

We need to hear from non-American Christians. We need their true voices, not some parroting of Americanized theology. We need to see what they make of things coming from their own histories and cultures. We need to be challenged—provoked, even—because Christ came as a marginalized person, and because we are the citizens of the most powerful nation the world has ever seen. I think it's nearly impossible that we fully and correctly understand the gospel.

James Baldwin, in testimony before Congress in 1968, said, "If we are going to build a multiracial society, which is our only hope . . . then one has got to accept that I have learned a lot from you, and a lot of it is bitter, but you have a lot to learn from me, and a lot of that will be bitter."[38]

When it comes to missions, this educational exchange remains lopsided, because most white American evangelicals prefer to only partake of its sweet fruit and retain the power to pick and choose.

Part III

The Myth of Saints

7

The Untouchables

Allie misses the rain.

If you, like Allie and me, have experienced them, you know that African rains often burst out of a sunny day and come down in a symphonic torrent. They are best enjoyed under a metal roof nursing a cup of tea, allowing the cool, clean air to open up the cramped spaces in your mind. No wonder Allie misses the rains down in Africa. (I know the correct Toto lyric is "bless the rains." But that makes no sense, and I think we can all agree my edit is an improvement.)

For Allie's family, with no running water in their house, the rains were a call to action. "We stopped everything to collect it," she recalls. She fondly remembers running and dancing in the refreshing showers, streams of water running down her face, and emptying buckets into rain barrels as they filled up.

Her father had built their cement house in a remote area in West Africa when Allie was eleven years old. Before that, the family had lived in a "regular house" in a larger town, but still with no other Americans nearby. Visitors needing directions to either place would simply inquire after the "white people's house." In the more rural location, "people would come like tourists to see us," Allie says.

Despite being so awkwardly conspicuous, Allie and her siblings immersed themselves in village life. They were home-schooled, so had little choice if they wanted any friends. Her family largely eschewed interaction with other missionaries in their organization who lived elsewhere in the country, skipping regional conferences and visits to the closest mission station, which Allie called "Little America." Unlike most MKs, she didn't have many, if any, MK friends other than her siblings. Her family was her main source of friendship.

She and the local kids ran freely around the village and played on the swing set Allie's dad built. As she got older, the troubling realization that she was irrevocably different from the other kids began to creep in. The others' fascination with her. The obeisance they showed her. The special treatment their parents gave her. "I realized at around ten years old, that, wow, I am really powerful," she recalls. But it was not a good feeling. She wanted to belong.

This caused conflict with her parents, who were content with their elevated place in the community. "They didn't need or want to belong," she says. She felt like her parents' more distant relationship with locals reflected poorly on her in the eyes of her African peers. And she strongly resisted her parents' attempt to move back into town when Allie was sixteen.

The following year, however, they gave her no choice but to transition to life in America, where she lived on her own with legal guardians and struggled to find her place. Now in her late twenties, Allie says it's still difficult to find a sense of home. In her absence, her parents moved the rest of the family from the village into town, as they had wanted to do. "They felt they were losing their kids to Africa," she says.

As my interview with Allie winds down, I ask her what I have asked almost all the MKs with whom I've spoken. "It sounds like you had a great childhood," I say, trying for a gentle approach. "But just as a formality, and only if you want to discuss it, I do ask folks if they were a victim of or witness to any abuse or trauma."

Allie shifts uncomfortably, and her bright, generous smile drops. She hesitates.

"Well . . . my dad is a pedophile. Some of us were abused."

I stop breathing for a moment.

She goes on. "None of us remember it. The only way we know is that he confessed several years ago." She explains that she had told me about her childhood "as I experienced it," with no memory of the abuse.

Since then, Allie has had no contact with her father, who is now divorced from her mother. She has gone to therapy and is trying to sort through what she still considers a happy childhood. She has no idea why she and her siblings don't remember the abuse, whether it took place when each of them was very young or if they have dissociated from the experience, a common trauma response.

I pause before asking, "Do you know if he also abused local kids?"

She shrugs, then says quietly, "I don't know."

* * *

As a child in Kenya, I sensed my family's importance acutely. Everywhere we went, we were a big deal. Being a white person in small-town or rural Kenya gives one insight into the life of a boy band member at the height of its popularity—perhaps a slightly scandal-plagued one, because it's equal parts people falling all over themselves and hushed stares and pointing.

When our car went by, children ran beside it smiling, waving, yelling, "Mzungu (White Person)!" In churches, the pastor often brought my parents to the front to say a word. We got front-row seats (I did not see this as a perk) and sometimes gifts, which were undoubtedly a financial sacrifice for the givers. Everyone generally acted as if they had just encountered their favorite movie star. One church member tried to give my dad his last chicken in the midst of a drought; it was one of the rare times he turned down a gift. Awestruck children sat behind me gently stroking my long blond-ish hair, a common MK experience of unwanted touch (one person I interviewed connected this to a message that one's body is not important and doesn't belong to them). The attention always made me uncomfortable, and not only because there's pretty much nothing worse for a prepubescent girl than a room full of strangers staring at her.

I understood clearly that people revered my parents. They sought their advice, weighted their opinions, followed their example. Even though my dad was not a trained pastor at first and his sermons usually required translation, he got frequent requests to preach in local churches. Many Kenyan friends still call my parents Mom and Dad.

My parents are good, talented people. But the adulation always struck me as way over the top, far in excess even of the likewise gratuitous praise they received from American

Christians and more than what was healthy. "There are a million Bettys and Chips running all over eastern Congo," an MK friend half-joked about the legacy of her parents. "I mean, I loved my obstetrician and was grateful for his care, but I didn't name any of my kids after him."

Our entire presence in Kenya was, in a way, premised on an implied superiority. My parents had come here, presumably, because they had something to offer, something more, something Kenyans didn't have. They had come to do things Kenyans couldn't do and teach them things they didn't know. Why else would we be there? We had come to save the day. We were the heroes of our story.

* * *

American missionaries aren't uniformly adored in every country around the world, of course. As scholar Melani McAlister pointed out to me, American foreign policy in some places has poisoned the well of opinion about the United States.[1] But I heard this mainly from MKs from Europe. MKs from Latin America, where one might expect that US Cold War interference left a bitter taste in many mouths, told me that people nonetheless generally idolized their parents. Or they appeared to, anyway; in the presence of inequalities, it can be hard to distinguish between genuine affection and savvy calculation. The fact is, love her or hate her, America is the power center of the world. Abroad, American citizens carry that power with them in varying forms and to varying ends.

This power—cultural, spiritual, economic—means that missionaries are almost never peers in the communities they serve. And that imbalance, combined with the institutional weaknesses of those contexts, has major implications for accountability on the mission field. Missionaries provide aid, connections, and in many cases scarce employment. In the 2023 documentary *Savior Complex,* the Ugandan employees of missionary Renee Bach—who did the work of a medical doctor for malnourished children despite having only a high school diploma—said they were bothered by some of her practices and by her disregard of their own medical expertise. But they needed the work in a country where jobs for even well-educated people were hard to come by, and Bach literally signed their paychecks. Not only do locals see missionaries as bearers of tangible help and opportunity, they often attribute to white people superior expertise and even moral authority. In the same example, a Ugandan social worker related how mothers with ill children flocked to the clinic upon hearing that "a white lady" was administering care. Her qualifications to do the work were of no concern. The mothers assumed whatever she was offering was the best and that she herself was trustworthy. Bach's status as an American missionary told them everything they needed to know.

The lack of integration of missionary families into social, institutional, and legal structures raises the risks for abuse. Abuse happens in the United States as well, of course, but there is far more outside accountability to discourage and apprehend abusers. In the United States, most families are enmeshed in a web of state and community institutions that are undergirded by and subject to a strong justice system. Most children have contact with teachers, coaches, doctors, and other adults who are trained to spot abuse and legally mandated to report it to authorities. There are nosy neighbors and family friends who aren't beholden to or dependent on a child's parents. There is broad cultural awareness of and intolerance for abuse. In the

United States, there are multiple obstacles that an abuser must circumvent. And, sadly, we know they too often do just that.

On the mission field, most of these protections are frequently absent. Rule of law is often weak, institutions are sclerotic, and cultural norms don't define child abuse the way we do in America. Child marriage is legal in many countries, and domestic violence is sometimes a culturally acceptable way of maintaining household order. A child safety officer for Africa Inland Mission told me, "The reality is that in most of the countries we work in, the Child Protection mechanisms just don't exist—or if they do, they are unsafe, unreliable, or under resourced."[2] And MKs are often socially, if not geographically, isolated.

In Allie's case, if she had been cognizant of the abuse by her father, to whom could she have turned? There were no other missionaries nearby (and as we'll see, the missionary community presents its own accountability challenges anyway). State institutions were not trustworthy or dependable, and her parents were not the peers of local adults. For all she knew, her father was abusing their children as well.

Therapist, podcast host, and MK Caleb Adams explains how vulnerable social isolation leaves children. In these mission field locations, he says, "It's like you and your family [are] in this little lifeboat together, and you have to be close because you're going through a lot." He goes on to spell out the implications for accountability, when "kids are so attached to their parents, and the family unit is so tight." In addition, he says, "[Our] parents' reputation was our currency . . . it paid the bills . . . We were acutely aware of how any loss of reputation would put us out on the street."[3]

Of course, MKs aren't the only ones who suffer from a lack of accountability. Local communities and children have probably been victimized more than we know, because there are even fewer avenues for victims to come forward and even less incentive for mission boards to investigate or atone for such abuses. The example of a missionary I will call Russell is a case in point.

Russell and his family lived among a highly traditional, isolated African tribe. A story about his ministry in his mission's magazine described the community as wary of outsiders. Russell and his wife, the story reported, had worked diligently and successfully to earn their trust. Two years later, the family was "sent home," a phrase that often obscures as much as it discloses. I heard from one source within the missionary community at the time and two additional sources since that Russell had engaged in "affairs" with local "women" (given the common practice of child marriage among the tribe, it is possible, if not probable, that Russell's relationships were with underage girls). By his own telling—in an interview I heard in which he related an inspirational story of God's deliverance from his demons—he had ongoing problems with addiction of various kinds when he was appointed a missionary. Before finding Jesus, he had been in jail for drug use and drunk driving. He continued to struggle with sex addiction after his conversion and after becoming a missionary.

It's unclear how Russell was finally caught; based on the interview, it seems his wife may have reported him to mission authorities. It is highly unlikely anyone else would have. Years later, the tribe remains a traditional, insular community, removed from government presence, in which women have few protections and child marriage is common. Sexual abuse by a missionary is unlikely to be understood as such by this community (or, frankly, by American evangelicals, as demonstrated by how frequently evangelical leaders characterize these situations as infidelity or blame the victim for "seduction"). It is unlikely to be reported to mission authorities and unlikely to result in any sort of accountability.

The fact that I have anonymized this account is telling itself. Although Russell's case was widely known in my circles—I have heard about it from at least three missionaries or MKs—and although I located other circumstantial evidence that lined up with what I knew, the investigative journalists I consulted advised me I would need to speak directly to the victims themselves in order to report his identity. But it would be nearly impossible to locate his victims, many years later, among a remote community that is distrustful of outsiders and may have never found any fault with Russell's behavior. So, Russell will no doubt continue to work in a ministry setting, as he has done since he was sent home from the mission field. I sincerely pray he has changed, as he claims he has, because he remains in a position to do enormous damage if not.

Multiple MKs I interviewed told me their fathers or other missionaries they knew similarly engaged in "affairs" with local women, often household help. These events occurred in more modern, urban communities than the one in which Russell worked. But the reality has always been that, depending on the particulars, such relationships can be a gross abuse of power, similar to clergy-congregant relationships, which are now outlawed in some US states. Especially in the case of remote, traditional communities, it's difficult to construe such relationships as purely consensual, given the high place American missionaries occupy in these contexts.

Missionaries are just like all other human beings, who require accountability through formal mechanisms and by being members of a community. But they often live in environments where they never really belong as a peer. Especially in the absence of strong institutions and rule of law, this isn't normal or healthy or wise. As we will discuss in later chapters, important changes in US law and mission board policies have improved the landscape. But the cultural and social context of missions remains problematic.

Missionaries are still too untouchable.

8

One Big Happy Family

Christopher Cole just got back from Indonesia, where he took his elderly parents to say goodbye.

"In Indonesian culture, it's important to distinguish between 'see you later' and 'goodbye forever,'" he says. "This will be their last trip."[1]

His sister went too, her first return since 1995. She gorged herself on her favorite mangosteen fruit and filled her purse with what she couldn't eat. They saw their old dorm, now an office building for the mission, at the international school his mother helped to start. The rambutan tree they used to sit in, blissfully eating its "hairy" fruit, is much larger now. Old Indonesian friends, one of them now a wealthy businessman, turned out to see them. Christopher could see the passage of time everywhere and nowhere. Throughout the trip, vivid memory mingled with new experience in the bittersweet, warmed-over grief that eases into nostalgia.

Christopher, more than many MKs with whom I've spoken, experienced his adopted country and its people fully and richly while growing up. His was a truly multicultural, cosmopolitan upbringing in a vibrant, sizable city, something he finds most Americans, who often think of missionaries living in a jungle somewhere, don't understand. Many of his friends were Indonesian, albeit mostly from elite families whose children attended his school—"my alumni group is a Who's Who of Indonesia"—where twenty-six nationalities and multiple religions were represented.

He had what he calls a "second family," the family of their Indonesian housekeeper. I've heard many missionaries and MKs claim locals as "family." But often when you drill down just a bit, the disparities and hierarchies become clear, and you wonder whether the locals, if they were being honest, would define the relationship in the same way. But this family lived with Christopher's. Christopher shared a room with one of the housekeeper's sons. They are all still deeply enmeshed, decades later.

Christopher knew the gifts of the MK life. But he also knew its pain.

He thinks he must have been one of the last of his cohort of MKs who knew the unspeakable truth of his Southern Baptist missionary community. He found out as a teen, when some of his friends told him to stop listening to a cassette recording of William McElrath, a.k.a. "Uncle Mac," singing the children's songs he loved when he was younger. He asked them why.

"Mac does bad things to children," they told him, incredulous he didn't already know. They told him about girls who were fondled. Boys, too. And much worse. It had all been going on for twenty years or more. The older MKs tried their best to keep the younger ones away from him. But it was hard. McElrath was like a pied piper to kids, with his funny songs, autoharp playing, and engaging stories.

Christopher was shocked. His interaction with McElrath had been more limited than that of some of the others. His family lived on a different side on the Indonesian island where McElrath resided, and he mainly saw him at mission meetings.

But Christopher lived in a dorm with some of McElrath's victims and saw the fallout, even before he knew what he was witnessing. Traumatized, brittle kids, full of anxiety, unable to trust. Some of them were the "troublemakers."

He believes there were Indonesian victims, too, but he doesn't know that for a fact. He cites MKs after his time being abused by Indonesian adults in the area where McElrath worked who would have been children during that time; abusers are often child victims themselves. Certainly, McElrath would have had ready access to many Indonesian children. Despite multiple reports to IMB authorities starting in 1973, McElrath was considered "THE missionary to children," according to Christopher.

No one did anything. For thirty years.

One survivor, Linda Davrath, recounted to the *Houston Chronicle*, which investigated this case, that she told her father about the abuse in 1977. Her father reported it to an IMB official in Indonesia. Nothing happened. And that was after McElrath had already confessed to molesting another MK several years earlier. Davrath told the *Chronicle* that "all the adults knew about it, and no one did anything."[2]

Christopher and the other kids didn't say anything. They had internalized the message that "God's work" was too important. They needed to present a saintly face of missionary service to the American churches who funded the IMB. If things got out, lost people would go to hell. The missionary kids believed that. And they didn't want to distract or burden their parents.

Years later, some of the missionaries wrote letters of apology for their silence to the survivors via the IMB. According to Christopher, IMB attorneys forbade mission personnel to forward the letters onto McElrath's victims.

It wasn't until adult MKs repeatedly approached IMB executives that McElrath was finally fired, in 1995. Christopher's parents, who apparently knew nothing about the abuse, called to tell him the news.

Christopher grimaces at the memory of that phone call. "Oh, you guys finally found out about Mac?"

* * *

My mission field home, and that of many MKs, was quite different from Allie's isolated village life in West Africa. Our family was part of a mission "station," a small community of mission families and households living in close proximity to one another. We also didn't live far from and interacted frequently with other families in our larger Kenya mission. Especially in earlier days of missions, stations might be a literal compound of mission houses, often in conjunction with a hospital or school or other mission enterprise. Our mission station was not that formal—we lived in houses spread out across the bustling Kenyan town of Nyeri, nestled in the chilly highlands between majestic Mt. Kenya and the densely forested Aberdare Mountains.

It was a tight-knit missionary community by design. We were "in this together," whether or not we actually liked each other or got along. Indeed, one of the dirty little secrets of the mission field is that missionaries don't always get along. In fact, they can put a bunch of middle school girls to shame, what with the cliques and power struggles and backstabbing. I recall my parents trying to mediate between two families in our broader circle, whose matriarchs hated each other for unclear reasons. While one of the families was on leave in the United States, the other family fired their beloved cook, who had been with the furloughing family for twenty years, and had him returned to his native Tanzania.

Reading João Chaves's history of Southern Baptist missionaries in Brazil, which confirms that missionary knife fights date back over a century, I found myself chuckling with recognition. "It is not well for everyone to know this," wrote missionary D. L. Hamilton to his family in 1908, "But it is a fact that foreign missionaries have no wings."[3] And it's perhaps no wonder. The kinds of folks who volunteer as missionaries are usually pretty pugnacious, to put it diplomatically. It takes a certain amount of moxie and determination to become a missionary in the first place, qualities that don't always translate into playing well with others.

Despite the personalities and conflicts involved, these communities of missionaries do lean on each other and form a family of sorts that I certainly experienced as a child. MKs call other missionaries "aunt" and "uncle," and I mostly loved mine. There was Aunt Janet, who taught me piano and was my fourth-grade science teacher at a local primary school. I have an enduring image of her running down the road with a giant blue bucket on her head to protect her carefully styled hair when it started raining on our field trip to a nearby stone quarry. She and Uncle Jim were the center of our community, hosting potluck breakfasts after Easter sunrise services on their front lawn, overlooking Mt. Kenya, and festive Christmas Eve teas before we all trekked to an old Anglican church high up on the mountain for candlelight services. Christmases spent with the Nyeri crew are some of my warmest memories. My sister and I spent hours at Aunt Janet and Uncle Jim's home playing with their two sons, who somehow had every single Star Wars action figure *and* the Millennium Falcon.

When I was a senior in high school, we moved to a different town, and a nearby missionary family, the parents of one of my best friends, took me in when my mother had to be medically evacuated to the United States. They took me along on their family vacation, and Aunt Jane sewed my dress for the junior-senior formal banquet at school. I think I might have even made their family Christmas photo that year.

But there were also missionaries in my orbit with whom I felt uneasy. There were those whose behavior could be unpredictable and unsettling. There was one missionary who seemed to consider me her special spiritual renovation project, constantly correcting my behavior and criticizing my personality well beyond what was appropriate for a friend of the family. But we *were* a family. Or at least that was the message. Certainly, we were the only family, the only resource, the only safety net available. Certainly there was no avoiding them.

I heard similar things from other MKs, including one who told me that upon arriving on their mission compound in central Africa, her family felt like they were "living in a fishbowl." They lived in a wing of another missionary family's home at first, and their hosts routinely went through their things while they were gone. That family closely monitored their whereabouts, even in the absence of any significant security concerns and even after they moved into their own home. Another MK from Latin

America said, "It was clear that all the adult missionaries thought they were the parents of all the MKs." This MK considered their interference and punishments "physical and spiritual abuse."

In communities that are insular and interconnected, when abuse occurs, it's hard to uncover, even as it is never contained. Its impact spreads like dye in water, leaving its mark on everyone. There are typically multiple victims and even more people who know but take no action. Accountability is fraught, not only threatening the "family" but jeopardizing the all-important mission, the work. And for impressionable kids, being abused by trusted adults scrambles their understanding of love, sex, friendship, and boundaries. In my discussions, I heard of a few cases of MKs, one quite young, abusing other MKs. One of my subjects confessed that after older boys inappropriately touched him when he was around ten, he did the same to friends his age. Another MK told me she found out later that the girl who molested her was herself a victim, of the girl's own father. Research indicates that children who abuse other children are usually themselves victims.[4] That doesn't excuse their harm of others, but it does demonstrate how abuse can mushroom, particularly in families and self-contained communities.

* * *

I have found it difficult to get MKs to discuss these "mission family" situations in any detail. There is understandably a desire to protect one's parents, whether or not they themselves were abusive or complicit in a cover-up. Even a discussion of their colleagues and friends is feared damning or embarrassing to an MK's parents. There is also the common MK instinct, as previously discussed, to protect parents from emotional distress. This was a pervasive theme in most of my conversations and why almost all my subjects remain anonymous.

In addition, the bonds of missionary community are tight, complex, and long-lasting, woven like intricate baskets. One MK who told me of being embroiled in a web of mission field abuse asked me not to discuss it in any identifiable way, because "my story touches on the lives of so many others": people who don't want to talk about it, people who are still important in her life. If you are an MK who was abused, your abuser might be the brother of your best friend or the husband of your mother's best friend. Your own story of abuse might also involve the abuse of a sister or close friend who can't bear to revisit it or has never spoken about it or who is still close with the wife or the daughter or married to the brother. The missionary world is small enough that your parents might recognize a story of abuse that happened on the other side of the world involving a family whose child is married to the child of dear friends. Then, when you consider that many missionaries are second, third, even fourth generation, you can see how the link charts can become a tangled, messy cloud—one that hides a library of stories, stories many people know but no one talks about at any volume.

Breaking these bonds is costly, certainly on the mission field, but even long after leaving. D. L. Hamilton, of historian João Chaves's study, resigned nineteen years into his service after being ostracized by the missionary community for his attempts to ensure better financial management, to uncover another missionary's sexual misconduct, and to advocate for more local autonomy for Brazilian Christians.[5] Southern Baptist missionary Dee Ann Miller and her family also felt they had no choice but to leave the field after her dogged attempts to seek the removal of a fellow missionary who assaulted her and abused others in the community, including an MK. Even the MK's parents were hesitant to take any action due to their relationships with the man's family members.[6] I heard from an MK whose family was shunned and eventually fired because his physician father would not assent to what he considered medical malpractice at the mission hospital where he worked. His supervisor told him the hospital's patients were "lucky we are here providing any medical care at all."

MKs who speak out about mission field abuse and misconduct might even be attacked by other MKs. Even MKs in the same family can have radically different mission field experiences, and for those who had happy childhoods—or else can't bear to face their own pain—hearing about abuse or trauma threatens to destroy a precious remnant of a much-cherished identity. Other MKs have gone on to become missionaries themselves and are deeply invested in the system of missions. I heard from two MKs who told me that discussion of abuse on mission school alumni Facebook groups ignited an MK war of words.

Letta Cartlidge, who attended Hillcrest Academy in Nigeria, watched her alumni Facebook page break apart in 2021 after a former principal at the school confessed on the forum to molesting two students while at Hillcrest. She estimates that 30 percent of commenters responded with anger or stories of their own, while 70 percent wanted to immediately "extend grace" to the man. When the majority began attacking the minority, Letta started a new group for survivors and allies. The volume of reports of abuse on the new page prompted members to form a steering committee to seek accountability.[7]

For MKs, the mission field is their only home, and the missions community remains their family in many ways. Their identities are wrapped up in having an enduring place in these networks. Exclusion and the loss of relationships can be extraordinarily painful. Although more and more MKs are coming forward and speaking out about the shadow side of missionary life, it always comes with risks. I have a feeling that, when this book is published, I may find this out for myself.

But like so many features of the mission field, its insularity is a more pronounced version of what is found in American evangelicalism writ large. Especially as they have become a cultural minority, American evangelicals have increasingly tried to wall themselves off. The implications for fostering a system that tolerates abuse are multiple: it makes outside accountability less possible, magnifies an external threat over an insider one, and discourages victims from speaking up because doing so would threaten their place in the only community they know.

In America, however, evangelicalism's walls are thinner. There are other community resources to employ. There are other physical places to go. There are sometimes other extended family nearby. Certainly, there are other friends to be made and other belonging to be had. It may not be easy, but you can walk away. You don't even need a passport.

9

A Breeding Ground for Abuse

Caleb Adams and Kyumin Jang don't want anything to be wasted.

They are both alumni of Faith Academy in Manila, Philippines, one of the largest mission-run schools in the world, with more than five hundred students K–12, both day students and boarders. The students are mostly American MKs, with an increasingly large contingent of Korean MKs. Although MK boarding school attendance has declined sharply in the last 20 to 30 years, 30 of the 150 mission schools around the world still offer a boarding option.[1]

Caleb, a therapist, and Kyumin, a pastor, had the idea of starting a podcast about MKs after Caleb attended a class reunion in 2021. He had become newly aware of the mixed meanings and impacts of his childhood experiences, at once cherished and traumatic, humorous and disturbing, typical childhood fare and the truly bizarre. After the reunion, he reconnected with Kyumin, from a different graduating class at Faith, who was similarly rummaging through the luggage of his life to see how he might incorporate it into his present self. Many of Caleb and Kyumin's classmates, as well as MKs from other times and places, including myself, have joined them on their *Life Unwasted* podcast to process, reminisce, laugh, cry, and just enjoy chatting with some of the only other people who understand the truly weird life of an MK.

I've listened to the stories of many Faith alumni on the podcast and collected a few myself. I hear so many familiar emotions in their voices, though our schools were half a world away from each other: the exquisite nostalgia, the fond memories, the longing for a lost home and a sense of self that, in hindsight, was squeezed too tightly into the tight space of a controlling religious culture.

Some of the particulars are unique. I never swayed gently in a hammock enveloped by the tropical dusk on a dorm balcony, or leaped off the jagged boulders of a Pacific island into the sea, or searched for World War II detritus on a field trip. There are accounts of commutes on rickety public transport, run-ins with violent crime in Faith's urban setting, and comedic stories that in hindsight are actually "not OK." In fact, "some of the f---ed-up stuff is the funniest now," Caleb says. Like the time Caleb's pet pony hung itself jumping off an embankment. The pony had been a blind MK's service animal that Caleb inherited when the family went back to United States after suffering various mishaps, including one of their children being bitten by a boa constrictor while using the outhouse. Caleb's parents had the pony's meat sold at the market, and Caleb used his share of the money to rent a car for Faith's version of prom. "Now that's horsepower," he jokes. "The Pony Story," as it's widely known among Caleb's peers, just may be one of the strangest MK tales I've ever heard. And that's saying something.

But some of the Faith MKs' stories are not the stuff of sardonic retellings years later. They are instead the stuff of corrosive memories. Children who were mercilessly, physically bullied by other students with few consequences from the adults in charge. "Creepy" teachers who looked down girls' shirts. An emotionally disturbed dorm parent who badly needed mental health treatment instead of being put in charge of twenty-odd children. Children, with parents distant in more ways than one, yearning to be special to someone. And supposedly sainted adults, called by God to care for them, who could sniff out the most vulnerable, dangle the attention they craved in front of them, then go in for the kill.

Annie Abernethy attended Faith Academy for her entire childhood.[2] Initially, her parents served as dorm parents at Faith. But when she was twelve, they took on a new assignment at a sister school in the south of the country. She wanted to stay at Faith, which she thought of as home and where she had friends and activities she loved. She loved Faith. So she moved into a dorm supervised by missionaries "Uncle Rich" and his wife.

Although Annie had lived with her parents up until then, their family life existed alongside the dorm children of whom her parents were in charge. "It was not a normal family home life," she explains. There was "not as much attachment" to her parents, whose attention she shared with many other kids. Another daughter of missionary dorm parents whom Caleb and Kyumin interviewed also discussed the resentment and frustration of sharing her parents with twenty dorm boys and awkwardly navigating adolescence in that environment.[3]

As a dorm kid, Annie felt newly important. Her dorm parents were dorm life rookies, whereas she had spent years watching her parents do the job. As she helped them learn the routine and lapped up their attention, she "felt seen for the first time," Annie says. Especially by Rich, who showered her with affection. She recalls thinking, "This is nice, I've never felt this before."

He soon began seeking her out by herself, usually when the other dorm girls were getting ready for bed and his wife was doing the same for their young child. He became increasingly physical with her. Then one evening, he beckoned her to sit with him in a papasan chair and told her he just wanted her to "feel loved." "Everything went black for me," she recalls. "There was a tangible sense of darkness . . . I remember thinking, Satan is here."

Yet the attention was so confusing. On difficult days, when she would be crying about something, he would comfort her. "Some of those memories have the potential of being sweet," she says. And I understand what she means, because it brings to mind the times my own dorm parents were there for me in my own distress. But none of them ever took advantage of me or broke my trust. "I've had to remind myself that he was predatory," she says of her enjoyment of his attention. "It began to be very sensual for me." The abuse robbed her of other relationships, as she completely fixated on Rich to the detriment of peer friendships. Other kids bullied her for being his "favorite" and called her his "girlfriend" behind her back.

She decided to tell her parents about what she perceived as a "dark spiritual experience." But when she mentioned she had been sitting in Rich's lap, her mother exclaimed, "You were doing what?!" "I knew I was in trouble," Annie remembers. "I realized then that something was wrong, and it was probably me, not him. I was a dirty, sexual girl, and all of my feelings were indecent."

Her dad ended up coming to Faith to confront Rich and talk to school administrators. At the time, she wasn't sure what happened next, only that her parents took her home with them for the rest of that year. But the next year, she went back. Rich now kept his distance from her. She felt confused, embarrassed, depressed, and rejected. She had lost her "special status." She confided in another Faith teacher, a sympathetic woman who listened to her, prayed for her, and offered words of support. But she did nothing else.

It was only as an adult that Annie realized the full extent of the damage Rich had caused. After curtailing his abuse of Annie, Rich had moved on to other girls, some of whom complained to school administrators about his inappropriate behavior. Faith administrators interviewed some of the girls at the time about how they had been "getting fresh with Uncle Rich" and the trouble *they* were causing. Administrators also talked to Rich, who told them the girls were "practically jump[ing] into my lap." They believed him, and he stayed in the dorm. He taunted the girls who turned him in, making a show over not being able to hug them or show them any attention.

Annie still thinks of Faith as "home," she said in a podcast interview. She holds in her heart the good friends she made, the fun they had, the small gifts of the place itself. "I remember the sound of rain, the frogs and geckos, the clanging of the flagpole hooks on a windy day," she wrote to me in an email. But the abuse severely weakened her confidence in her own judgment and a healthy sense of attachment. It's all jumbled up in her mind—"a nostalgia so poignantly off-kilter, you know?"

She has had to reevaluate the concept of God with which she was raised. "He's a pretty bad father," she says of that God. "[But] what I believe is not a system or a religion . . . it's a person . . . and Jesus has been a real presence to me."[4]

* * *

I so easily could have been Annie.

By the time I graduated from Rift Valley Academy (RVA), seven years after I arrived, it was my whole world. I loved my friends, some of whom I had lived with since my arrival. Sometimes it was full-on *Lord of the Flies*, and sometimes it was the true story behind the novel, in which the stranded children survive through cooperation and community. I loved the incomparable view of the Rift Valley floor and its resident dormant volcanoes, a sublime, majestic stage for an unending display of shifting light, shadow, and tint. I loved going to sleep at night to the sound of the train going by high up on the escarpment, click-clack, click-clack, click-clack, or the wind rushing down to the valley, or the rain tapping out a lullaby on the tin roof. No place has ever filled me with such wonder, the beauty seeping into my soul like a healing salve. It was my friend when I was lonely, my parent when I felt abandoned, and my God when religion failed to do him any justice. It would become my true home.

But that took time, and looking back with the wisdom of age, I can see that it was an inadequate home and that my friends—my peer-parents—were an inadequate family. At only ten years old, I spent my first year with that uneasy, on-edge feeling of not being at peace, never able to relax, always a bit on guard. I lived stuffed with fear, through clenched jaw and shallow breath, as if too much movement would shake loose everything I was holding inside in a grotesque, public humiliation. I was bullied some, tellingly for being a "teacher's pet," as receiving more than one's fair share of adult attention was a guarantee of being despised by other attention-starved children. As one MK I interviewed put it, at boarding school, you had to find ways to get love without being perceived as favored, because "[that] was a good way to get bullied." At that risk, I desperately cultivated scarce adult affection early on, even faking illness to get into the infirmary, where you could be looked after by the sweet nurse whose name was literally Mrs. Loveday. But I was not severely bullied or abused. I simply wasn't loved beyond the generic fulfillment of needs, general toleration, or institutional care. I wasn't special to anyone.

After my first year, I got used to the rhythms of boarding school life, made friends, and began to appreciate the camaraderie of being one of a group. I learned the hard way that I wasn't the center of the universe. I learned to compromise and adapt. I learned to be low-maintenance and likable. And those are all good skills to have. But ideally you learn them from a place of generosity, empathy, and knowing with certainty you are unconditionally loved. And I can't say that I knew that.

My relationship with my parents dwindled the way the weave of unfinished cloth gradually frays. I was home with them for a combined four months of each year. The remaining two-thirds of the year, we had little communication. There were no phones, or at least none of the type invented after 1885. I'm not even exaggerating. The phones at RVA had no numbers, just a big crank on the side, as if you weren't so much calling someone as aiding in the construction of an oil pipeline. You cranked the crank and subsequently heard the voice of a usually cranky operator on the other end. Needless to say, I only called my parents in dire emergencies that boiled down to *I have died and am contacting you posthumously to ask that you collect my body and bury it somewhere nice.* That happened only a few times in seven years. When we were home together, we had great times as a family. But after I went to school, it wasn't my normal life; it was more of a suspension of normal life. Nor was it the stuff of day-to-day parent-child relationship. We did not deal with the reality of each other, and we did not forge the trust that is born from conflict.

No matter how well I adjusted to boarding school life, there was always a hole inside of me, an aching need that the harried adults, trying to manage dozens of kids, and my similarly starved adolescent friends couldn't meet. I was a groomer's dream, had one found me; mercifully, none did. But we were all vulnerable, in a way: completely cut off from our parents, the emotional bonds with them underdeveloped if not broken. Children who desperately needed to feel seen. Living in a completely isolated, insular community with no oversight by local institutions or authorities. A highly controlled and controlling religious environment where submission to authority was spiritualized. Not even a phone to use. Nowhere to go, no one in whom to confide, except other members of the same self-contained community of people you believe have been called by God to be there. The Lord's chosen people for the special mission of coming to Africa. I mean, it was a predator's Disneyland.

With mission-run boarding schools, "what you have just now created is an absolutely flawless, perfect breeding ground for abuse of every shape and form and flavor," MK survivor and advocate Daniel Robinson says.[5] It's no wonder that there have been documented cases of abuse at nearly every missionary boarding school in the world.[6]

Especially after hearing survivors' stories, some from my own school, I feel thankful I was spared. I now know that one of my teachers at RVA, who served as a counselor there for over a decade, abused boys. I had no idea. With all I know now, I view in a new light some of the "creepy" behavior by staff members that I witnessed, that my friends and I joked about, and I wonder. I wonder, too, what I would have done if a staff member had abused me. I can't know for certain, but I feel fairly confident that I, like so many others, would have buried it in as deep a mental recess as I could dig.

MKs have also experienced physical abuse at boarding school. Changes in school discipline and better faculty have thankfully made it far rarer. But in the "bad old days," corporal punishment was the norm, blurring the line between discipline and abuse and resulting in severe beatings.[7] By the time I was a student in the 1980s, this was mostly unheard of. My punishments were work details, such as carrying logs from the wood pile to the dorm or extra cleaning assignments, some of which could be construed as age-inappropriate but were generally fine by my estimation. Another change is that teachers at missionary boarding schools over the last several decades have specifically volunteered for their roles, whereas in the more distant past, these individuals were often "washed-up" missionaries, those with mental health issues or other problems that the mission organization reassigned. And who better to be put in charge of a whole bunch of children than people with untreated mental illness?

I had one teacher at RVA whom I would characterize this way. She slapped one of my classmates across the face in class one day, and she once threw a chalkboard eraser at me, covering my face in dust and humiliating me in front of the class. I couldn't tell that anything was done about her behavior (I didn't report it, and I'm not sure if anyone else did), and she continued to teach for many years.

But most of my teachers were competent and kind and did the best they could to care for us. Some of my dorm parents were as dear to me as anyone has ever been, such as Miz, whose death at age thirty-nine broke my heart as few losses have. And Mr. and Mrs. B—who made us laugh and encouraged us think for ourselves and subtly subverted the evangelical party line—are still a beloved presence in many of our lives. And so many others.

My negative experiences at school almost all resulted from neglect. And again, as an exhausted parent now myself, I have a lot of grace for the individual staff members who tried their best to not just keep us alive but to genuinely care for us. It's just that it's an impossible job. We were generally left to our own devices, which sometimes included severe forms of bullying and unsafe pranks. I have heard of multiple cases of severe physical abuse of MK boys by classmates that caused enduring harm. We girls preferred gossip, teasing, and exclusion, which, in a boarding school setting where your peers are your only source of comfort and peace, is excruciating. As a sometime boarding school bully myself—one time I put baby oil in my roommate's shampoo, a prank as cruel as it was brilliant—this is a difficult truth with which I've had to wrestle.

As an example of how unsupervised adolescent behavior can go awry, in ninth grade, some dorm mates and I engaged in a multi-phase battle with one of the boys' dorms that went on for an entire school term. It culminated with one of RVA's most epic stories (in my humble opinion), in which the boys snuck into our dorm during a school-wide movie screening and hid hundreds of locusts they had spent a week collecting in every nook and cranny of our room. They put them in our pillowcases, inside our folded clothes, in tampon boxes, shoes, packed suitcases. It was extremely yucky but harmless and funny. (Later. At the time, I thought I might hyperventilate from disgust.)

But an earlier episode probably crossed the line. The boys physically restrained us, tied us to the porch columns of their dorm, and filed by in a relentless wave, dumping bucket after bucket of water, one after the other, over our heads, until I felt I couldn't breathe and my brain raced with panic. Many years later, as I was reassessing this incident and wondering if my adult horror at it was overblown, I had dinner with one of the boys, who has turned out to be a wonderful man. Out of the blue, he asked, with some chagrin, "Hey, do you remember that time we waterboarded you guys?"

The boys' dorm parents, by the way, sat just inside, where they could see the whole drama unfold not ten feet away.

10

Sent Home

Owen never got to say goodbye.

Bolivia was his home until he was sixteen years old. His mother was a hospital training nurse, and his father was a mission finance officer. Owen ran around with neighborhood kids, including a Bolivian girl who went on to become a dentist. Much later, when he returned for a brief internship as an adult, she extracted Owen's wisdom teeth.

He felt like he belonged. He attended both Bolivian and mission schools, but his friends were mostly Bolivian. Tall and blonde, he knows now he stood out, but it didn't feel that way growing up, although he was conscious of the surrounding poverty and understood his privilege. "I was aware I was much sought after," he recalls.

His reserved, midwestern parents also thrived in Bolivia. On trips back to the United States, they seemed remote and self-contained. But in Bolivia's inviting culture, they were "more alive." They were pragmatic, modest, and compassionate people, who preferred to spend time with Bolivian friends than with other missionaries.

Owen knew he was gay in junior high, which was a problem for the son of evangelical missionaries. When he was in eighth grade, he told his parents. "They were sad," he recalls, "but it was fine." They sent him to counseling, and he continued on with his adolescence, coming to terms with his sexuality. He had some brief, consensual physical encounters with other boys, but generally tried to resist what he saw as temptation.

Two years later, the family went on furlough and attended a mandatory debriefing with their mission's counselor and other mission leadership at the headquarters. Going into his counseling sessions, Owen's strategy was to say as little as possible. Which is what he did at first. He told the counselor all was well, no big drama, nothing to see here.

But his conscience wore on him, and the counselor seemed caring and kind. And Owen believed he had the assurance of confidentiality. He trusted the counselor. So he told him the truth, that he had, in evangelical parlance, "same-sex attraction" and had had some physical contact with other MK boys.

And that was when his life as he knew it ended. Suddenly, without warning, and for good. The counselor went directly to mission authorities and reported what Owen had told him. The reaction was swift and fierce.

Like what it should be when a mission organization is told of a missionary's abuse. Like what should happen to all the adult missionaries who have proven themselves dangerous to children and youth and other adults but who continued in their roles, for years, while sending agencies looked the other way.

But Owen wasn't a missionary. And he had not abused anyone. He was a gay kid trying to figure himself out. And now he'd be doing it in the midst of grief and disorientation.

Because the mission refused to let his family go back home to Bolivia. Not even to say goodbye.

The next several years plunged the whole family into despair. Owen watched his capable, intelligent father lose all confidence in himself. His dad, who held an MBA, didn't even try to get a job that would use his professional skills, instead choosing to work menial jobs. He seemed completely defeated.

Owen blamed himself. Like many MKs, he had internalized the mission from an early age and put on himself the burden of its success. The family loves to tell the story of a five-year-old Owen, during a visit to a supporting church, asking an elderly congregant, "Are you gonna pray or are you gonna give?"

And now, he thought, he had wrecked everything. He had robbed his father of meaningful work. And he had lost the only home he had ever known. He began self-harming and dabbling in what he describes as "dark magic." At one point, he ended up in an outpatient facility for treatment.

Owen eventually found his way. But he considers himself a permanent migrant, someone who can't stand to be in one place very long. His brother is the opposite, staying put in one American city his entire adulthood.

The varying "wings" and "roots" responses to MK grief is typical, according to MK advocate Michèle Phoenix.[1] Some MKs immediately dig deep roots where they are planted, while others embark on lives of unrelenting wanderlust. But either way, the grief is real. And feeling like you have some closure—some control over the terms and timing of your departure from the mission field—doesn't prevent that grief, by any means. But at least it's something to hold onto.

* * *

As Owen told me his story, I struggled to hold back the tears. Because I understood. His description of his grief in leaving dragged me back into my own. The grief of an MK returning to their passport country is not the kind that most people acknowledge or understand. There are no flowers or casseroles. There's just you, stripped of an entire life, an entire self, thrown out to sea. But at least I got to say goodbye. I got to cherish the last little bit, to be warmly embraced by the rituals of an ending. It was a tiny lifeline as I bobbed on the waves.

Decades after my own departure from Kenya, I wept over the RVA class of 2020, sent home "for a few months" in March of that year due to COVID and never to return, as it turned out. Sometimes I still worry about the students in that class, and I wonder whether they are OK.

Owen lived my worst nightmare. It was a scenario I saw happen so frequently that there was a terminology for it. If a family was "sent home," it meant that someone did something wrong—usually the parents, but perhaps the children. Possible offenses ranged from the horrific (sexual or physical abuse, or violence; again, I knew a suspected murderer), to the corrupt (misuse or embezzlement of mission funds), to the personal (marital problems, infidelity, homosexuality, noticeable mental health issues). There were usually few details offered publicly but a lot of whispering behind the scenes.

In some cases, the reasons for the departure were advertised, if there was some larger lesson the community needed to hear or if the offender did not have friends in higher places. Caleb Adams told me that, while he was at Faith Academy in the late 1990s, school leadership announced at chapel one day that two female teachers had been "sent home" for homosexual behavior. Caleb thinks there were actually only some affectionate emails between the women, not even a physical relationship. But a gay MK I interviewed, who was also present that day, got the message loud and clear. He was terrified. "Being gay was pretty much the worst sin," Caleb surmised when I asked him about the wildly divergent reactions to mission field offenses, from public shaming to sweepings under rugs.

More sympathetic responses were given to leave-takings described as "having to go home." When someone "had to go home," it could mean one of the family or their elderly parents in the United States had severe health problems. It could also encompass mental health problems, although depending on other factors, that person might be "sent home" instead. For missionaries who had to raise their own support, "having to go home" might mean their funding had dried up or that the country in which they lived had become too unstable. Or it could mean the family just "couldn't cut it" on the mission field, that they didn't have what it took. Or it meant one of their children was a problem. Bad behavior, mental health issues, acting out, addiction, eating disorders, self-harm, being severely bullied at school, being a victim of abuse: all of these were MK "problems" that often necessitated leaving the mission field. "People would just disappear," said one Faith alumnus. "You never saw them again."[2]

These days, mission organizations and schools have more resources to support missionary families. RVA now has several trained therapists on staff, as well as relationships with psychiatrists in Nairobi. I personally know of students in more recent years getting the help they needed to successfully remain in school—although one RVA alumnus told Caleb on his podcast that when she sought help as a student there in 2010, the message she heard was to "stop being a problem."[3]

Tanya Crossman of TCK Training believes the broader scope of "member care"—as mission organizations' support structures are called—is a mixed bag. "Too often, member care is modeled more on human resources than mental health care, seeing missionaries as employees, and the organization with a reputation in need of protection," she says. "It's a well-meaning hybrid that can inflict unintended trauma through strict processes that leave little space for unique realities."[4] Counselors are often not well trained, and, as Owen's case demonstrated, they aren't bound by confidentiality standards and are encouraged to report to mission authorities. There can be unpredictable outcomes that may deter honesty.

Most MKs dread leaving the mission field more than almost anything else. They not only don't feel a strong connection to the United States (it's definitely not "home") but many have had intensely negative experiences there. I simply didn't know who I was in America. And I didn't really want to know. I thought leaving Kenya would be a kind of death. And when I eventually did have to leave, to return for college, I found out I was right.

So, a lot of us learn not to make any waves. Evangelicalism generally doesn't like waves anyway. That culture likes sweet stories that inspire and confirm belief. It likes tales of redemption and forgiveness that get neatly wrapped up. On the mission field, though, telling the wrong stories will annihilate your entire life. Many MKs internalize the message: whatever you do, don't rock the boat. Don't divulge. Don't tell. Don't be a victim. If you see something, say nothing.

Everything is fine.

* * *

Of course, as we have seen, some missionaries have been allowed to stay and stay and stay, even after abuse was repeated, reported, and known. Their victims often left before they did. Or abusers were "sent home" quietly, without further consequence, without further warning to other missions or ministries or churches.

Who got "sent home" and who got to stay seemed to have little rhyme or reason even within the same mission organization. Looking at multiple cases within multiple organizations, we can see that clear, uniformly applied policies were not the norm in missions before the last fifteen to twenty years. As Caleb Adams pointed out, the offense mattered somewhat—homosexual activity was deemed worse than heterosexual. But William McElrath in Indonesia also abused boys, and there are similar cases in which the perpetrator was allowed to stay. If I were to guess, I'd say it probably came down to the personal: who the abuser was, how well connected, how well liked, how talented a missionary they were, how many converts and baptisms they could claim. But even that doesn't explain every case. Dee Ann Miller, the Southern Baptist missionary who was assaulted by a colleague, says her assailant was not well liked or respected in the mission. But still he was protected.

"In hindsight," Miller says, "based on what I know about institutions in general, keeping his criminal behavior under [wraps] was . . . because he was an embarrassment to the system."

Regardless of whether a mission board allowed a perpetrator to stay or sent them home, they almost always remained silent. Once "home," abusers in most cases have faced no legal action, and many continue in ministry. Few, if any, questions are asked by onward employers—mission field experience is seen as a plus in evangelical settings—and there has often been no intervention by mission boards to ensure a perpetrator is not allowed to continue in ministry or work with children.

In the cases of which I have personal knowledge, the missionary suspected of murdering his wife and Russell from chapter 7, both the alleged perpetrators went on to further ministry, at least for a time. In Russell's case, he continued in ministry not despite his conduct but *because* of it. He was specifically platformed as a "recovered sex addict" by the pastor of a megachurch who had met Russell on short-term mission trips. The pastor reached out to invite Russell, fresh out of rehab, to head up a new counseling ministry at his church. As if that isn't outrageous enough, the pastor himself was later credibly accused of assaulting a congregant, and he sent his own victim and her husband to counseling at Russell's center.

As journalist Kathryn Joyce has pointed out, the "sprawling, disparate world" of evangelicalism makes it easier for abusers to move on to the next thing, reinvent themselves in a new role, and evade accountability.[5] This is especially the case with missionaries from the many small, nondenominational mission boards who raise their own support from individual donors and churches. These mission boards aren't tied to a network of churches or governing structures. Small mission boards also have fewer resources for human resource management, accountability structures, and policies. Still, you would think prospective employers, Christian or otherwise, would check references and contact mission boards and that boards of any size would provide pertinent information on the person's job performance and character.

What is perhaps most outrageous—though perhaps not surprising, given the documented cover-up of hundreds of sexual abuse cases within the Southern Baptist Convention—is how routinely the largest, most bureaucratic of mission boards, the Southern Baptists' IMB, has quietly "sent home" problematic missionaries and apparently done nothing to stop their ongoing ministry in Southern Baptist churches and organizations in the United States. This practice apparently goes back over a century. Historian João Chaves and his coauthors have documented cases of problematic Southern Baptist missionaries in Brazil in the late nineteenth and early twentieth centuries quietly reassigned or "sent home," according to missionary correspondence.[6] More recently, other cases have been detailed by journalists.

After the IMB fired McElrath in 1995, he joined a Southern Baptist church in North Carolina, where he served as a deacon and taught English classes to recent immigrants. The church's pastor was aware of McElrath's past, according to a bizarrely matter-of-fact confession letter McElrath wrote to the church in 2002 and the pastor's subsequent statement. The two men had agreed when McElrath joined the church that he would not work with youth or children, although in the 2002 letter, he acknowledged "occasionally accept[ing] one-time requests to share with children or youth" in conjunction with his wife. As if his revelation to his church was no big deal, akin to dipping a few bucks out of the offering plate, McElrath said he planned to continue teaching English classes to adults as part of the church's ongoing "mission" to new immigrants and students. The church's pastor assured the congregation that McElrath would have no contact with children.[7] And that was apparently that.

In the case of Tom Wade, a missionary in several African countries in the 1970s and '80s, the IMB kept credible allegations that he was abusing his daughter *from his own wife.* She only discovered he was abusing children after their return to the United States, three years after the IMB knew about it. She turned her husband in to the police, and he was convicted and sent to prison for the offenses committed in the United States. The IMB denied her request for compensation and counseling because she and her husband had "both" resigned.[8]

I asked Dee Ann Miller where the breakdown in accountability occurred. Since resigning from the mission board more than thirty years ago, after a year-long fight to get her assailant "sent home," she has become an advocate for mission field survivors and for reform in religious organizations across the board. Was it a failure of the church or ministry where the abuser went on to serve to do a proper background check? Had they not contacted the IMB at all or disregarded incriminating information provided? Or was the IMB failing to provide complete and accurate information about the former missionary's record? What was happening, exactly?

"I wish I knew," she told me. "Let me know if you find out. Quite possibly all of the above."

Miller's assailant went on to serve in a series of Southern Baptist churches and ministries in the United States. She says that after the *Houston Chronicle* detailed her story in 2019, a middle-aged woman reached out to Miller. More than three decades earlier, the same man had assaulted the woman after his return from the mission field. She was fourteen at the time.[9]

The IMB has conducted various internal investigations on these matters over the years, most recently in 2018, after public disclosure of the IMB's mishandling of a case involving Mark Aderholt, a missionary in Hungary who assaulted a then-teenaged Anne Marie Miller (no relation to Dee Ann) before being appointed by the Board. In 2007, Miller informed the IMB about the abuse, and the Board found her allegations to be credible. But it allowed Aderholt to return quietly to the United States, where he subsequently served at two Southern Baptist churches. He was finally charged with assaulting Miller in 2018 and eventually pleaded guilty.

The IMB's 2018 policy review, conducted by a law firm, concluded with recommendations for major policy changes, including hiring an abuse prevention and response director and requiring that all allegations be reported to local and US authorities. The IMB says it fully implemented all recommendations by 2021; the IMB never publicly released the 2018 review's full findings. When I initially contacted the IMB for comment in 2022, however, the IMB website said the organization would report allegations to authorities only if an internal investigation found it was "warranted," and that it "encourages victims to report their cases to the authorities."[10] Two years later, in a belated response to my repeated requests for information, the IMB said it had updated its policy to include: "Our default stance is to take the necessary actions, to report a credible report of abuse to appropriate authorities, and to remove offending individuals from IMB employment."[11]

The IMB has issued no public reports of any internal IMB investigations nor any public detailing of missionaries fired for abuse. In a letter to one MK victim's family, former IMB President Jerry Rankin—who served with McElrath in Indonesia—wrote,

"I see no constructive purpose by making a general accounting of [this] matter to all our missionaries and to Southern Baptists in general."[12]

* * *

Other mission organizations, too, have resisted publicly acknowledging past abuses and identifying perpetrators. As of this writing, Faith Academy has never publicly acknowledged its investigation of Annie Abernethy's abuser. I reached out to the school requesting information and was told they could not give me information about any specific case. They provided me with their child protection policy and said, "Faith Academy continually improves its child safety policies and response procedures by following emerging best practices, including trauma-informed care."[13]

Annie Abernethy says she sat for hours with investigators—she even gave them access to her therapist and mental health-care records—only to receive a terse three-page report sent only to her that did not even name her abuser, as well as a generic cover letter of apology sent to all the survivors.

Africa Inland Mission (AIM), which runs RVA, commissioned an investigation of my former teacher in 2008, after he had already moved back to the United States. They claimed it was external, but it did not meet those criteria as defined by victims' advocates, such as attorney Boz Tchividjian.[14] AIM's child safety officer (CSO) told me AIM reported the findings of the investigation to his victims or their parents if they were still minors (it's not clear how they identified those victims) and reported him to authorities in the US state where he lived after leaving RVA. But otherwise there has been no public acknowledgment of this case "because investigations are done to a standard of preponderance of the evidence, which is a standard very different from a criminal conviction," according to the official.[15]

I can understand the impulse to protect an individual before there is credible evidence of wrongdoing or in the absence of criminal conviction. However, as AIM's CSO herself acknowledged to me, criminal conviction for overseas abuse is "a huge challenge . . . [because] evidence and testimony is often lacking [and] there are multiple jurisdictions."[16] In addition, in many cases the abusive acts may not be illegal in the country where they were committed. Last, there was no US federal jurisdiction for overseas child abuse until 2003. So, in the interest of preventing future abuse in a ministry context or providing healing for victims, I wonder if criminal conviction should be the standard for public disclosure of mission field abuse. If an investigation concludes there are credible reports of abuse, particularly if there are multiple victims, most advocates think sunlight is the best disinfectant. A public acknowledgment of abuse is a lifeline to survivors, who may be hiding in the shadows, afraid they won't be believed. They may or may not hear of an investigation through the grapevine.

The refusal to release full findings is only one of the faults MK survivors and advocates find with most missions' investigations into past abuses. They say the only credible investigation is a wholly external one conducted by a firm completely independent from the organization in question or other missions or missions-adjacent organizations. The first investigation into abuse at a school run by New Tribes Mission (now called Ethnos360), for instance, was performed by victims' advocate Tchividjian and his organization, Godly Response to Abuse in the Christian Environment (GRACE). The final report of abuse at a New Tribes school in Senegal was public, detailed, lengthy, and horrific. It named names of both perpetrators and those complicit in the cover-up.[17] The mission had no control over where the investigation went nor how the findings were released.

Not surprisingly, New Tribes Mission subsequently opted for in-house investigators and legal counsel for other inquiries—there have been findings of pervasive, widespread abuse at multiple New Tribes schools—and have closely guarded their conclusions.[18] According to MK survivor and advocate Richard Darr, most of the twenty-four denominational and interdenominational mission agencies involved in reports of abuse his organization has received from MKs have had "inadequate" responses, including "ineffective internal investigations."[19] Tchividjian wrote in 2021 that Christian organizations' claims of conducting "independent investigations" were more "fashionable" than credible. He argued the motivation behind most investigations mission organizations have conducted is "institutional self-preservation," and the way they are done meets the criteria of an internal investigation, in which the organization remains "in the driver's seat," controlling the investigators, process, and findings.[20]

The efforts of alumni survivors of Hillcrest School in Nigeria are illustrative. The Hillcrest Survivors Steering Committee, with the support of MK Safety Net—a resource and sounding board for MK survivors that strives to educate the broader public about the issue of mission field abuse and trauma—has been trying to get the school to authorize an independent investigation since 2021. The school's superintendent has denied that Hillcrest is responsible for the abuse that occurred there, instead blaming the consortium of missions who funded and staffed the school.

She has also cited as a reason for the school's inaction the small volume of historical records, mainly yearbooks, that might verify the employment of teachers and hostel parents at Hillcrest. The yearbooks do not identify the mission affiliations of staff and, given that students were sometimes not aware of their teachers' affiliations, the Steering Committee has had to painstakingly research this information. Multiple cases of missions that have since changed their names or divided have further complicated their efforts.[21]

The Steering Committee has contacted each of the fifteen-plus mission organizations who have seconded staff to Hillcrest over the years. Some of them have been cooperative, despite not having had personnel at Hillcrest for many years. The United Methodist Church and the Evangelical Lutheran Church in America, upon discovering the volume of allegations of abuse—from the Steering Committee, not from Hillcrest—immediately agreed to support an investigation. The Steering Committee subsequently secured cooperation from nine more organizations. The IMB, which had teachers at Hillcrest for years, has thus far refused to join the coalition of mission boards cooperating with the Steering Committee and stopped responding to their emails after issuing a "statement of support" for the survivors in September 2023.[22]

It's important to note here that MK survivors have gotten far more accountability from mission boards than have local victims of missionary abuse. I know of no investigation of such cases authorized by any mission board, nor of any acknowledgment or compensation for these local victims. Christopher Cole does not believe the IMB investigated the possibility that McElrath may have abused Indonesian children as well.[23] Nor, to my knowledge, was there any subsequent investigation by Russell's mission board into the well-being of the woman or women with whom he "had affairs."

MK survivors' and advocates' takeaway from involvement in these processes has been that mission organizations are motivated by self-preservation rather than by repentance and a desire for change. In a recorded conversation posted on MK and advocate Lindsay Rodriguez's website, Lindsay and Annie Abernethy noted the eerie similarities between the cases of abuse at their two boarding schools, half a world and many years apart and involving different mission organizations (Lindsay attended a New Tribes school in Panama and had friends abused there). In each case, Annie observed, there was a "circling of the wagons, and we're the fools that get caught in the middle." Mission organizations seem to believe they can't completely come clean without jeopardizing donations and their "sacred" work.

"Apparently God needs lawyers," Annie deadpans during their conversation.

"Why does this deity need the protection of fragile humans?" Lindsay asks. "Is that deity even worthy of your worship?"[24]

11

Fighting for Change

Dianne Darr Couts will not be quiet.

It's just not in her constitution. She credits her parents' encouragement to speak her mind, but she says it's also "just sort of the way I'm wired, to just have it be out there. I'm quite extroverted, as you can tell."[1]

I can tell. She speaks bluntly, and her eyes flash with fire. It's the same spunk I could see in photos of her as a child, decades ago, as an MK in what is now Mali. She has one of those faces that is easily recognizable as the same person throughout their lives.

She has needed that fire to survive and to fight for the survival of others, starting with her three younger brothers, for whom she tried her best to care through the upheavals of their childhood, when their mother was sick, and when they were horribly abused at boarding school.

Dianne's introduction to the mission field was swift and cruel. When her family arrived in the late 1950s, her parents left her and the oldest of her three brothers in the care of another missionary family in Dakar, Senegal, while they traveled into the remote interior to set up a house. Dianne was just turning nine when her missionary "uncle," Ron, began molesting her.

A few months later, their parents returned to move the family to the small village of Kenieba, where they lived in two thatch-roofed huts connected by a veranda with an outdoor toilet and shower.

Another missionary family lived on the compound, too. And that missionary "uncle," Don, also began molesting Dianne, as well as her brother, David. Ron's family came to live on the compound, too, for a brief time, before he was killed in a fire.

Dianne told her parents about Don a year later (she only told them about Ron as an adult). "They believed me, right away," she says. "My dad was amazing . . . he was tender hearted. But, boy, you did not push him over a certain line."

Her parents immediately contacted their mission board, but when officials confronted Don, they were satisfied with his apologies and his promises never to do it again. "My parents were asked to forgive him and move on," Dianne writes in her memoir. When her father demanded Don be removed from the mission field, the mission board accused her parents of trying to "ruin Don's ministry."[2]

Dianne's parents changed mission affiliations, and Don remained on the mission field. Years later, after Don continued to minimize what had happened and even accused Dianne of seducing him (she was nine at the time), mission board authorities confronted him again. He finally signed a full confession, admitting what he had done.

The Darrs' new mission organization required all their missionaries to send their children to boarding school at

Mamou Alliance Academy in Guinea, run by the Christian and Missionary Alliance (C&MA). The youngest of Dianne's brothers was just five years old. They and many other children endured horrific physical, sexual, emotional, and spiritual abuse by multiple staff members, spanning at least twenty-five years. This story is presented in heartbreaking detail in the 2012 documentary *All God's Children.* Dianne's brothers and other children were beaten, humiliated, forced to urinate on themselves, and sexually and physically abused by older boys. Dianne was not assaulted at Mamou, but other girls reported being raped repeatedly by a dorm parent.

All the while, of course, they attended multiple Bible classes and services every week. Every Sunday was a "confession" service, with an altar call at the end, during which time the children were encouraged to come forward and repent of their sins.

"Remembering my years at Mamou is complicated," Dianne writes in her memoir. Obviously, she remembers the abuse and spiritual manipulation. She says her brothers have suffered immensely due to their time there. But, like many MKs when reflecting on the difficulties of their childhood, she was comforted by the beauty of the place. "My eyes well up with tears when I long for just one more glimpse," she writes. "But deeper than that are the scars . . . that will never heal this side of heaven."[3] Those scars are physical, in Dianne's estimation. She attributes to her childhood trauma decades of severe gynecological problems that eventually required a hysterectomy. "The body *does* keep the score," she tells me, referencing Bessel van der Kolk's book on the physical effects of emotional trauma.

Dianne also cherished her friends from Mamou. And it was out of those bonds that a movement was born. In the mid-1990s, the Mamou alumni began reconnecting with each other and connecting the dots. As they shared their experiences, they realized that what they had suffered was much more severe and systemic than any of them had known individually. The wisdom of age and experience also strengthened their resolve, and they decided they had to do something to get justice for themselves and protection for MKs going forward.

David and Richard Darr, two of Dianne's brothers, and others formed a steering committee, conferred with an attorney, and began to press the C&MA denomination, which ran Mamou, for an inquiry. Dianne's father, who was a former president of their mission agency, the Gospel Missionary Union (GMU), also began pressing the GMU for an investigation of Mamou, where the mission had required its personnel to send their children, and of Ivory Coast Academy, another mission-run boarding school that faced multiple allegations of abuse. Rev. Darr got "a response of inaction."[4]

In 1995, Dianne and five other Mamou alumni set up a lonely picket line at the C&MA's annual meeting in Pittsburgh. They handed out homemade fliers detailing the abuse they had suffered, and they prayed together. At first attendees were curious about their presence, but when they realized why the group was there, they turned hostile, yelling at the alumni group as they streamed into the conference. Despite its small size, the protest and the story behind it got national media attention. American evangelicals were finally confronted with what had been going on for decades.[5]

The following year, the C&MA agreed to conduct an independent investigation. It found seven missionaries guilty of abusing dozens of children over a twenty-year timespan. That was the first of many investigations of missionary abuse that have followed, as well as a wave of policy changes by mission boards and missionary boarding schools.[6] In 1999, the Mamou steering committee became the advocacy group MK Safety Net.

Dianne is the current president of MK Safety Net, and she is gratified by what she sees as real reform and greater awareness. But as a survivor and an advocate, she isn't satisfied. "When we went to Pittsburgh, we really thought there would be change. I had no idea I'd still be at this thirty years later," she tells me. "The younger people need to take this over. It is hugely stressful for me . . . to see it repeat and repeat and repeat," she says wearily. "And the victims, survivors doing all the heavy lifting."

She says that present action is at least better than mission boards' handling of historic abuses. She and other survivors have told me they have never gotten the kind of apologies they deeply want, apologies in which mission boards completely and earnestly take responsibility for enabling and mishandling abuse. They long for the organizations with which their parents served to grapple with the culture and belief systems that bred this immense moral failure and how those ideas continue to undergird missions.

"To be blunt," she concludes our conversation, "I really feel they're just waiting for us to die."

* * *

The determined lobbying by MK survivors and the resultant public shaming of mission organizations have no doubt been a major impetus for changes in policy. But Dianne and other advocates also point to crucial changes in US law. They consider the 2003 federal PROTECT Act a watershed in addressing mission field abuse.[7] Before 2003, mission boards could quietly send abusers home because missionaries essentially operated in a legal no-man's-land, with no applicable US jurisdiction and complicated or inadequate foreign ones. In many of the countries in which missionaries serve, the criminal justice system is not equipped to handle such cases, and cultural norms and even laws themselves too often excuse abuse of women and children (and as survivors know all too well, justice is hard-won even in the United States).

The 2003 law allows the federal government to prosecute American citizens for sex crimes and child sexual abuse committed overseas (it has no provisions for other forms of child abuse). The perpetrators that the law's architects probably had in mind were international businessmen who take despicable detours to Bangkok or shadowy purveyors of child sexual abuse material. But several missionaries have now been successfully prosecuted by the Department of Justice under this statute. And mission boards now have a clear legal path to report missionary abusers to US authorities.[8]

Equally important, the law also removed the statute of limitations for criminal child abuse. A 2022 law eliminates the statute of limitations for a minor victim to file civil suits in these cases, removing an impediment that, for example, derailed a 2021 civil suit against the SIM mission brought by Hillcrest and Kent Academy survivors. This doesn't help Dianne or others who were victimized before 2003. But going forward, missionaries and mission boards are legally liable no matter how much time has passed. After the 2022 law was passed, advocate Boz Tchividjian tweeted, "Mission agencies . . . be on notice!"[9]

Another positive change is that the deference shown to missionaries in many developing countries is beginning to erode with the rise of educated professionals who are aware of the historical and cultural dimensions of Western philanthropy and who are more committed to the rights of women and children. Missionaries have been charged or civilly sued in Uganda, Belize, Kenya, and the Philippines.[10] However, charges were dropped in the Belize and Philippines cases, demonstrating the ongoing difficulty of securing convictions. Legal deficiencies in most countries also remain. Data compiled by the group End Child Prostitution in Asian Tourism (ECPAT), which tracks and lobbies for efforts to end the sexual exploitation of children around the world, indicates there are massive gaps globally; most countries do not even have a legal age of consent.[11]

The case of missionary Gregory Dow, who was eventually prosecuted by the US Justice Department, likewise shows the weaknesses of child protection mechanisms in many countries. Dow, who was a registered sex offender in the United States when he arrived in Kenya in 2006, was able to establish an orphanage and abuse dozens of Kenyan children for over a decade before the Kenyan police took any action. Orphanage employees reported Dow to various Kenyan authorities several times over the years but were told to "leave [Dow] alone" because the orphanage was "a small America in the village." When authorities finally did issue an arrest warrant, he was able to slip out of the country. A Kenyan court convicted his wife and sentenced her to a fine and time served in remand. Catching Gregory Dow took the dogged efforts of a Kenyan American woman, Margaret Ruto, who heard about the case while visiting family. She painstakingly gathered testimony from multiple victims, alerted American authorities, and secured his arrest in the United States.[12]

With advances on the legal front, including the possibility of facing civil action, and more MKs speaking out, mission boards and schools have uniformly adopted child protection policies and other accountability standards over the last fifteen years. Many of these policies have been crafted under the guidance of the Child Safety and Protection Network (CSPN), an organization founded in 2006 by mission agencies, faith-based NGOs, and international Christian schools to help such organizations create policies and to offer training to their personnel on abuse prevention and response. CSPN's growth, from thirteen founding member organizations to 130 today, speaks to how the concern for child protection on the mission field has increased. The CSPN recommendations and the mission board and mission school policies I've read include definitions of different forms of abuse; the appointment of child safety officers and the establishment of email addresses or hotlines for reporting abuse; improved screening procedures, including background checks, for all personnel; initial and ongoing training for personnel on how to recognize and report abuse; response procedures for investigating and reporting abuse; and "member care," which includes mental health check-ins and care for mission families.[13]

Advocates say the establishment of these policies is a major advance in mission field accountability. But they also point out enduring gaps. For example, MK Christopher Cole, who himself served as a Southern Baptist missionary, lauds the IMB for improvements in its policies, which his family experienced firsthand, such as mandatory abuse prevention training for all missionaries and age-appropriate versions for children. But he thinks the policy contains too much wiggle room for not warning future churches and ministries about missionaries terminated for misconduct.[14] He has pointed out that the IMB policy as written seems to put the onus on the hiring church or ministry to request information from the IMB, although senior IMB officials have more recently told Cole that the Board does notify churches if they discover a fired employee has been subsequently hired in a ministry position. But the IMB doesn't actively keep tabs on fired personnel and doesn't have a proactive plan regarding their subsequent non-ministry employment. The IMB policy also requires former IMB employees to sign a release of personnel records before the Board will pass them onward, a measure Cole calls "simply unacceptable."[15]

The IMB's guidelines for reporting to authorities also raise questions. The policy offers a phone number and email through which to report to IMB officials and states that the IMB will forward reports of overseas abuse to Child Protective Services or police in the alleged perpetrator's home state "if the IMB believes that any personnel has committed child abuse." But I wonder why the IMB doesn't report the information to the FBI, instead of local or state police or child protection officials, as the appropriate American authority, given the federal jurisdiction under the PROTECT Act.[16] Susan Bissell, the former chief of child protection for UNICEF, told me that in her reading of the PROTECT Act, any suspected cases of child sexual abuse by an American citizen overseas should be reported to the FBI via a US embassy.[17] She added that she doesn't "have a lot of faith" in any internal reporting mechanism, regardless of the organization. "It doesn't work," she says, "And it implies . . . being beyond the law."

Africa Inland Mission's child safety officer (CSO) was honest about the incredible complexity involved in navigating domestic and foreign legal systems, as well as the mission's conduct code. She says that the specific authority to whom AIM reports would depend on where the offense is committed, the laws of that country, and the nationality of the offender (AIM has many non-American personnel). If local laws were violated, AIM would report the person to local authorities. She, however, detailed concerns about how local authorities would treat victims, as forensic practices and cultural mores may not meet American standards for victim protection. If AIM's code of conduct but not local laws were violated, then AIM would go through American CPS in the state where the offender is from. I asked her why AIM would do an investigation before onward reporting, and she said that in most of the countries where they work, CPS mechanisms are not adequate and that the threshold for a breach of AIM policy is much lower than for criminal liability.[18]

But once again, given that US federal law since 2003 applies to Americans committing abuse overseas, I am unclear why any mission board must conduct an internal investigation before contacting American authorities. I'm also confused about why a mission board would report to state police or CPS officials instead of going directly to the FBI. The CSOs of both AIM and Faith Academy, as well as the IMB's abuse prevention and response director, seemed unclear about when and how they could and should report abuse to the FBI. I reached out twice to CSPN, of which both RVA and Faith Academy are members, to ask what guidance they give on this matter, but I received no reply.

Current US law does not mandate that mission organizations report abuse at all. There are still no mandatory reporting requirements for American entities and citizens overseas. In the United States, teachers, doctors, ministers, and other people who work with children are required by law to report any allegation or even suspicion of child abuse directly and immediately to police or to CPS. But mission agencies are still bound only by their own policies, most of which require an internal investigation before onward reporting. Boz Tchividjian and other advocates have tried to secure passage of a law that would extend mandatory reporting to US authorities, which Tchividjian says is "critical" for protecting children, and Americans working in these roles around the world. The Kimberly Doe Act, named for an MK raped by a missionary in Bangladesh, was introduced in 2015, but never made it out of a House committee.[19]

Advocates also have more general concerns about the implementation of mission agency policies. CSPN, on which most agencies and schools rely for guidance and training, ended previous regulatory and oversight requirements for membership in 2017, according to MK Safety Net's Sarah Bucy Klingler.[20] Currently, all of its resources, trainings, and conferences are optional for membership.[21] The CSPN website makes clear that it is "not an accrediting or regulatory organization and membership does not signify that CSPN has concurred with each organization's child safety program."[22] Klingler and other advocates worry that, in the absence of oversight, membership in CSPN can provide organizations with an unearned facade of diligence.

As an example of how policy adoption does not necessarily translate to implementation, Dianne Darr Couts points to a recent investigation of abuse at a Missionary Aviation Fellowship (MAF) training facility in the United States. She says the MAF investigation was well done, meeting the standards of an external, independent investigation. But it revealed that none of the MAF employees knew that MAF, a founding member of CSPN, even had abuse prevention and reporting policies, much less how they were implemented.[23]

On the positive side of things, I have witnessed firsthand at least some changes to child safety policies while visiting RVA. RVA implemented its child safety policies in 2014 in cooperation with CSPN, and the most recent version, revised in 2021, appears in full on RVA's website (I found that RVA is an exception; most organizations and schools are only forthcoming about the existence of a policy or with a very broad strokes summary). While visiting staff member friends on campus in 2023, I was surprised when one of my friends told me she was "on duty" monitoring the student center that evening. In days of yore, not only were staff apparently uninterested that some male students were physically restraining and "waterboarding" female students, most of the time there was no adult presence anywhere to be found past a certain hour, when staff families generally retreated to their homes. There were always a few enterprising staff members who enjoyed hunting down student couples violating the strict rules against physical contact. But otherwise, they couldn't be bothered.

"On duty?" I asked, totally confused.

"Yeah, we have a staff member at each of the areas of campus where the kids congregate. Just to make sure everyone is safe."

"Huh," I said. "Well, that's a change."

12

Theology Trumps Policy

Becca just wanted to be a good person.

When her parents, who were physicians, told her they felt called to serve as medical missionaries in Kenya, she "felt like the rug was pulled out from under me." She was in sixth grade and happy with her school and life in New England. She spent a few months angry and upset, to the point that her parents almost put off going. "But then I saw how it was hurting them," she recalls. "I felt myself being selfish." So, she wrote an essay for her parents, laying out all the reasons why they should go, citing the Great Commission and Jesus's parable of the talents. She told them medicine was their talent, and they were obliged to use it to bring people to Christ.

She doesn't know whether it was her parents' personal decision or their mission's policy, but the family spent their first few months living with a Kenyan family. The family was wonderful, she told me, but their lifestyle was not what she was used to. They had no hot water, and bathing was difficult. She and her brother got scabies. Looking back, she's thankful for the experience, although it was a huge adjustment having come straight from the United States. It was an adjustment for her parents, too; she recalls her vegetarian father watching their hosts kill a goat to roast, a common way to welcome guests or celebrate other special occasions in Kenya. He ate some of the goat without comment.

Once in their own home near the hospital where her parents worked, she settled in. She loved RVA, which is just up the hill from the hospital. She was thus able to attend school as a rare day student, and she succeeded in every way: academically, socially, spiritually. She felt "closer to God" in the school's devout environment. She got baptized. And she started dating in the way RVA allowed, which came down to furtively holding hands at school-wide movie screenings or kissing in a darkened corridor.

Becca was at RVA at the height of the purity culture boom of the early 2000s, which took long-promulgated evangelical strictures against premarital sex and the shame and fear used to enforce them—with which I was raised a decade or so earlier—and intensified and formalized them in curricula and practices like purity rings and purity balls. Purity culture rituals and products all made the long journey to Africa and to other mission fields around the world, from MK schools to True Love Waits rallies for indigenous Christians. Becca and other women of her era with whom I spoke told me that RVA separated the boys and the girls for a purity-based program in tenth grade. While the boys went camping and did "manly" things in the outdoors, the girls went on a "princess retreat," where they picked the petals off roses and tore up paper hearts to illustrate what happened when a hypothetical girl did anything approaching premarital sex. By the time the girl got married, "she had nothing left to give to her husband," Becca remembers.

She kept one worksheet they used that had a list of physical acts with corresponding rankings. A woman who was "pure" on her wedding day—who had engaged in none of the acts—was "priceless china," while further down the list she might become "a ceramic mug" or a "styrofoam cup." "It didn't actually take much to become one of those," Becca recalls. This, and an alarmist video on the physical and emotional consequences of sex outside of marriage, was the only sex ed she got at RVA.

Even during my time, RVA had a strict dress code mainly targeted at girls' modesty. Staff could stop and ask you to kneel on the ground to measure any skirt that appeared too short to see if it met the requirement of no more than two inches above the bend of the knee. Then there was the mandatory swimsuit inspection before the senior beach trip, which was like a Miss America contest from hell. You donned the swimsuit or swimsuits you planned to wear on Senior Safari and paraded in front of an esteemed panel of female staff members. You had to walk toward them, away from them, bend over, squat, bounce, and do some light calisthenics. The judges carefully assessed whether there was any indication that you were an adult human female, and if there was, that swimsuit was a no. I was fortunate enough to bear little evidence of sexual maturity myself, but my more buxom friends basically had to wear a wetsuit.

I can laugh about this now, but the rest of Becca's story shows how harmful patriarchal theology, which puts full responsibility on women and girls for upholding sexual ethics, can be. When she was in tenth grade, Becca and her boyfriend were called into the Dean of Men's office based on reports they had violated school rules (someone had seen her boyfriend's arm around her). He lectured both of them for a few minutes before dismissing her boyfriend. He then continued to berate Becca, telling her that, based on this incident and another, similar one with a previous boyfriend, she "had a problem." She was causing boys to "stumble," and she needed to reflect on her behavior.

"I was so ashamed," she tells me through tears. "I didn't want to tell my parents; I thought they'd think the same thing about me." She felt like she had a "permanent mark" on her good record, and in fact, she was subsequently denied admission into the National Honor Society due to "character issues." She doubled down on trying to be a good person. Already very committed to her faith, Becca "got more serious" about it, fasting one day a week and refraining from all dating.

She finished up at RVA with many positive experiences, too. She still considers it her "beloved school." But a year after graduating from college, Becca was sexually assaulted, and all the shame, guilt, and fear resurfaced like an overflowing septic tank. "My mind flashed with images of teacups, ceramic mugs, and styrofoam cups," she wrote in a 2018 letter to RVA authorities, urging change, as part of a review the school commissioned after several incidents of sexual and racial harassment in which alumni were invited to have input. "I was now forced into being the styrofoam cup that I had always dreaded becoming."

She continued, "I believe fear is too central to the culture at Rift Valley Academy. Fear of breaking school rules . . . Fear of being judged . . . Fear of asking questions . . . If the culture of fear continues, there will be more girls like me who will remain silent . . . They have gotten used to the idea that adults are not necessarily safe to confide in. They have gotten used to being judged."

* * *

The culture assessment that RVA commissioned and that prompted Becca's letter yielded some tangible change. To its credit, the school released the full findings and recommendations to students, parents, and alumni, and it implemented some reforms. The stringent dress codes are gone. The purity curriculum is gone, although the school still promulgates traditional, conservative sexual ethics. There is more female representation in leadership.

The 2022 document detailing RVA's responses to the audit, however, references "diversity" in staff viewpoints on gender issues and admits to a lack of "a unified and overarching goal to ensure attainment of gender equality. . . . An absence of coordinated effort and focus on the attainment of gender equality is likely to limit sustained systemic change."[1] As the 2019 audit had explained, "RVA exhibits many of the characteristics of a conservative, white, United States (US), male-centered culture that has been perpetuated through the generations, supported by doctrinal teaching, which has resulted in a culture in which some women and many girls do not have a healthy understanding of their value and significance, and in which there is the perception of high levels of male power and control."[2]

And that is what we call the rub. Policy changes are fantastic. Better mental health support is great. Clearer legal remedies are vital. And good implementation, when it occurs, is laudable. But unless you address the underlying beliefs that have allowed abuse to happen, you haven't solved the problem. As MK Safety Net's Sarah Bucy Klingler told me, ultimately, "theology trumps policy."[3] And the same theology that has fueled abuse crises in the United States has done the same in American missions overseas. But the mission field context makes accountability even harder. The isolation and insularity.

The emotional and sometimes physical separation of MKs from their parents. The racial and economic power structures and weak rule of law in many countries that advantage Americans. The difficulties of investigating and collecting evidence. All of it is challenging, as anyone involved in ensuring child protection overseas will tell you.

But deeper than that, at the very heart of the matter, is that American evangelicalism, as a system and culture of belief, has little place for a narrative of abuse. Or even just human frailty. Especially not involving its missionary "saints."

Much has been made of the patriarchy piece of things: the idea that women are under the headship of men. The media is flooded with stories illustrating the unhappy marriage between patriarchy and abuse in evangelicalism. Marie Griffith, a scholar of American religion at Washington University who is currently studying parallels between the Catholic and Southern Baptist abuse crises, told me that patriarchy is "a crucial key for understanding how abuse works in both of these settings."[4] When I last consulted her in 2024, she was still collecting and analyzing data comparing patriarchal to egalitarian religious organizations on the prevalence of abuse, but based on her initial review of her findings, she believed it would support that assertion.

I think it's telling, for instance, that in the case of the Hillcrest School investigation, the most cooperative missions have also been the more theologically liberal, non-evangelical ones that ordain women pastors and include women in leadership structures. Political scientist Brian Klaas demonstrates more generally that homogeneous accountability mechanisms and leadership pools—which exclusively male-led evangelical institutions have by design—are more susceptible to corruption and abuse.[5]

But patriarchy is just one piece of the puzzle, in some ways more of a manifestation than a driver. Patriarchy is what psychologist Dave Verhaagen, an evangelical Christian himself, identifies as a response to deep-seated anxiety and fear that, according to data he has analyzed, pervades evangelical culture and leads to an overemphasis on control and unquestioned authority. Since the 1960s, if not before—religious historian Diana Butler Bass roots it in the social humiliation and mockery of fundamentalists beginning in the 1920s—American evangelicals' sense of embattlement and persecution has fueled a pessimistic view of the world and those outside its sphere.[6] This view has become more pronounced as evangelicals separate themselves in an ever more insular subculture. Much of the doctrinal rigidity, literalist biblical interpretation, and stringent cultural mores, particularly those surrounding sex and gender, can be seen in this light. Evangelical leaders may not be able to control the larger culture—although the rise of white Christian nationalism is an attempt to do just that—but they can police their own and shore up their own bases of power within the group. "If you can order your environment," Verhaagen writes, "you can feel safer and in control."[7]

An overemphasis on control is just one feature of the "collective narcissism" Verhaagen identifies in evangelical culture.[8] Evangelicalism attracts individual narcissists looking for a compliant power base; it also promotes a group culture of narcissism through a belief system that tells adherents they are special, chosen, enlightened, and heroic. I'm not here to dispute orthodox Christian beliefs, but I can't help but notice how the idea of Christian exclusivity—our way is the only way, and everyone else, even other kinds of Christians, is lost and hell-bound—slides easily into such a narrative. As historian Alan

Scot Willis puts it, in discussing Southern Baptists' struggle to overcome racism, "[The] belief that one's own religion is superior to another person's presented a difficulty."[9] And American evangelicalism has developed an additional nationalistic layer, as we have seen.

Most white American evangelicals conceive of themselves as a group of warriors for God, fighting against the forces of evil "out there" (look at the amount of energy spent on the culture wars). There is little room in this framework for the existence of abusers "in here" and certainly not for the concept of systemic abuse, which could strike at the heart of one's faith and doctrine. Historian Jesse Curtis quotes one Southern Baptist in the 1950s, who admitted that some of his denomination's reassessment of its racial views had "shaken" his faith. Because "if Southern Baptists have been wrong for over a hundred years [on race], could they not be wrong as to many other things?"[10]

In fact, the evangelical emphasis on individual faith and aversion to historical inquiry helps insulate evangelical culture from the impact of failure. When abuse or some other moral disaster happens in evangelical environments, it is invariably seen as an isolated, contained, personal issue—something that happened "back then" or "over there" or within that one life. The collective isn't responsible and doesn't need to examine themselves or their belief system. "This idea of the depravity of man only applies to the people outside the group," Dianne Darr Couts told me. "Inside the group, it's, 'It was a mistake. He was tempted once, and he yielded to temptation.'"[11]

The framing of abuse like this prevents a proper response. It absolves the organization and larger culture, the success of which is still seen as essential to the cause of Christ, and it fuels the instinct to quickly and quietly dispense with the episode via spiritual means. "Since it's a [personal] moral failure, a sin, the way we resolve it is by another spiritual practice called forgiveness," Dianne says.[12] The abuser repents, the victim forgives, and everyone joins hands and sings "Kumbaya" around a campfire. The naivete and obtuseness of this response is why many survivors refer to forgiveness as "the F word." The group culture's need for a redemptive arc to avoid its own culpability and shame—the disruption of its grandiose sense of self—is deeply wounding to abuse victims. It is spiritual abuse on top of any other they have experienced. But the victim's very existence is problematic and threatening to a narcissistic culture because, as Diane Langberg, a psychologist who is an expert on church abuse, explains, "acknowledging the truth will completely disrupt the system."[13]

In abuse prevention, too, the emphasis on individual, instantaneous conversion or redemption is detrimental. American evangelicals love a feel-good story. The more messed up the person was before he "got saved," the better. The worse the trauma someone experienced, the greater the healing. As with evangelicalism's handling of race, its approach to abuse functions as a spiritual bypass, which is what Verhaagen calls a short-circuit processing of pain and guilt to avoid unpleasant emotions and experiences.[14] MK and therapist Caleb Adams calls it "hitting the Jesus wall."[15] I have, less expertly, called it "redemption porn" or the "Bible colander," for the way all experience is strained through a latticework of pat belief and simplistic biblical interpretation to fit the evangelical cultural narrative. In this story, a sex addict can be "healed" and go on to be a missionary. A "fallen" pastor can be "restored" to ministry. Trauma and grief can be overcome in short order, as victims find "freedom in Christ."

It's a nice story that is sometimes true. But most evidence runs to the contrary. Abusers tend to re-offend, and more people are harmed. Survivors spend decades recovering from the damage. And the true miracles of change and healing, repentance and forgiveness, tend to be less flashy, less dramatic, and more complex than in evangelical fairy tales. The miracle of grace is more often a day-to-day, touch-and-go, non-linear slog. It requires individual effort, but it is also a community enterprise that asks difficult questions, addresses underlying issues, and engages with and repairs historical harm. Such miracles unfold over lifetimes, if not generations.

* * *

You could argue the mission field is the ultimate spiritual bypass for the dominant white American church. From the beginning, around the time Southern Baptists were sending missionaries to Africa while upholding racial oppression at home, missions have reinforced American evangelicals' inflated sense of self and allowed them to flee from their failures. It's no wonder that missions have been cited repeatedly by evangelicals—most notably those ultimate missions-boosters in the Southern Baptist Convention—in perpetuating and defending their cover-up of abuse. Missions, after all, are the grandest expression of evangelical grandiosity. What could be more heroic, adventurous, special, and extraordinary than winning the world—the entire thing!—for Christ? Crossing oceans and mountains and deserts to find every last lost sheep before they plunge over an eternal precipice? And how can we possibly risk such vital work with bad publicity brought on by a "few bad apples"? What does it say about us, and our beliefs, if the rot goes deeper? We don't want to know. Our cause can't afford it. Our God can't afford it (and yes, he needs lawyers).

From talking to survivors, I think the disappointment and hurt they feel with regard to the responses they've gotten from mission organizations result from hitting the kind of "Jesus wall" that evangelical culture too often erects with the aim of self-protection. Survivors pick up on a refusal—sometimes subtle, sometimes brutally explicit—to acknowledge the reality of what has happened to them, its full extent and reach, its wide net of complicity. They intuit any attempt to compartmentalize their story away into the dark corner of a basement, to remove it to a place far from all the other good things the organization is doing and all the other good people in its service. More than one survivor has noted the interesting parallel between how their abuse was handled and how white evangelicals engage America's racial history: contain it, personalize it, separate from it. Like that of Black Americans, abuse survivors' very existence shakes white evangelicalism's sense of self by embodying its complicity with evil.

MK survivor Annie Abernethy articulated it to me well when I asked her: What do survivors want? What haven't they gotten yet? "There needs to be a vulnerability and a humility that says—systems are always going to get it wrong. Systems are not spiritual," she says. "Every organization has to be able . . . to wake up every morning saying, 'It's OK if this system crumbles today' . . . No system can be held higher than the love and compassion that Jesus showed."

"I just think Jesus is throwing tables, really," she continues, referencing the biblical account of Jesus angrily turning over tables of moneychangers taking advantage of others' faith by doing business in the sacred space of the temple. "He's saying that this was . . . never about a system."[16]

It was never about saints, either.

Part IV

The Myth of Indispensability

13

Getting Out of the Way

Sam got out of the way.

He wanted to be a different kind of missionary than what he typically saw growing up in Kenya in the 1980s. His parents, trained nurses who worked in community health and agricultural development, offered a better example. He accompanied them frequently into villages, visiting with people in their homes and touring the small farm plots Kenyans call *shambas*. While many other MKs (like me) preferred to stay bubble-wrapped, Sam loved venturing out with his parents as they worked.

Sam's dad, in particular, actively tried to break through the racial and economic disparities—of which Sam was all too aware, even as a kid—that stubbornly fueled the deference that the families they visited doled out along with the more normal hospitality of tea service. Shirking the typical American bias for action and quick solution, Sam says his father "always discussed at length with them whatever the challenge or problem was. He asked them what they thought, deferred to their expertise, and acknowledged their ideas." He instructed Sam to always view Kenyans as equals who had much to teach them. Sam says his father was ahead of his time.

That hadn't always been true. As a young man, Sam's father had a "radical conversion" on the issue of race. He had come from a "redneck" family, Sam says, and worked as an EMT in Indiana in the late 1960s. During those tumultuous times of racial violence and protest, rioters damaged his ambulance on more than one occasion. But then he felt God calling him to go to Africa as a missionary. "But I hate Black people," he thought. The calling, and the conviction it brought, did not abate, until eventually he was overwhelmed, drove to a majority Black part of town, and began repenting to whomever would listen. Sam's parents went to work at a mission-run hospital in Kenya.

When Sam felt called to missions—which in his view entails "discovering God's heart for the vulnerable"—he knew he wanted to do something radically divergent. So, he moved into a slum in Nepal with an organization called Word Made Flesh, carrying only a backpack. "We had no system, no program, no strategy," he says. "I wasn't a church planter. We just lived in the community. We addressed needs as they came up." Eventually he got married to another American missionary, and they had children while living in that same slum. They shared a small house with another family.

Five years in, they agonized about buying a fridge to ensure better sanitation for their children, something they did in consultation with the other family. Sam pushed back on my concerns for his kids living in such conditions. "I wouldn't take older kids from America to live there," he says. "But my kids were born there. That was their home. That was their community."

Over time, Sam's relationship with Eautam, the father of the Nepalese family with whom they lived, deepened into a joint children's ministry. Although it was Eautam's idea, Sam says Eautam doubted his own abilities and tended to look to Sam for leadership. But then it was time for Sam's family to return to the States. Their oldest child had special needs that could not be addressed in Nepal. Eautam took over the ministry, which took off. Years later, he and others have planted thirteen churches in the area. "He has no funding," Sam says, "He just *is*."

"I used to think partnership was the way," Sam reflects. "But now I think it's developing local leaders and getting out of the way. We carry too much; it gets in the way." Even if it all fits in a backpack.

One of the things Western missionaries and ministries too often can't shed is a sense of their own righteousness, and sometimes the greater the sacrifice, the greater the tendency to slide into narcissism. And sadly, Sam experienced how this can happen even in more "enlightened" mission models. He says the culture of Word Made Flesh as an organization over time grew toxic and abusive, and its director, Chris Heuertz, became enamored of his own cause and leadership. On its website, Word Made Flesh in 2020 posted an acknowledgment of and apology for Heuertz's "harmful acts," including "manipulation, bullying, psychological, and spiritual abuse of power."[1]

* * *

When it comes to winning the world for Christ, it doesn't have to be us anymore, if it ever did. We might consider that American Christians aren't indispensable. We might consider that we never have been.

I'm not saying American missionaries have had no impact; clearly they have, as I've already discussed. In more recent times, as we've seen, the American evangelical machine—the cultural, economic, and political force of American evangelicalism, which I would distinguish from Christian faith—has had massive, global reach. But the gospel message and its spread has had a life and a story separate from that of America.

To state the obvious, Christianity existed, thrived, and expanded for almost 1,800 years before the founding of the United States and before the first American missionaries went anywhere. It started from a handful of marginalized Jewish men and women struggling under the thumb of an empire. It was passed on by monks living ascetic lives, through mystics and pilgrims, and in the midst of wars and plagues and persecutions. The Christian story continued in spite of entanglements with corrupting political power and violence by believers who didn't trust God enough to let go. One MK who grew up in Ethiopia imagined the insult and frustration of orthodox Ethiopian Christians watching American evangelists arriving to convert them: "We've had Christianity for 1,700 f---ing years."

Even many of America's missionary triumphs were more of an indigenous project than often acknowledged, then or now. According to historian Dana Robert, American missionaries rarely worked in truly "virgin territory," nor could they function without indigenous partners. In the final analysis, she and other scholars consider those partners more effective evangelists to their own kind, particularly if they came from marginalized communities.[2] Jay Riley Case deconstructs multiple examples of American missionary triumph and finds the hidden, local believers who played even more important roles. The American church has credited the Judsons, for example, for the birth of

Christianity in Burma, but Case finds that, in reality, Christianity first took off among the oppressed Karen community there, a group with whom the Judsons hardly interacted. It was a Karen believer named Ko Tha Byu who spearheaded that movement.[3]

Similarly, the typical origin story of World Vision, the Christian aid behemoth, emphasizes the role of American Bob Pierce. But in fact Pierce built on—some would say co-opted—the work of a Korean Christian named Kyung-Chik Han, about whom American Christians rarely hear.[4] History is also full of cases in which Christian movements gained steam after Western missionaries left, the Chinese church being one example.[5] American missionaries and organizations are often centered in the stories of global Christianity because they usually have been the ones telling them. To quote an African proverb, "Until the lion learns how to write, every tale of the hunt will always glorify the hunter."[6]

It is deeply embedded in our self-concept as Americans that we *are* essential—a unique, special, blessed, exceptional people, "the indispensable nation," to quote former Secretary of State Madeline Albright. In the realm of foreign policy, I'm one who generally believes that's true; American power is unavoidable and often beneficial, and the absence of American engagement has as much impact as its presence. But in a spiritual sense, American exceptionalism is a dangerous concept for the American church. And believing in our own indispensability becomes its own cause and builds its own self-perpetuating, self-protecting infrastructure.

That, in a nutshell, is what has happened with the aid industry, which is the biggest sector in some economies.[7] In South Sudan, a state practically created by the aid industry, foreign aid is equal to around a third of its GDP, according to

World Bank data.[8] It's not like such assistance does no good, and certainly its withdrawal would have a devastating economic and humanitarian impact, at least in the short-to-medium term. The aid industry—and the missionary one, with which it often coincides—brings medical care, vocational training, clean water and food, and employment. But its critics say it is a Band-Aid, not a cure, and one that is inefficient, poorly informed about the root causes and daily reality of poverty, and more invested in the employment and lifestyles of Western do-gooders than meaningfully changing recipients' lives.[9] By meeting many of citizens' basic needs, critics argue, aid also helps shield corrupt political elites in developing nations from taking responsibility for and responding to the demands of their people through sound policy, fiscal integrity, and the building of strong institutions. African nations have received over $2 trillion in aid over the last fifty years, and although the poverty rate on the continent has fallen significantly overall, the pace of progress has not been as rapid as that of other developing regions that have received far less in aid.[10]

Meanwhile, the private aid industry has ballooned in size, with more non-governmental organizations (NGOs) starting up all the time, employing educated Westerners (and many locals, although at lower pay) to live, often quite well, in foreign capitals like Nairobi and Kampala and Kigali—all lovely places—while claiming to do transformative work. One reason for the sector's explosive growth is that, since the early 1990s, Western governments and multilateral donors have preferred to distribute aid via contracting with NGOs instead of through budgetary support for the typically corrupt governments of developing countries. The growth rate of the aid industry globally has rivaled that of private business, and NGOs are now worth over $300 billion and employ over nine million people.[11] In Kenya, the aid industry is so massive and ubiquitous—and in some cases, absurd—it inspired a hilarious *Office*-style TV show called *The Samaritans.* The show followed the multinational staff of a fictitious NGO called Aid for Aid, whose "mission" boiled down to raising money to give to other NGOs—minus the cost of a sleek office and Western-educated experts apparently needed for such an enterprise.[12]

As the industry with its multiplicity of organizations grows in size, it also grows in complexity and, like any bureaucracy, tacitly adds its own survival to its overall mission. Eventually, "the structures become more important than the work itself," in the words of Kenyan journalist and former United Nations officer Rasna Warah.[13]

Evangelical missions overlap with the secular aid industry and are part of that discussion, because many NGOs are religiously based and many missionaries do charity work. But evangelical missionaries primarily use charity as a platform for proselytization, and ultimately, the aid they distribute is Christian faith (or more specifically, evangelical faith). On that front, too, missions have become a high-dollar, entrenched industry that uses many of the same strategies, practices, metrics, and marketing as secular businesses and charities. And they can be plagued with the same absurdities and inefficiencies, in which expansion is always progress, more is better, and expensive bureaucracies and experts are justified by ambiguous claims of results.[14]

Missiologist Andrew Walls calls this "Missions Incorporated" and points out it had its roots in the growth of American industry and the business revolution of the early twentieth century. "The whole climate of American Christian thinking was conditioned by expansion," he writes. "The linking of entrepreneurial activity, efficient organization, and conspicuous financing which was characteristic of American business became characteristic of American Christianity."[15] Just as in other industries and with other institutions, the larger the growth, the more money is involved and the more consumed with its own protection the organization or enterprise becomes. Is it any wonder that the Southern Baptists' IMB—with an annual budget of almost $300 million—has apparently deemed full transparency with regard to abuse too risky? Almost certainly this decision is made with the advisement of counsel on staff. "The IMB has developed an attitude of 'too big to fail,'" Baptist historian Carol Ann Vaughn Cross told me, assessing the Southern Baptist Convention's allergy to accountability. "Southern Baptists think they 'can't be wrong' because of missions."[16]

One reason that missions (and secular aid) are so expensive is because mission boards continue to send Americans overseas well past the point in time that this is necessary. American missionaries aren't rich, but their needs and lifestyle expectations are far in excess of those of local workers. And in fact, when missions and NGOs employ locals, they usually pay them substantially less *even when they are performing similar work*—something journalist Lara Pawson has called "a charitable apartheid."[17] In the secular aid industry, the disparity is more egregious than in missions; many American missionaries live on what would be poverty wages in the United States. But in developing countries, even those missionaries in most cases enjoy a standard of living far above the average local. And some of their basic requirements—like American health insurance and airline travel back and forth to the United States—are things a local would not require.

Andrew Walls contrasts the missionaries of today with their predecessors, who left everything behind (of course, that included their children, which is definitely one way to reduce costs), to live simply and permanently in the field. "Nowadays Missions Incorporated generally makes it possible to maintain life at a tolerable level," he writes, noting that missionaries often live in a wholly different realm than their national colleagues.[18] Add to the infrastructure of support for today's missionary the new edifices of well-intentioned "member care" that provides needed mental health assistance but also, as we've seen, functions to protect the institution in a human resources capacity. According to its 2022 financial statement, the IMB spends $264 million on overseas programs, $159 million of which goes toward missionary salaries, benefits, and travel. And that doesn't even include the US-based supportive bureaucracy, another $42 million in 2022. Bubble life is expensive.

But career missionaries are a bargain, especially over time, given the expertise they build up and comparative impact they have, compared to short-term missions, which are a boondoggle in almost every case (likely exceptions being people with medical or other highly sought-after expertise). According to author Mekdes Haddis, two million Americans go on short-term mission trips annually at a cost of about $4 billion per year, a figure equaling Haiti's annual budget.[19] Once in the field, they usually perform work that more skilled indigenous Christians are already doing or could be hired to do at a fraction of the cost. For example, Ben Marsh, who pastors a church in North Carolina, described a mission trip he once took to the Dominican Republic that entailed correcting stucco work on a church that a previous mission team had botched the week before. His team performed no better, however, and the church eventually hired a local "who did the job [in] half the time, and it cost less than one flight that we took to get there."[20]

Or how about an American visitor, who just arrived in the country the day before, doing evangelism, accompanied all the way by a local pastor who has been living and working in the same community for years and knows the people and their culture and speaks the language? Not only does this strike many missions observers as ludicrous, it reinforces locals' racial and economic biases by implying a service or message brought by a white American is somehow better, as Haddis and other non-white missionaries have discovered. While translating for an American group in her native Ethiopia, Haddis says community members told her to "get out of the way" because they preferred to interact with the white visitors.[21]

As we've previously discussed, mission-sending organizations have made greater efforts in recent years to emphasize cultural sensitivity and respect for indigenous Christian workers, counter "white saviorism," and present mission trips as opportunities for American Christians to learn rather than to have meaningful impact. But I've never had a conversation with or heard a presentation of a short-term missionary that didn't emphasize the good work they performed, the service they offered, the sacrifice they made. A woman I interviewed who spent her youth doing summer missions recalls her church community's excessive praise for the "sacrifice" of her summers for the Lord. "We were like the travel soccer team, or some kind of elite athletes," she says. Sacrifice and heroism are what sell; that's how you raise money for missions. Are people going to pony up cash so you can go "learn" in a country like Kenya (and maybe take a safari afterward, as most short-term missionaries there do)? And as we have discussed, there's little evidence, based on their views, that white evangelicals as a collective have learned much from their participation in missions, except insofar as the lesson reinforces their own sense of righteousness.

* * *

The sending of American missionaries around the world seems even stranger when you consider the now massive pool of current and potential indigenous missionaries who are educated, skilled, and devout, and whose work is far more cost-effective. In almost every country in the world, there is now a sizable professional middle class with more means and access to do the kind of missions work that meets American evangelicals' standards. And most of the world's Christians—even evangelical Christians—live in the Global South, according to data tracked by the Center for the Study of Global Christianity (CSGC) at Gordon-Conwell Seminary.[22]

Indeed, as American Christianity has hit the skids, global Christianity has taken off. In fact, thousands of non-American Christians—half the total of missionaries worldwide—are already doing missions with or without Western support. According to the missions reform group The Return Mandate, indigenous ministries are twenty-three times more cost-effective than American-led ones, and the cost of sending one American missionary to the field is fifty times higher than supporting a local pastor. "And yet, the vast majority of our funds go to sending Western missionaries to places with many existing churches and Christians," the group says.[23] The United States still sends more missionaries by far than any other single country, the same number as all other countries combined, according to CSGC data.[24]

Indigenous missionaries, unlike American ones, are often bi-vocational, following the "tent-making" example set by the original missionary, Paul, who actually did make tents and perform other tasks to fund his mission. (The IMB would probably have a study commissioned to examine the results of this program and determine that its missionaries win more souls per year. And that Southern Baptists make the best tents.) Consider my family friend Philemon, whose vocational work for decades has been as a government chaplain at a prison in western Kenya. About twenty years ago, he and his wife, Agneta, felt called to start a ministry for prisoners as they were released. They taught them vocational and domestic skills, preventive health care, and Bible study. He baptized many of them and saw them become productive members of society. Some of them were from Kenya's remote northern region, and through these connections, Philemon and Agneta began going as missionaries to the Pokot community—the Joshua Project considers them a "partially reached people group"—several hours north, where the verdant highlands dip down into a dusty plain. They go up there multiple times a year, bringing food aid, public health information (in partnership with local government), vocational training, and Christian education.

Philemon told me they want to bring the gospel message, but they also hope to end "the cycle of poverty and crime" that he sees in his prison work. His adult children have also joined the family cause. One of them is training as a dentist and another as a social worker, skills they hope to use in a missions capacity. Philemon has received some training and assistance from an organization called Community Health Enterprise (CHE), and he has a few small donors in the United States. But otherwise, his is a self-sustaining, family-based effort, funded by his own income, from one Kenyan to another. And he doesn't need strategy reports, cultural or language training, or "member care" to do his work.

American Christians and mission boards are paying more attention to such indigenous missionaries than they used to, perhaps because they can't ignore them anymore. The word *partnership* is ubiquitous these days in missions-related literature, as mission boards respond to growing calls for Americans to cede ground. Missions books published over the last ten years are more likely to urge missionaries to avoid paternalism, elevate local voices, and, like Sam's family, live at the level of locals (few American missionaries do that).[25]

And some actual ground has been ceded. The IMB began reapportioning (and slightly decreasing) its overseas staff and, in heavily evangelized countries, handing over control of institutions to national conventions in the 1990s. More recently, the IMB launched its Globalization project, which seeks to work "with our non-US national partners to help them embrace the Great Commission."[26] In countries like Brazil, many evangelical churches, denominations, and mission boards operate independently from American ones and send out missionaries themselves (although there are still a number of American missionaries in Brazil).[27]

But critics say the incorporation of more non-American workers into missionary work and marketing literature is primarily window-dressing that can mask and enable continued American control. Missions "partnerships" in response to the growing assertiveness of Global South Christians are akin to the creation of "color-blind" theology in response to the civil rights movement: a shift in messaging and small-scale activity that deflects criticism while preserving power structures. In fact,

American missionaries and mission boards have been pledging "partnership" since the mid-nineteenth century, when the "Three-Selfs" model of missions—establishing churches that were self-governing, self-supporting, and self-propagating—was dominant.[28] All the while, American mission boards and missionaries have held onto control with both hands, sometimes waging years-long battles with local Christians, as João Chaves describes in his history of Southern Baptist missionaries in Brazil.[29] Yet, as we have already discussed, American institutions still mostly own the money, ideas, and organizations that fuel not only missions but global Christianity writ large. And for all the talk of "unreached people groups," the majority of missionaries, American and otherwise, continue to go to predominantly Christian nations with well-established institutions and leaders, according to CSGC data.

When American missions do partner with locals, they often devalue their expertise, question their theology, and generally treat them as subordinates. "Often I hear indigenous leaders' frustration about how they are confined to roles that are beneath their educational and skill level while the Westerners leading the organizations have neither the level of education, nor the skillset these leaders possess," Haddis writes.[30] According to non-American missiologists like Harvey Kwiyani, American missions' emphasis on partnership is mostly "lip service," an effort by American evangelicals to stay in the game—and stage-manage it—as the shape of Christianity changes.

* * *

I have heard many reasons over the years as to why maintaining that control is essential, and why American missions' partners can't manage without their supervision. The biggest one, which is not without basis, is corruption. And it is true, in developing countries, where people are barely getting by, handling church or organization money can be a temptation. Then again, all we need to do is think of any number of American megachurch pastors and televangelists to know that corruption abounds all over the world.

The second reason I hear over and over is "bad theology." And, well . . . [waves hands at the American church's dalliances with racism, misogyny, and Christian nationalism]. In my estimation, American evangelicals have lost all moral and theological authority on that front. Remove the entire forest of giant sequoias from your own eye before you go speck-hunting elsewhere.

Then you get to methods and results. I have heard American missions supporters find fault with the work ethic, strategy, rigor, and commitment of indigenous Christians and churches. Ultimately, the concern is that there is no substitute for American missionaries in terms of results and that more people will go to hell as a consequence. The messaging and marketing of American missions and Western aid groups always emphasize the dire emergencies to which they respond and compile various statistics proclaiming good results in order to justify their continued existence. In the aid context, there are real and heartbreaking photos of suffering communities and hungry children. Missions groups dangle the worst fate imaginable, eternal damnation (the IMB's latest annual report laments "173,451 dying daily without Christ"). Taking at face value evangelicals' sincere beliefs, this is a worthy cause.

But measuring results in both contexts is tricky, and it's impossible to prove counterfactuals—that is, what would happen if we didn't do our work. Aid groups can at least count the number of patients treated or meals served or bore holes dug, even if they can't show how they are rolling back conflict and poverty. But can anyone really count the number of souls saved? I mean, you can't send an investigative team to the afterlife, first to verify its existence and then to tally up all the people in heaven due to missionaries. The IMB has certainly tried (figuratively speaking; I don't think they've managed a round-trip fact-finding mission to heaven. Yet.). They've rigorously counted sinner's prayers prayed, baptisms performed, and churches planted. Such methodology is questioned even by some evangelicals, who say you can't measure true discipleship, not all conversions are the same in terms of effort and sincerity, and reducing the gospel to metrics is distasteful.

But the biggest reason, I believe, American evangelicals are reluctant to loosen their grip on missions is because missions are too integral to their own identity. More than change itself, certainly more than how it occurs or how deep it goes, American Christians want to be the change agents. They want to "make a difference." They want to see people like them doing extraordinary things.

This same dynamic plays out in secular charity work as well, and it is in fact human nature. Our altruism is pretty evenly matched by our egocentricity. It's why charities continue to use inefficient methods to raise money and distribute aid even though economic research has suggested that giving out cash directly to needy people, whether in crisis or poverty, is much more cost-effective and produces better, more deep-seated results than offering goods and services. Research from Give Directly—a charity created by a group of economists that dispenses cash payments to poor people around the world and studies the results—demonstrates that cash payments, especially in a large lump sum, made people more productive and financially secure after two years. But people aren't as inspired by this model, and they don't trust the poor to make good decisions. (And sometimes they don't. And sometimes rich people also use money really badly. I mean, Donald Trump presumably paid someone to make Mar-a-Lago look as if flamingos vomited up gold on everything.) So, charities like World Vision continue to use less efficient models, such as child sponsorships, that center the giver.

Full disclosure here: I've sponsored a World Vision child for my entire adult life. Like most of my financial support for missions, I'm tied to the work through personal connections. In the case of World Vision, I do think the organization on the whole does good work (and I, too, like having a picture of a cute kid on my fridge). World Vision tried to phase out sponsorships in the mid-1980s, but donations plummeted, so they soon brought the program back, at least as a marketing device. In practice, the organization pursues a community development model, which is more effective than individual sponsorships.[31] Many other charities use the child sponsorship model, too, to the tune of a collective $3 billion a year in contributions from sponsors looking for a personal connection with "their" child. The organizations end up spending additional resources and money on "'servicing' donors," with personalized reports, letters from their children, gift deliveries, and visit facilitation, basically securing their continued contributions with ego strokes.[32]

Mission organizations, too, are highly attuned to the fact that American Christians are consumers searching for significance, meaning, and adventure. "Mission trips are in fact about the goer not the receiver," Haddis writes. "The instant gratification and long-term impact of achieving self-actualization help the goers sustain a self-image that keeps them going as they pursue their American dream."[33] The IMB calls one of its current recruitment campaigns "The Great Pursuit" and invites Christians to become Missionary Explorers: to "journey to the edge of lostness" in order to share the gospel with more than 3,000 communities the IMB has identified as "unengaged, unreached people groups."[34] The website includes a statement from one such Explorer—name and location concealed for their protection—that reads like Magellan's log or something out of Indiana Jones:

> I'm hiking very deep into a jungle region, a place apparently no foreigner has gone before. . . . I am in a village of about 200 people where there is no church, no Christians, and they are very closed to hearing or learning about the gospel. . . I have also found some families of one of the unengaged, unreached people group(s) I traveled here to find and spoke with locals and gathered information on where they may be. I will walk that direction and try to find them two days from now. We are going to sleep now on sheets of plywood. Goodnight from here.[35]

Not only is this an invitation to individuals to do something heroic and thrilling, it's also faith-affirming for American evangelicals as a culture, so invested in certainty, to spread its particular form of Christianity.

The perpetuation of an American-dominated missions culture assumes that "the gospel in its purest form is found in the Western church," in Mekdes Haddis's words. While white evangelicals look for ways to keep going, sending, leaving home—perhaps with more enlightenment than in the past—Haddis suggests God may be telling them it's time to stay. "Surely we can't believe that God is so small that he awaits Western theology . . . to reach his people around the world," she writes.[36]

Evangelicals from other countries argue they are better positioned at this point in human history to take up the missionary mantle. In their book, *Africa to the Rest*, missiologists Yaw Perbi, Sam Ngugi, and Joshua Bogunjoko argue persuasively and with an infectious enthusiasm that the future of missions is African. Not only are the majority of the world's Christians now African, Africans are spreading out all over the globe anyway, in a large diaspora driven by a search for opportunity, education, family reunification, and stability. In fact, there are already African missionaries in many places, but their methods look different from those of white Americans. They are usually bi-vocational, like the apostle Paul was, and instead of being guided by strategies and data, they are, in the words of Perbi and his coauthors, "centered on relationships, belonging, community, togetherness, mutuality, solidarity," things the authors say come naturally to Africans.[37]

Perhaps most importantly, power is not a tool in the African missions and service kit. Historically, people from the African continent have been marginalized, exploited, and abused. They engage in missions from the perimeters, just like generations of missionaries did before Christendom arrived on the scene and distorted the picture.[38] Not only did Christianity begin and rapidly spread from the margins of human society, in today's global context, non-American, non-white Christians may be less conspicuous, have more access, and face less hostility and danger in many parts of the "unreached" world where being an American isn't an advantage but a target on your back. In fact, numerous American missionaries have been kidnapped or killed since 9/11, usually necessitating American military involvement and diplomatic effort and sometimes costing additional American lives.[39]

The margins are not a place white American Christians know much about. We are a global superpower, and we've created a cultural empire that includes missions. We are the rich men whom Jesus warned would struggle to enter the Kingdom of God. I've heard white evangelicals argue that God has used power and even its exploitation—through slavery, colonialism, racial hierarchy—to spread the gospel, a notion I find deeply offensive.[40] The real, true gospel has traveled far and wide and through time in mysterious ways and on the engine of God's grace. If anything, our power-wielding has impeded that in ways we can't even imagine, for control and empire are antithetical to the good news.

In general, American Christians desperately need to pursue what The Return Mandate calls "a theology of humility."[41] Maybe we do need to get out of the way. Or maybe it's less the going and sending that is problematic and more how we frame it in our own minds and use it to avoid our own hearts.

Beyond what we've already discussed, however, there's another reason why we haven't gotten out of the way and probably won't. A more complicated explanation lies at the heart of the MK story.

14

Searching for Home

Ian is still a bit adrift.

He and I knew each other somewhat as children. But mostly, we recognize in each other the slippery grief, the intense dislocation, the pervasive feeling of lostness that almost every MK I have ever known, and the vast majority of those who responded to my survey, has experienced upon leaving the mission field. As an MK, one's sense of belonging is so highly specific—not quite American, definitely not part of the host culture—that once gone, it is difficult to replicate and relocate, like sifting through a barrel of buttons looking for the one that will match. We mourn something that never really existed, we wish to recover something we never really possessed, and we lose ourselves like something replaceable and cheap. And a lot of us, though we might look successful on the outside, stumble around in a fog for years after, quietly running into walls, knocking over glasses, and stubbing toes.

But Ian didn't even look successful. He left his home in Kenya after high school already in mental distress. After a blissful early childhood in what he called "a boy paradise," full of freedom and outdoor adventure, and even a relatively smooth adjustment to boarding school at a young age, puberty set off a cataclysmic chemical reaction in his brain. He plunged into major depression, punctuated by periods of suicidal ideation, that no one around him seemed to notice or know how to manage. He did talk to a counselor at boarding school, but she wasn't well trained and just told him he needed to express his feelings more openly. His parents were completely out of their depth and, of course, at a physical distance. After he left Africa, things only got worse. Ian made new friends who introduced him to the self-medication of drugs and alcohol. "I was sad all the time," he recalls.

So, he became a missionary. You may not have seen that plot twist coming, but it didn't surprise me at all. At first, he went as a temporary assistant for his dad, coordinating the large numbers of short-term mission teams that worked in the Nairobi slums. And he did pretty well. He found a sense of purpose trying to figure out how to do short-term missions in ways that weren't condescending to Kenyans and empowered locals' own work. But he readily acknowledged that he really wasn't needed at all. "I told the mission board a Kenyan could be doing my job," he says.

He met a bright, altruistically ambitious woman on one of the mission teams. They kept in touch, and though they didn't know each other well, he eventually returned to the United States to marry her. She deeply wanted to be a career missionary and seemed to pick him out as an appropriate partner. But the marriage did not go well. She was emotionally abusive and narcissistic. Ian's mental health soon went into free fall, and he returned to drinking. But the couple was too laser-focused on getting out to the mission field to confront any of their own problems. And the mission board was too distracted by his wife's clear sense of calling and evident gifts and Ian's MK pedigree. They both skated by the board's psychological screening.

Once back in Kenya, Ian spiraled out of control, going to nearby bars almost every night and driving home drunk. One night, his luck ran out. He crashed his car into a tree, and the truth of his situation came tumbling out. The mission board quietly sent them home, enrolled him in a treatment program, and sent letters out to their supporters telling them to stop their contributions and end all contact. And that was that.

Ian finally got help for his underlying depression, the couple got divorced, and he went on with his life, trying to figure out its purpose away from the mission field.

* * *

Kara is a true believer.

When we speak, she is at a friend's house in Germany, where she has fled after Russia's invasion of Ukraine in early 2022. She had been in Kiev less than a year, working as a missionary and teaching English, when the war began. She doesn't know when or if she will go back, and she is worried for her new Ukrainian friends. She strikes me as earnest and kind-hearted, and her care for people comes through clearly.

She was fourteen when her parents became missionaries to Russia, and she wasn't happy about it. "I didn't feel personally called to missions," she explains. The first year was challenging. But then "God broke my heart," she says. "I fell in love with Russia." Soon she had mastered the language and felt she belonged.

Kara threw herself into their ministry at a well-established church started by Russian Christians. She helped organize a Christmas concert, played instruments, and worked the sound booth during services. Her family formed relationships with people in the community, although those were hard-won. Though Kara's family looked and lived similarly to ordinary Russians, locals were "a little standoffish." Her dad's evangelism efforts were much easier with the Chinese students they encountered.

Though she says the original church where they worked "didn't need our help," she passionately believes Russia does. Despite the presence of the Russian Orthodox Church, she says Russia is "very closed" to Christianity and proselytizing is illegal—something the many American evangelical fans the Russian government has cultivated over the last twenty years may not realize. Kara also points out that many Russian pastors are bi-vocational and aren't paid at all for their service. Missionaries can supplement their work.

After college at Bob Jones University, Kara immediately returned to the mission field, this time to an Asian country, where her parents had moved.[1] Her dad, a carpenter who never attended seminary, started a Bible college, where Kara taught English and other subjects. She had hoped to return to Russia, but her mission organization mandated that single women be paired with missionary families, and there were no opportunities in Russia.

Even though her new home was, on the surface, a "warmer" culture that emphasized community, she found it harder to form meaningful relationships across the wider cultural and economic chasm. Locals, at least around missionaries, were conflict averse and more likely to show deference, calling the missionaries "Teacher." Another challenge was that "people were always needing things," and she and the other missionaries worried they were only coming to church to see what could be gained.

She worked five years in Asia before going to Ukraine, and I can tell that's where her heart is. Culturally and linguistically, Ukraine is similar to Russia, but freer, more open, and more Christian. The church in Ukraine is larger and stronger than in either Russia or the Asian country where she served. She was just settling in when the war broke out.

Kara loves missions, but she also sees some problems. "Missionaries are kind of on a pedestal," she says. "It's very uncomfortable. I appreciate everyone's prayers, but I don't like people talking about sacrifice." She saw her parents, "very humble people," try to push back on these notions, but she has seen other missionaries "put themselves on the pedestal," including one who took credit for her dad's work.

She also thinks there needs to be more support for missionaries. She's working on a counseling degree and hopes to help others who may struggle. "In my organization, there is no intentional plan for mental health," she says. Instead, furloughing missionaries meet with a group of male leaders, with whom "I don't feel I can be honest."

I ask her about her organization's abuse prevention and response plans, and she's not sure it has any. "I would hope so," she says, but shrugs. "But I'm not sure US authorities could do anything."

* * *

Of all the MK hardships I've taken in while writing this book and experienced for myself, the one that is most common—and for many of us, the most painful—is its conclusion. When it's time to move on and say goodbye, some of us never can let go.

Caleb Adams says at Faith Academy, the grief descended with the glide of elevator doors at the Robinsons Galleria Hotel in Manila, where seniors gathered on graduation night for a party. One by one, they filed out: doors opening, doors closing, friendships and identities and lives as they had been disappearing down a shaft. "All of a sudden it was over," he tells me. "It just ended." He describes the next few years of his life as "an out-of-body experience," and "the traumatic death of who you were." "We adapted as hard as we could," he says.[2]

At RVA, senior year is a litany of farewell rituals, a long meditation on goodbye designed to comfort and bring humane closure, but one tinged with mounting dread. It all culminates at graduation, year after year, class after class. The choir sings the same songs, with a few variations—always a song called "Mayibuye," and these days, a choral arrangement of Toto's "Africa."

"Mayibuye" is a haunting, *a cappella* South African piece that I have never heard outside of RVA. But I do know the Xhosa word *mayibuye* was a common rallying cry in the struggle against apartheid. It means something akin to "Let it come back," or "Bring back what was lost." In that context, *mayibuye* referred to Black self-determination and the return of ancestral land. In classic MK style, we claimed as our own something that didn't belong to us. In our context, ironically sung by a bunch of predominantly white kids, it was a song of mourning, longing, and loss. It expressed the hope that we would not completely lose this part of ourselves, that we might return to that place, and to this place, over and over again, that somehow it would be ours to keep. As a member of the choir, I had practiced it over and over, but it never lost its emotional gut-punch. I held the hands of the girls on either side of me the day of graduation and choked back tears as I reached for notes beyond my ability.

And then it was over. I was given my diploma and shown the exit. The final hugs and waves were anti-climactic. In some cases, I knew they were not final. But everything would be different. I would be different. As it turned out, I would be deeply, hopelessly lost, my vision obstructed by grief and confusion for years to come.

That day, as my parents drove me away from RVA, I couldn't know that in less than two years, I would be married to a man I didn't love, sinking ever deeper into suffocating sadness. But though I had no concept of the specifics, I could see my general fate clearly, with no idea how to save myself. I knew I wasn't going to be OK. And for a long time, I wasn't.

There were the mundane and practical challenges of adjustment. In my case, my older sister took me back to the States to college. My parents had just returned to Kenya in time for my graduation from RVA, after a medical evacuation, and so my sister stood in for them in helping me move onto my college campus. She set up a bank account for me, took me to Walmart to outfit my dorm room, and tried unsuccessfully to talk me out of buying an ugly comforter because it was on sale. She showed me how to pump gas into our shared car, which I could barely drive.

I technically had a driver's license, after taking a driving class during a previous furlough. But I hadn't driven at all since, in almost two years. Frankly, I was a danger to society, mitigated only by my terror of putting any pressure on the gas pedal. At one point, I had to get a dorm mate I had never met to re-park my car after my repeated attempts positioned it about an inch away from its neighbor. Having spent so many years in a former British colony, I also drove on the wrong side of the road once; fortunately, the other drivers froze in confusion, and everyone lived.

Multiple MKs mentioned driving—the pun "crash course" came up repeatedly—as a major challenge upon their return. American grocery stores, particularly the cereal aisle, also got numerous shout-outs in my conversations with MKs. The mesmerizing array of choices delighted some and caused others paralyzing anxiety.

Here are some of the many responses to my survey question about the MK transition back to the United States (I've strung them together):

> Devastating. Overwhelming grief. Isolating. Still in transition after thirty years. I never felt understood. I felt lost. No closure. The sense of being without roots, misunderstood, or lost never quite leaves. I felt prone to restlessness. Overwhelmingly difficult and lonely. Manifested as physical issues. It took six years to start feeling like an American. I had no support. I was forced to pretend it never happened. It was like starting a new life from scratch. My parents weren't around. I got married too early. I felt my heart had truly broken and the best part of my life had come and gone. I cried myself to sleep. I have deep longing for home. Not mentally or culturally prepared. Traumatic. My heartstrings kept pulling me home. Slipped into depression. Had a very hard time figuring out my place in the world.

Over three-quarters of the respondents to my survey said their transition back to the United States was either extremely difficult or difficult. This response by a young MK, still in the throes of the grief I remember all too well, made me want to track them down and adopt them (if they are reading this and need support, I hope they will reach out): "I'm in college and I hate it. Every day I want to go home. I hear people complain about spending a whole week with their parents or going back to their hometowns, and I literally want to scream. I have to mentally shut down until I am out of the context to refrain from losing my mind or crying. I wish I could go home. Every day I just wish I was home."

I just wish I was home. Longing for home, trying to recapture a feeling of belonging, not knowing how or where or who that entails: this is homesickness for a land of make-believe. It's grief for a life, not a death. MKs' yearning for home is hard to describe for people who can hardly describe it themselves. I don't know how to explain it to you, even here, on this page. Please understand, I hope you can cover the gap for me. We hope you can cover the gap, meet us halfway.

It is a grief that stays with us, a longing for something that was never ours. If it had been ours, we could have brought it along. But it wasn't ours, and we weren't part of it, not really, not if we're honest. It causes some of us to dig deep roots into the first ground our feet can find. It gives others of us indefatigable wings, flapping furiously in shifting skies, lifting us up to a vantage point from which we can scan the earth, searching for a place to land, never finding it. Onward, onward, to the next place. How about that one? No, that one. Some of us burn all the bridges and firebomb the roads, not bearing to look back, either because we love or fear too much.[3]

Some of us hop the next plane back to the "field" as fast as we can, however we can manage it. We go as teachers and doctors and businesspeople and aid workers and diplomats. But mostly if we go, we go as missionaries, like our parents before us, and like some of their parents before them, and even some of their parents before them. One missionary told me he estimates about 30 percent of American missionaries are MKs. Because that's what we know. That's where we know ourselves, and that's how we know ourselves. We're nesting dolls, stacking ourselves inside of culture and place. We try to burrow ourselves into a small, specific world, within a bigger one, within the whole. Maybe it's a location or a community or just an identity that's our actual home. And so we go home, or we try. And sometimes it feels like it, and sometimes we are disappointed. It's not the same. You can't go home again. Not to ours.

But we keep trying. And we keep going. When we become missionaries ourselves, we don't say out loud that we want to go home—not even in an anonymous survey by a fellow MK. We know that no one will fund a home-going. So, we say we are "called." We say it's "ministry." And sometimes, maybe a lot of the time, we are, and it is. Because I do believe that God speaks through our lives and our experiences—and through our yearnings—yes, even those. And we bring all of it with us. We bring our knowledge and our skills and our desire to find a place. And sometimes we bring the pain, too, and it spills out across the field and sows the ground with its poison seeds, such that another generation harvests the bitter fruit.

And sometimes we even change the missionary game, mostly for the better, because we want it to continue. But we also keep playing it. Well past the final buzzer, we keep playing. We love the game. We *are* the game.

We and it are essential. We can't bear for it to stop. We can't bear to become spectators while the next team takes to the court. "All my cousins want to go back," one MK tells me. His parents and his grandparents and his aunts and his uncles and many of his friends are missionaries. Some, if not all of them, are doing good work; I don't know that for a fact, but I have hope that they are.

But he gives them no credit. "They want the lifestyle, it's so much more comfortable," he says. Reflecting on his own childhood, he confesses, "It didn't feel like we were doing much but patting ourselves on the back."

He doesn't say it, but I silently think, "And hoping to belong."

* * *

Nora is not a missionary.

She speaks to me from her home in the West Bank, several months before the October 7, 2023, attacks and the outbreak of the Gaza war. She teaches English and history at a Palestinian school. It's not a mission school or even a Christian school. It's just a school, the goal of which is English fluency and preparation for university. It is US–accredited, but all the students are fairly wealthy Palestinians.

Nora knew she wanted to go back overseas. Her family spent a few years in the United States while she was growing up, in the early 2000s, between mission stints in Mozambique and Namibia. She never really made friends in the United States, mainly hanging out with immigrant kids, although she didn't quite fit in with them either. "I realized my privilege," she said, in describing the difference between their experiences.

But she didn't feel completely at home in Africa, either. At least not in Mozambique. The family lived in a medium-sized city in an apartment building with Mozambicans, where Nora did not feel safe. "I was scared of the kids," she recalls. "They were more aggressive." Once when she and her brother tried to play with them, the other children pelted them with rocks. She remembers a birthday party to which her mother invited the neighborhood kids. "I hid under the table," she says.

Thieves attempted to break into their apartment numerous times, and she could hear men beating their wives and kids through thin walls. Even the nearby beach wasn't a respite. Sewage seeped into the ocean, sending used tampons bobbing on the waves like tiny rafts. "We still swam in it," she smirks. Shelled-out buildings stood like makeshift memorials to Mozambique's violent past. "Nothing was beautiful," she says.

Namibia, one of Africa's most developed countries, was a much better experience. They lived in the cosmopolitan, multiracial capital city of Windhoek, where Nora felt she was safe and belonged.

Both her parents were also MKs, and they had had their own struggles. Her mother grew up in an unstable country and went to boarding school very young. Her father suffered numerous severe physical injuries and PTSD from being attacked with a machete by thieves before Nora was born. He had regular nightmares and times when he was overwhelmed with anxiety, which fueled Nora's own. But there was really no question that her parents would become missionaries. In families in which missions were "deeply entrenched," "it was just the next logical step," Nora explains.

Despite her love for her family, Nora is vehemently anti-missions. She's seen "so many negative aspects," including "clearly unstable people working with no assistance." She has also studied African history as an adult, and she is troubled by the comingling of missions and the colonial mindset. Her parents share many of her concerns, but these aren't views she can discuss with her extended family. "There's no space for critique or examination," she says. She thinks her family members "over-identify" with Africa, claiming ownership of it without realizing how and why that's been made too easy for white Americans to do.

Her new life in the West Bank has its frustrations and drawbacks. Her superiors and coworkers are all Palestinians, whose communication and administrative styles are decidedly not American. She sometimes weathers anti-American comments and has a list of forbidden topics that governs her teaching. But she finds it all "refreshing," even the anti-Americanism, which she contrasts favorably with the uncomfortable deference she always felt in Africa.

"I don't feel like an envoy of a better culture," she tells me. "I'm not here to prove anything or justify why I'm here. I feel free to make real friendships and experience Palestine."

Then she describes what I think is a fundamental MK hope for their lives: "I just feel normal."

* * *

As for me, I'm feeling pretty normal these days, too (well, grading on an individualized curve). Mostly by letting go. Of who I am, who I want to be, how I am understood. Of what I believe. I've learned to bob gently in a sea of ambiguity and ambivalence, to become part of the waves and the flow of the tides.

Jesus said if you want to keep your life, you give it up. And maybe if you want a home, you stop searching.

The truth is, you don't have to be sure about who you are or who God is, or even if God is, to form community with others. In fact, it helps to not be entirely sure. If you keep your edges a little bit frayed, they are more easily woven together with other fabrics.

I spent so many years of my life trying to fit. As part of the hardest core of a hardcore religious culture, I clung with all my might to a religious certainty that I didn't really have. I feared that loosening my grasp for even a second might allow it all to slip through my fingers and pull me down with it, like water sucked into a drain.

After I left Kenya, I built a fortress around my identity in an attempt to define it for myself. I was special, I was enigmatic, I was not a "regular American." I was Kenyan, I was international, I was something else entirely. I didn't know what I was, but I knew what I wasn't. I laid claim to what I hadn't earned and laid down in a bed someone else had made. I held on so tightly, my fingernails etched grooves into my palms. I refused to make common cause with anything or anyone that might steal it away.

I liked to think I was different, but I also hated being different. When I told my story, did I want you to wonder at my strangeness or see yourself in me? Did I want you to understand or not? If you can't fathom who I am, I remain a singular figure, the citizen of a one-person nation that exists as long as I do.

I doggedly chose to stay lonely. I chose to maintain a death grip on what I thought I could keep. But it was never mine. And I kept my hands so full of nothing that I missed out on holding so many other hands for far too long.

One of the things I love about living in Washington, DC, is that there are people here from all over the world. My international upbringing is not especially unusual, and it bridges more than it divides. I often run into Kenyans here, and I've had to learn to contain my glee regarding their origin. Without any context, a white American asking someone of color where they are from, assuming they aren't fully American, is understandably offensive.

When I meet Kenyans, here or anywhere in the world, I tell them I grew up in Kenya and how much I love their country. I might add, "But I'm not a real Kenyan." I don't want to be presumptuous. I don't want to equate my privileged, Americanized experience there, my bubble-wrapped life, with whatever authentic culture they embody or hardship they have endured. I don't want to pretend I am not so typically American, now or then. I don't want to steal from them by claiming what is theirs as mine.

But they often offer it to me with grace and generosity. Their faces light up with recognition, and their brows furrow with the kindest of rebukes. "No! No!" they insist, "You are a real Kenyan! You *are*!"

That's their call.

Conclusion

For the retired parents of missionary kids, as for many of their children whom I interviewed, transitioning back to "civilian" life can be difficult. After being on the front lines of what your religious culture has told you is an epic struggle for the world's salvation, and after years of being greeted here and there as a minor dignitary, it can seem dull and even decadent to sit in a padded pew with other soft-bellied American believers, passing velvet-lined offering plates to fund a new generation of missionaries. It can feel mundane to drive a sedan to a well-stocked grocery store instead of a Land Rover over rutted, rural roads in search of lost souls or struggling lives. Conversely, many returning missionaries, who lived in relative socioeconomic privilege and comfort in developing countries, struggle financially in the United States, some having to get menial jobs to make ends meet.

Former missionaries usually find some new calling or ministry, because that's just how they're built. They are people of action and generosity. They take casseroles to the sick and mentor school kids and teach Sunday School and Vacation Bible School and—a favorite, for obvious reasons—work with refugees and connect with recent immigrants. Sometimes they get to dust off rusty language skills to help newcomers find jobs and navigate bureaucracy. Or just to help them feel more at home.

Retired missionaries have the task of revitalizing relationships with elderly parents, siblings, and old friends after many years away. And then there's the struggle to reconnect with grown children—some with giant axes to grind, and many more who don't know how to meet the relational needs of parents who taught them not to need parents. Many of their kids, frankly, don't have the emotional energy to try. "They were not there for our transition back, but they expected us kids to help them with theirs," one MK told me.

At day's end, or even periodically throughout the day, many of our missionary parents turn on the television. It's unlikely to be BBC or Al Jazeera or to present even one in-depth story about the country where they served—or any other country, really. Instead, like almost all their evangelical friends, fellow churchgoers, and generational cohort, they are probably watching Fox News, OAN, or NewsMax, sometimes for hours a day. The missionary parents are likely imbibing, on a daily basis, the domestic, secularized version of a narrative that accompanied their work overseas. America is the indispensable Christian nation. American evangelical Christianity is the one true version. And it's all under attack from the forces of evil, at home and abroad. It's up to you, white evangelical American, to lay claim to America and by extension to save the world. And by reaching the world, you show yourselves worthy of that claim and solidify its hold.

It's also a narrative that explains away and relieves responsibility for any new hardships or strained relationships they may be experiencing. It's all persecution, it's all Satanic attack, it's all part of the immense sacrifice they made for the cause of Christ. They aren't sure why their kids can't see that. Why they don't call more often.

And many of those retired missionaries, at least of the ones I know—good people who have done many good deeds—have voted for Donald Trump, the man who called their former homes "sh*thole countries," tried to end the US refugee program, and labeled immigrants "invaders." A man who is not even remotely Christlike or Christian by any definition. A man who, were he a Nigerian or Brazilian, they would certainly call a heretical pretender, a con artist, whose seduction of the church endangers the cause of Christ. But many of these missionaries voted for him every time. I reminded one retired missionary, who said they had to support Trump because of abortion, that most African dictators are vehemently "pro-life" (well, when it comes to the unborn. The born they have killed with impunity).

America is different, they think. America is special. In America, the stakes are higher. God can't do without America. God can't do without American Christians having control.

Tim Alberta, in his book *The Kingdom, the Power, and the Glory: American Evangelicals in an Age of Extremism*, includes a discussion he had with an evangelical woman named Nancy, who insisted to him that Democrats were coming after the church and, among other things, allowing immigrants (with the help of the Catholics) to spread disease around the country. "I was struck by her tone—and by the fact that Nancy had been involved with supporting missionaries," Alberta writes.[1] Elsewhere, Alberta chats with Southern Baptist Daniel Darling, who bemoans all the negative stories about his denomination, acknowledging, sure, the "crazy" antics that have attracted so much attention. He pleads his case to Alberta by rattling off all the money Southern Baptists have sent here and there and all the wonderful ministries it has funded, arguing, without irony, "Anywhere you see human suffering in the world, you see Southern Baptists, you see evangelicals."[2]

On first glance, it does seem like quite a disjuncture, people serving Christ earnestly with one hand while stabbing him in the back with the other. Of course, the missionary parents don't think they are stabbing Jesus in the back. They think everything they do is part and parcel of the gospel: a holistic defense of a God who apparently needs defending. The good distracts and subtracts from the bad. The good creates a self-image that can withstand its alter-ego evil twin. Deep down, white American Christians have always known their fears and failures have led them to dance with devils and demons: slavery, segregation, and brutal violence, bigotry, nativism, and misogyny. They know, but they can't face it. In the words of Navajo Christian writer Mark Charles, white America has "traumatiz[ed]" itself with centuries of "dehumanizing injustice."[3] So we have constructed alternate universes and stories to avoid reckoning with the reality of ourselves.

When I look at white evangelicalism and its missions—particularly with a mind toward the MK experience—I keep coming back to the opening salvo of 1 Corinthians 13: "If I speak in the tongues of men or of angels, but do not have love, I am only a resounding gong or a clanging cymbal. If I have the gift of prophecy and can fathom all mysteries and all knowledge, and if I have a faith that can move mountains, but do not have love, I am nothing. If I give all I possess to the poor and give over my body to hardship that I may boast, but do not have love, I gain nothing."

And what is love? I'll tell you what it is not: "There is no fear in love, but perfect love casts out fear" (1 John 4:18). And whether voting for a wannabe authoritarian because he will defend "Christian interests," quietly cheering for people storming the Capitol in an attempt to overturn democracy, insisting on a rigid doctrine of theological certainty, shutting down alternate views and voices, putting mission above people, idolizing heroic calling over everyday faithfulness, or using power to maintain ownership of the gospel, American evangelicals, in their intense need for control, demonstrate a fair amount of fear. In a University of Maryland survey cited by Alberta, 78 percent of white evangelicals said they would support a formal declaration of the United States as a Christian nation, even as our pluralistic, democratic system has allowed Christianity, along with all religions, to thrive.[4]

"Many American evangelicals cannot let go," Alberta writes. "They cannot detach themselves from national identity or abandon the notion that fighting for America"—and I would add propagating American Christianity around the world—"is fighting for God."[5] "Humility doesn't come easy to the American evangelical," he explains, "The self-importance that accompanies citizenship in the world's mightiest nation is . . . augmented by the certainty of exclusive membership in the afterlife."[6] Both of those impulses—as well as genuine faith, none of it precludes that—have accompanied American missionaries overseas for more than two centuries now.

But American Christians need to imagine that God has never needed America, and God doesn't need them. In many ways, they have waved God off and told him to move on, even as they try to keep him on a leash. Whoever or whatever God is, God has never needed any one person or country or government or organization or enterprise or church. God has moved through history and progress and politics and medicine and technology and relationship and everyday encounters and random flukes. Through people of every faith and no faith at all. Sometimes, even many times, God has moved in opposition to white American Christians, shoving them out of his path, kicking and screaming.

But mostly, I think, God has moved through love, the invisible force that holds everything together and is part of everything good, that beckons us to rise above our innate instinct for self-preservation and begs us to trust, to believe, and to rest, knowing all will be well in the end. I believe God invites us to trade control for faith, power for community, certainty for peace. God's gonna be just fine. And I believe we will all eventually be fine, too—even missionary kids, no matter how lost and lonely we may feel.

The MK experience has a lot to teach the American church, but it has lessons for us all. The missionary kids know more than most how tenuous our grasp is on the things we try to own: identity, place, belonging. None of it was ever ours, and none of it will ever be ours. What we all have in common—MKs or not, evangelicals or not—is that we cheat ourselves of love over and over again in our attempts to hold on. And we give ourselves over to love when we stop trying.

ACKNOWLEDGMENTS

First and foremost, I am incalculably indebted to the eighty or so missionary kids who agreed to speak with me so honestly and at length, as well as to the hundreds more who responded to my survey. I cherished every one of these conversations, which felt almost sacred to me. Not only did these MKs make this book possible, but their stories helped illuminate and validate my own. I've come away with a deeper understanding of myself and my experience, which is pretty much the best gift another person can give you. I'm so honored by their generosity and trust, and I hope they are honored by the results.

Next, I must thank my agents, David Bratt and Laura Bardolph, who took a chance on an unknown writer and gently guided what started as a memoir toward something far more profound and relevant. They envisioned this book before I did and coaxed it into existence. If I were still an evangelical, I'd say their entry into my life was a "God thing." As an exvangelical, I'll just say I'm incredibly grateful for it.

My editor at Broadleaf Books, Valerie Weaver-Zercher, is another exquisite gift. An MK herself, she connected to this project on a deep level, believed in it completely, and expertly ensured its message rings clear and true. It's been a joy to work with her.

Many thanks to the scholars, writers, journalists, and other experts who lent me their learning, wisdom, and connections, including David Hollinger, Melani McAlister, Mekdes Haddis, Harvey Kwiyani, João Chaves, Paul Putz, Michèle Phoenix, Tanya Crossman, Carol Ann Vaughn Cross, Jesse Curtis, Kimberly D. Hill, Joey Cochran, Grant Jones, Jennifer Christian, Dave Verhaagen, Jon Ward, Mona Charen, Jonathan V. Last, Jim Swift, and Diana Butler Bass. I am especially grateful to those who helped me navigate issues and connect to resources related to abuse in religious contexts, child protection, and/or overseas legal jurisdiction, including Rebecca Hopkins, Benjamin Wittes, Susan Bissell, Marie Griffith, Nancy French, Sarah Stankorb, Sarah Bucy Klingler, Letta Cartlidge, Richard Darr, and Dianne Darr Couts. You all helped me climb a steep, and sadly necessary, learning curve.

I am blessed to be surrounded by so many people who love and believe in me, but I want to thank those who have encouraged and supported my writing most directly. Lorene Burroughs, LaToya Deans, Chanda Creasy, Lauren Victor, Pamela Fierst, Amy Polishuk, Maggie Ray, Erin Hitchev, Char Beales, Alison Faupel, Gary Williams, Dale Sawaya, Charlcie Steuble, Linda Skaggs, Jennifer Lahaie, Sarah Lawrence, Patricia Petty, Thyra Smith, Jon Desenberg, Charlotte Savage, Rachel Shew, Sarah Eppler Janda, Heather Clemmer, Linda English, Tammy Tangen, Aly Hawkins, Beth Taggard, and Carol Friend come most immediately to mind. Christina Hillsberg, Sarah Fletcher, Christina Hoffmaster, Elisa Evans, Beth Hoffman, Anne Jones, and Caleb Adams read the first draft and offered valuable feedback.

There are no adequate words to describe, much less properly honor, how my husband's love and support has empowered me in all things. I would never, ever have had the courage to write without you, Kevin. The failures along the way have barely registered because of your steadfast insistence on my talent and worth. That's the force of unconditional love in a life, and I'm completely overwhelmed to have it in mine.

Thanks to my kids, Charlotte and Lawson, for putting up with a mom who is more interested in the world of ideas than in any of the mundane realities of everyday family life. I love you to the moon and back. And I'll pay for your therapy, I promise.

Finally—Lilo, I love you, but you get no thanks. You did everything you could—yelping during interviews, jumping in my lap, drinking my coffee, knocking my laptop to the floor, expelling all manner of bodily fluids in inappropriate places, being way too adorable—to distract me from my work. If I didn't know better, I would peg you as an agent of the Southern Baptist Convention. But in truth, I know I have no one but myself to blame.

NOTES

Introduction

1 See, for example, "A Little Respect for Dr. Foster," *New York Times*, March 28, 2015, https://www.nytimes.com/2015/03/29/opinion/sunday/nicholas-kristof-a-little-respect-for-dr-foster.html.

2 For example, see the Guideposts Solutions final report on the SBC investigation, 4, https://static1.squarespace.com/static/6108172d83d55d3c9db4dd67/t/6298d31ff654dd1a9dae86bf/1654182692359/Guidepost+Solutions+Independent+Investigation+Report___.pdf.

3 Russell Moore, "This Is the Southern Baptist Apocalypse," *Christianity Today*, May 22, 2022, https://www.christianitytoday.com/ct/2022/may-web-only/southern-baptist-abuse-apocalypse-russell-moore.html.

4 This definition is essentially the same as the Bebbington Quadrilateral, a widely accepted analysis of evangelicalism first delineated in 1989 by British historian David Bebbington.

5 Voice memo to the author, November 28, 2022.

6 Later editions included contributions from his son, Michael, and MK Ruth Van Reken. David C. Pollock, Ruth E. Van Reken, and Michael V. Pollock, *Third Culture Kids: Growing Up Among Worlds*, 3rd edition (Boston: Nicholas Brealey, 2017). TCK Training's 2022 paper on its TCK research includes a comprehensive bibliography on TCKs; see Tanya Crossman and Lauren Wells, "Caution and Hope: The Prevalence of Adverse Childhood Experiences in

Globally Mobile Third Culture Kids," June 2022, https://static1.squarespace.com/static/5c06a4337c9327f21e507621/t/629e936522290746aceafd18/1654559593835/Caution+and+Hope+-+TCK+Training+White+Paper.pdf.

7 Pollock et al., *Third Culture Kids*, loc 573 in the Kindle edition.

8 See Crossman and Wells, "Caution and Hope."

9 American Studies professor Melani McAlister documents the numerous ways missions narratives have served American evangelicals' self-image in *The Kingdom of God Has No Borders: A Global History of American Evangelicals* (Oxford: Oxford University Press, 2018).

10 See, for example, McAlister, *The Kingdom of God Has No Borders*; David A. Hollinger, *Protestants Abroad: How Missionaries Tried to Change the World but Changed America* (Princeton, NJ: Princeton University Press, 2019).

11 The TCK Training survey had almost two thousand respondents, with over half of those MKs. MK advocate and teacher Michèle Phoenix also shared her data from an informal survey of around one thousand MKs: https://michelephoenix.com/survey-for-adult-mks/. My survey of American evangelical MKs had more than three hundred respondents. My sample contains a good mix of ages/generations and a fairly good mix of regions, both of which my research and observation lead me to see as significant to understanding the MK experience. However, my sample skews more heavily toward Africa, given my own background and connections, and female, probably based on self-selection factors. Self-selection is another limitation of any such survey. It is probably the case that those who chose to respond have more on their minds and hearts.

Chapter 1: Accessories to Martyrs

1 Two Black Americans preceded him in the missionary endeavor; I'll discuss this more in a later chapter.

2 The Judson children's mortality rate wasn't much worse than that for children in the United States at the time, the first half of the

nineteenth century. But the Judsons actually fared better than most missionary families of their era.

3 Edward Judson, *The Life of Adoniram Judson by His Son Edward Judson* (New York: Edward G. Jenkins, 1883), 402.
4 *Rufus Hill: The Missionary Child in Siam, a Memoir Written by His Mother, Now in America* (Philadelphia: American Sunday School Union, 1854), 31.
5 Judson, *The Life of Adoniram Judson*, 402.
6 McAlister, *The Kingdom of God Has No Borders.*
7 Cecil B. Hartley, *The Three Mrs. Judsons, The Celebrated Female Missionaries* (Philadelphia: G.G. Evans Publisher, 1860), 159.
8 Joan Jacobs Brumberg, *Mission for Life: The Story of the Family of Adoniram Judson* (New York: The Free Press, 1980), 146.
9 Judson, *The Life of Adoniram Judson*, 404.
10 Hartley, *The Three Mrs. Judsons*, 250–253.
11 Judson, *The Life of Adoniram Judson*, 403.
12 Brumberg, *Mission for Life*, 146–147.
13 Judson, *The Life of Adoniram Judson*, frontispiece.
14 Andrew F. Walls, *The Missionary Movement in Christian History: Studies in the Transmission of Faith* (Maryknoll, NY: Orbis Books, 1996), 48.
15 Robbie F. Castleman, "The Last Word: The Great Commission: Ecclesiology," http://s3.amazonaws.com/tgc-documents/journal-issues/32.3_Castleman.pdf.
16 Jonathan S. Barnes, *Power and Partnership: A History of the Protestant Mission Movement* (Eugene, OR: Pickwick Publications, 2013), 45.
17 Dana L. Robert, *Christian Mission: How Christianity Became a World Religion* (Hoboken, NJ: Wiley-Blackwell, 2009).
18 Robert, *Christian Mission*, loc 478 in the Kindle edition.
19 Robert P. Jones, *The Hidden Roots of White Supremacy and the Path to a Shared American Future* (New York: Simon and Schuster, 2023); Mark Charles and Soong-Chan Rah, *Unsettling Truths: The Ongoing, Dehumanizing Legacy of the Doctrine of Discovery* (Westmont, IL: InterVarsity Press, 2019).

20 "The Doctrine of Discovery, 1493," History Resources, The Gilder Lehrman Institute of American History, https://www.gilderlehrman.org/history-resources/spotlight-primary-source/doctrine-discovery-1493.

21 Barnes, *Power and Partnership*, 75–78. Benjamin Harrison and Teddy Roosevelt also spoke.

22 Generally, historians have disputed that there were two distinct waves of revivals, called the First and Second Great Awakenings, and instead have described it as a continuous religious evolution. See Jon Butler, *Awash in a Sea of Faith: Christianizing the American People* (Cambridge, MA: Harvard University Press, 1992) and Nathan O. Hatch, *The Democratization of American Christianity* (New Haven, CT: Yale University Press, 1991).

23 Interview with the author, May 30, 2022.

24 See, for example, Steven Mintz, *Huck's Raft: A History of American Childhood* (Cambridge, MA: Belknap Publishing, 2006).

25 Holly Berkley Fletcher, *Gender and The American Temperance Movement of the Nineteenth Century* (New York: Routledge, 2012), 7–29.

26 Hartley, *The Three Mrs. Judsons*, 114; Judson, *The Life of Adoniram Judson,* 280.

27 Dana L. Robert, *American Women in Mission: The Modern Mission Era 1792–1992* (Macon, GA: Mercer University Press, 1997).

28 Joy Schulz, *Hawaiian by Birth: Missionary Children, Bicultural Identity, and U.S. Colonialism in the Pacific* (Lincoln, NE: University of Nebraska Press, 2020), 139.

29 Hollinger, *Protestants Abroad*, 18.

30 Mintz, *Huck's Raft.*

31 Schulz, *Hawaiian by Birth*, 98.

32 John Piper, "Risk Your Kids for the Kingdom? On Taking Children to Unreached Peoples," October 23, 2017, https://www.desiringgod.org/articles/risk-your-kids-for-the-kingdom.

33 Rachel Pieh Jones, "I'm Not Called to Keep My Kids from Danger," *Christianity Today*, November 13, 2017, https://www.christianitytoday.com/ct/2017/november-web-only/im-not-called-to-keep-my-kids-from-danger.html.

Chapter 2: A Very Special Calling

1 João B. Chaves, *The Global Mission of the Jim Crow South: Southern Baptist Missionaries and the Shaping of Latin American Evangelicalism* (Macon, GA: Mercer University Press, 2022), 93.
2 Interview with the author, April 27, 2022.
3 Dave Verhaagen, *How White Evangelicals Think: The Psychology of White Conservative Christians* (Eugene, OR: Cascade Books, 2022), loc 1200–1374 in the Kindle edition.
4 McAlister, *The Kingdom of God Has No Borders*, 212.
5 McAlister, *The Kingdom of God Has No Borders*, 21–23.
6 See for example, Peter Smith, "Agency: Haiti Missionaries Made 'Daring' Escape to Evade Kidnappers," *Christianity Today,* December 20, 2021, https://www.christianitytoday.com/news/2021/december/haiti-missionaries-escape-kidnap-gang-christian-aid-ministr.html.
7 McAlister, *The Kingdom of God Has No Borders,* 10–12.
8 Historian Kristin Du Mez has extensively documented the heroic narrative in American evangelicalism since World War II. Relevant to the mission field context is her detailing the false stories of supposed Islamic terrorists who converted to Christianity and became sought-after speakers on the evangelical circuit in the early 2000s. *Jesus and John Wayne: How White Evangelicals Corrupted a Faith and Fractured a Nation* (New York: Liveright, 2020), loc 3859 in the Kindle edition. Several MKs told me their parents or other missionaries they knew told exaggerated or fabricated stories to American churches.
9 The Southern Baptists' International Mission Board (IMB), to its credit, has typically been less willing than other mission organizations to allow its missionaries to go into or stay in dangerous situations.
10 As a side note, I should add that these types of missionaries can end up requiring a significant amount of US government resources. The US government is compelled to rescue them from such situations, at times at risk to American forces. Most recently, there has been a rash of missionary kidnappings by ISIS in West Africa that have resulted in dangerous rescue missions. See, for example, the case of Philip Watson, rescued by Navy SEALS in 2020 in northern Nigeria,

a hotbed of Islamic terrorism and under a "do not travel" State Department travel advisory. Danielle Paquette, "U.S. Special Operations Forces Rescue American Kidnapped in Niger," *Washington Post,* October 31, 2020, https://www.washingtonpost.com/world/africa/niger-us-rescue-kidnapped-seals/2020/10/31/2834f684-1b7a-11eb-8bda-814ca56e138b_story.html.

11 Rachel Held Evans, for example, related her own girlhood aspirations in these terms; see Evans and Jeff Chu, *Whole-Hearted Faith* (New York: HarperOne, 2021), 91. Kathryn Gin Lum documents how the term and archetype of the "heathen" has fueled a sense of American racial and religious superiority and its deployment in both religious and secular endeavors. *Heathen: Religion and Race in American History* (Cambridge, MA: Harvard University Press, 2022).

12 See John Donnelly, *A Twist of Faith: An American Christian's Quest to Help Orphans in Africa* (Beacon Press, 2012). He discusses short-term missions to Africa specifically in an NPR interview, "Missionaries in Africa Doing More Harm than Good?", July 20, 2012, https://www.npr.org/2012/07/20/157105485/missionaries-in-africa-doing-more-harm-than-good.

13 Joshua Project website, https://joshuaproject.net/help/definitions.

14 Joshua Project website.

15 Of the estimated 150 schools worldwide that serve missionary kids, no more than 30 still offer boarding. Sarah Eekhoff Zylstra, "Boarding Bust: Schools for Missionary Kids See Lower Attendance," *Christianity Today,* December 27, 2010, https://www.christianitytoday.com/ct/2011/january/3.12.html.

16 "Abbey," *Life Unwasted,* October 18, 2023, https://podcasts.apple.com/us/podcast/life-unwasted/id1620087617?i=1000631805205.

17 "Sarah," *Life Unwasted,* November 29, 2023, https://podcasters.spotify.com/pod/show/kyumin-jang/episodes/Sarah-e2ci7b9/a-aam0ohr.

18 Interview with the author, December 29, 2023; TCK Training, "Sources of Trauma in International Childhoods: Providing Individualized Support to Increase Positive Outcomes for Higher Risk Families," October 2023, 6. https://drive.google.com/file/d/1urHM

9v8We9iEUq7jGm2wRdifi7ERM6yq/view?_hsmi=279754667&_hsenc=p2ANqtz—sqT3ERWHXzrpe4AJ_cN_vyH2WTyEx6MounoDJnQmzk3b1QE5wrBEIaiqgAKNVvaO9OF9K9sZhKx0U-1JIPEzVW-3ZEQ.

19 Email to an MK he interviewed, forwarded to the author, December 1, 2023.

20 TCK Training, "Caution and Hope: The Prevalence of Adverse Childhood Experiences in Globally Mobile Third Culture Kids," June 2022, https://drive.google.com/file/d/1MNcaZrtDjO1V5vUoliV12qP8WXmDcIq3/view. In a variety of global studies, 8 to 13 percent of respondents answering the same questions had four or more ACEs.

Chapter 3: Jesus Is Their Favorite

1 Tanya Crossman, "New Data Shows How Missionary Kids Can Suffer. Here's What Parents Can Do about It," *A Life Overseas*, September 8, 2022, https://www.alifeoverseas.com/new-data-shows-how-missionary-kids-can-suffer-heres-what-parents-can-do-about-it/; Tanya Crossman interview with the author, December 29, 2023.

2 To be transparent, I know this story only secondhand, but from two separate, trusted sources who knew the family.

3 "Boarding School for Missionary Children," Focus on the Family, 2015, https://www.focusonthefamily.com/family-qa/boarding-school-for-missionary-children/.

4 Her work primarily deals with alumni of British boarding schools, which differ somewhat in culture and structure, but many of her findings rang true to me. *Boarding School Syndrome: The Psychological Trauma of the 'Privileged' Child* (New York: Routledge, 2015), loc 3010 in the Kindle edition.

5 Chefoo Reconsidered Book Committee, *Sent: Reflections on Missions, Boarding School and Childhood* (Melbourne: Thorpe-Bowker Identifier Services, 2020), 42. This entire collection of essays by boarders is heart-wrenching. Also see Ruth Van Reken, *Letters Never Sent: A*

Global Nomad's Journey from Hurt to Healing (Scottsdale, AZ: Summertime, 2012).

6 "The Tyranny of Shoulds," May 30, 2022, https://michelephoenix.com/2022/05/30/the-tyranny-of-shoulds/. She says that many other children who grow up in ministry contexts or just strict religious environments also experience these feelings. I think she would agree with me, however, that the pressures and pedestals of missionary life and the various dislocations that dilute other community supports elevate these feelings.

7 Interview with the author, February 23, 2022. He says anger scores have dropped over the years in his work, which he attributes to therapy that disentangles God from parents, making faith more of a constructive arena to process anger and other emotions.

Chapter 4: Bubble Boys and Girls

1 "He Reigns," by the Newsboys.

2 Joy Schulz, *Hawaiian by Birth: Missionary Children, Bicultural Identity, and U.S. Colonialism in the Pacific* (Lincoln, NE: University of Nebraska Press, 2020); for more on the missionary bubble, see Stephanie Vandrick, *Growing Up with God and Empire: A Postcolonial Analysis of Missionary Kid Memoirs* (Bristol, UK: Multilingual Matters, 2018).

3 Interview on February 9, 2022. Sadly, Jenny passed away only months after our interview.

4 Kathryn Gin Lum, *Heathen: Religion and Race in American History* (Cambridge, MA: Harvard University Press, 2022), 338–345.

5 Gin Lum traces this guilty/grateful dynamic through the entire span of American missions, arguing that contrasting their lives with "heathen" overseas reinforced white American superiority. *Heathen,* 196, 415.

6 Stephanie Vandrick also makes this observation; *Growing Up With God and Empire,* 89–98.

7 AIM finally handed over full control of AIC churches in 1971, after a protracted battle. F. Lionel Young III, "The Transition from the

Africa Inland Mission to the Africa Inland Church in Kenya, 1939–1975," Ph.D. dissertation, The University of Stirling, March 1, 2017; John Kamau, "Town Sells No Alcohol, No Cigarettes," *The Nation*, September 15, 2013, https://nation.africa/kenya/life-and-style/dn2/town-sells-no-alcohol-no-cigarettes—894470.

8 Dr. David A. Wells, Principal and Executive Consultant, Global School Consulting Group, "Rift Valley Academy—Culture Audit," January 2019, 7. The report was posted on the alumni Facebook page.

9 Stephanie Vandrick also identifies language acquisition, or the lack thereof, as a key indicator of the separateness of the missionary lifestyle. *Growing Up with God and Empire*, 80–88. I didn't realize how illuminating language was as a marker of separation until I had already deployed my survey, so I unfortunately don't have data on this issue.

10 Interview with the author on November 29, 2023.

11 Mekdes Haddis, *A Just Mission: Laying Down Power and Embracing Mutuality* (Westmont, IL: InterVarsity Press, 2022), 131.

Chapter 5: The Great (Race) Escape

1 I confess to using the word "wog" while at RVA. I had no idea it was derogatory or the colonial context of it. I just thought it meant "African."

2 "African–American Heritage Collection," International Mission Board, https://archives.imb.org/digital-collections/african-american-heritage-collection/.

3 Jason G. Duesing, "Pre-Beginnings," in *Make Disciples of All Nations: A History of Southern Baptist International Missions,* edited by John D. Massey, Mike Morris, and W. Madison Grace II (Grand Rapids, MI: Kregel Academic), loc 353–804 in the Kindle edition.

4 "Baptist Christianity in Nigeria," Religion in Public Life, Harvard Divinity School, https://rpl.hds.harvard.edu/faq/baptist-christianity-nigeria.

5 Jemar Tisby, *The Color of Compromise: The Truth about the American Church's Complicity in Racism* (Grand Rapids, MI: Zondervan, 2020), loc 1117 in the Kindle edition.

6 McAlister, *The Kingdom of God Has No Borders*; Hollinger, *Protestants Abroad*, 19.

7 Kimberley D. Hill, *A Higher Mission: The Careers of Alonzo and Althea Brown Edmiston in Central Africa* (Lexington, KY: University of Kentucky Press, 2020), 50.

8 Jay Riley Case, *An Unpredictable Gospel: American Evangelicals and World Christianity, 1812–1920* (Oxford: Oxford University Press, 2012), loc 2094 in the Kindle edition.

9 Hill, *A Higher Mission*, 127–143.

10 Rebecca Hopkins, "How Black Missionaries Are Being Written Back into the Story," *Christianity Today*, December 13, 2021, https://www.christianitytoday.com/ct/2022/january-february/black-missions-history-rewritten-protten-liele.html.

11 "Attendance at Religious Services by Race/Ethnicity," Pew Research Center, https://www.pewresearch.org/religion/religious-landscape-study/compare/attendance-at-religious-services/by/racial-and-ethnic-composition/. 47% of Black Americans regularly attend church, compared to 35% of white Americans.

12 Jesse Curtis, *The Myth of Colorblind Christians: Evangelicals and White Supremacy in the Civil Rights Era* (New York: NYU Press, 2021), 20–25; email to the author, January 11, 2024.

13 Haddis, *A Just Mission*, 193.

14 Haddis, *A Just Mission*, 196.

15 Thomas S. Kidd and Barry G. Hankins, *Baptists in America: A History* (Oxford: Oxford University Press, 2015), loc 2591 in the Kindle edition.

16 McAlister, *The Kingdom of God Has No Borders*, 12.

17 McAlister, *The Kingdom of God Has No Borders*, loc 2257 in the Kindle edition.

18 Frederick Douglass, *Narrative of the Life of Frederick Douglass* (Boston: Anti-Slavery Office, 1849), 93. Italics his.

19 Frances Fitzgerald, *The Evangelicals: The Struggle to Shape Society* (New York: Simon and Schuster, 2017), 49–94; David A. Hollinger, *Christianity's American Fate: How Religion Became More Conservative and Society More Secular* (Princeton, NJ: Princeton University Press, 2022), 45–67; Heather D. Curtis, *Holy Humanitarians: American Evangelicals and Global Aid* (Cambridge, MA: Harvard University Press, 2018), 179–212; David Blight, *Race and Reunion: The Civil War in American Memory* (Cambridge, MA: Belknap Press, 2001).
20 Hollinger, *Protestants Abroad*, 3.
21 Quoted in Gin Lum, *Heathen*, 216.
22 Gin Lum, *Heathen*, 251.
23 Chaves, *The Global Mission of the Jim Crow South*, 47–48, 58.
24 Fitzgerald, *The Evangelicals*, 149.
25 "Baptist Christianity in Nigeria," https://rpl.hds.harvard.edu/faq/baptist-christianity-nigeria; Alan Scot Willis, *All According to God's Plan: Southern Baptist Missions and Race, 1945–1970* (Lexington, KY: University of Kentucky Press, 2021), 84.
26 Willis, *All According to God's Plan*, 17.
27 Willis, *All According to God's Plan*, 17.
28 Verhaagen, *How White Evangelicals Think*, 144–145.
29 Quoted in Willis, *All According to God's Plan*, 171.
30 Quoted in Willis, *All According to God's Plan*, 172.
31 Gin Lum, *Heathen*, 29, 360; McAlister, *The Kingdom of God Has No Borders*, 144–158.
32 Anthea Butler, *White Evangelical Racism: The Politics of Morality in America* (Chapel Hill: University of North Carolina Press, 2021); other scholars' work previously cited.
33 Robert P. Jones, *White Too Long: The Legacy of White Supremacy in American Christianity* (New York: Simon and Schuster, 2021), loc 2833 in the Kindle edition.
34 Email to the author, January 14, 2024. This is not to suggest an equal comparison between Kenyan police, plagued with corruption and abusive behaviors, and American police, but rather to show a greater

openness to look at bigger issues of social justice in a non-American context.

35 Secular international charity provides a similar outlet more generally for Westerners. See Courtney Martin, "The Seductive Reduction of Other People's Problems," *BRIGHT Magazine*, January 11, 2016, https://brightthemag.com/the-reductive-seduction-of-other-people-s-problems-3c07b307732d.

Chapter 6: A Cultural Trade Imbalance

1 2020 Report on International Religious Freedom: Antigua and Barbuda, U.S. Department of State, https://www.state.gov/reports/2020-report-on-international-religious-freedom/antigua-and-barbuda/.

2 Gin Lum, *Heathen*, 110–184.

3 Zach Levitt, Yuliya Parshina-Kottas, Simon Romero and Tim Wallace, "'War Against Children,'" *New York Times*, August 30, 2023, https://www.nytimes.com/interactive/2023/08/30/us/native-american-boarding-schools.html.

4 Recent research by sociologist Robert Woodberry found a strong statistical significance between British missionary presence in certain countries in the nineteenth century and the current existence of stable democracies. Discussed by Stephanie Vandrick, *Growing Up with God and Empire*, 6.

5 Barnes, *Power and Partnership*, 45.

6 Lamin Sanneh, *Translating the Message: The Missionary Impact on Culture* (Revised) (Maryknoll, NY: Orbis Books, 2009). What Sanneh sees as Christianity's inherent translatability derived from its multilingual foundation and early jump over a major cultural chasm—from Jews to Gentiles—setting the stage for its effective global transmission. In Sanneh's view, Christianity is always indigenized; it's always tied to culture.

7 Donald M. Lewis and Richard V. Pierard, *Global Evangelicalism: Theology, History, and Culture in Regional Perspective* (Westmont, IL: InterVarsity Press, 2014), 225.

8 Sunny Bindra, "Men Behaving Badly," in *Missionaries, Mercenaries, and Misfits: An Anthology,* ed. Rasna Warah (Central Milton Keynes, UK: AuthorHouse UK, Ltd., 2008), 147.

9 "Nigerian Megachurches Draw in the Faithful, and Their Cash," *Deutsche Welle* English, September 20, 2018, https://youtu.be/knBzyEd_PEY?si=7AVuxbPR4GDs5Wbw. Christian religious expression in many cultures around the world does trend more charismatic, given its compatibility with many traditional religions' emphasis on the spirit world. (American missionaries, incidentally, often greet this with hand-wringing over "syncretism" diluting the true gospel.) But it's not so different from what you see in American charismatic churches.

10 It's also true that a strain of liberation theology, with its critique of Western power and capitalist systems, persists. This is true particularly in Latin America and in more educated parts of African Christianity. But elites in countries around the world have frequently seized this narrative as a way of deflecting criticism for their own use and misuse of wealth and power by keeping the focus on an outside enemy.

11 Jacob Poushter, "How People Around the World See the U.S. and Donald Trump in 10 Charts," Pew Research Center, January 8, 2020, https://www.pewresearch.org/short-reads/2020/01/08/how-people-around-the-world-see-the-u-s-and-donald-trump-in-10-charts/.

12 Du Mez, *Jesus and John Wayne*, 301. She notes examples of American evangelicals exporting aspects of a Christian nationalist ideology, including militant masculinity, to Uganda, India, Jamaica, Belize, Brazil, as well as the common ties forged between European and Russian nationalists and American evangelicals.

13 Email from Phillip Stargate, November 27, 2023.

14 Bernard Boyo, *The Church and Politics: A Theological Reflection* (Carlisle, UK: Langham Publishing, 2021), 7. Kenyan theologian Bernard Boyo has observed how this bifurcation of faith and politics, combined with the shedding of an African cultural context, has meant the church "has failed to be the conscience of society in giving appropriate direction on sociopolitical issues." He believes that

the church has often enabled corrupt political elites and neutralized popular discontent, thus making Africa's democratic development more arduous.

15 Anh Do, "Rick Warren's Saddleback Church Hosts Rwandan President, Spurring Outcry," *Los Angeles Times*, April 14, 2019, https://www.latimes.com/local/lanow/la-me-ln-rick-warren-saddleback-church-rawanda-president-20190414-story.html. Other examples: Evelyne Musambi, "William Ruto: How Kenya's New President Is Influenced by Religion," *BBC*, September 12, 2022, https://www.bbc.com/news/world-africa-62835681; Shashank Bengali, "Uganda at the Forefront of Africa's Boom in Evangelical Christianity," *McClatchy DC*, May 25, 2007, https://www.mcclatchydc.com/latest-news/article24454120.html.

16 Andrew DeCort, "Christian Nationalism Is Tearing Ethiopia Apart," *Foreign Policy*, June 18, 2022, https://foreignpolicy.com/2022/06/18/ethiopia-pentecostal-evangelical-abiy-ahmed-christian-nationalism/.

17 Interview with the author, January 18, 2024.

18 Interview with the author, January 18, 2024.

19 Mark A. Noll, *The New Shape of World Christianity: How American Experience Reflects Global Faith* (Westmont, IL: Intervarsity Press, 2013),189.

20 Isaac Sharp, *The Other Evangelicals: A Story of Liberal, Black, Progressive, Feminist, and Gay Christians—and the Movement That Pushed Them Out* (Grand Rapids: Eerdmans, 2023).

21 Carolyn Renee Dupont, *Mississippi Praying: Southern White Evangelicals and the Civil Rights Movement, 1945–1975* (New York: NYU Press, 2013), 37.

22 Interview with the author, January 18, 2024.

23 "Sarah," *Life Unwasted*, November 29, 2023, https://podcasters.spotify.com/pod/show/kyumin-jang/episodes/Sarah-e2ci7b9/a-aam0ohr.

24 "Jen," *Life Unwasted*, October 11, 2023, https://podcasts.apple.com/us/podcast/life-unwasted/id1620087617?i=1000631034785.

25 McAlister, *The Kingdom of God Has No Borders*, 1–14, 159–192.

26 McAlister, *The Kingdom of God Has No Borders,* 211–212, 268–285.

27 Harvey Kwiyani, "What Is Whiter than Missiology," *Global Witness, Globally Reimagined,* February 16, 2023, https://harveykwiyani.substack.com/p/what-is-whiter-than-missiology#footnote-1-102137553. Data on evangelical Christians is from Gordon Conwell Seminary, https://www.gordonconwell.edu/blog/evangelicals-worldwide/.

28 Interview with the author, January 18, 2024.

29 Hollinger, *Protestants Abroad,* 91.

30 Sharp, *The Other Evangelicals.*

31 Southern Baptist Convention, Baptist Faith and Message, https://bfm.sbc.net/bfm2000/.

32 Rebecca Y. Kim, *The Spirit Moves West: Korean Missionaries in America* (Oxford: Oxford University Press, 2015), 7, 11.

33 Yaw Perbi, Sam Ngugi, and Joshua Bogunjoko, *Africa to the Rest: From Mission Field to Mission Force (Again)* (Maitland, FL: Xulon Press, 2022), 133, 139.

34 Giovanna Dell'Orto, "A Green Card Processing Change Means US Could Lose Thousands of Faith Leaders from Abroad," *Associated Press*, September 29, 2023, https://www.yahoo.com/news/green-card-processing-change-means-120258067.html. More global, hierarchical churches are probably better positioned for "reverse missions;" for example, within the Catholic Church, more Global South clergy are filling positions in the United States, where the number of priests has plummeted. Grace Doerfler, "African Priests Fill American Pulpits as 'Reverse Missionaries,' Revitalizing Parishes," *USA Today*, December 26, 2023, https://www.yahoo.com/news/african-priests-fill-american-pulpits-121232393.html.

35 Fitzgerald, *The Evangelicals*, 479–482; Miles D. Williams, "White, Conservative, Religious . . . and Aid Skeptical," *Religion in Public* blog, January 21, 2021, https://religioninpublic.blog/2021/01/21/white-conservative-religious-and-aid-skeptical/.

36 Interview with the author, January 18, 2024.

37 Interview with the author, January 18, 2024.

38 Baldwin, testifying before a congressional committee in 1968, quoted by Jones, *The Hidden Roots of White Supremacy*, 233.

Chapter 7: The Untouchables

1 Interview with the author, December 1, 2023.

2 Email correspondence, November 7, 2023.

3 "Abbey," *Life Unwasted*, October 18, 2023, https://podcasts.apple.com/us/podcast/life-unwasted/id1620087617?i=1000631805205; email correspondence with Caleb Adams, January 30, 2024.

Chapter 8: One Big Happy Family

1 This account is drawn from two interviews with Christopher Cole, June 23, 2022, and December 6, 2023, as well as a post he wrote: "Richmond, we have a problem," *SBC Voices*, June 2, 2022, https://sbcvoices.com/richmond-we-have-a-problem-christopher-cole/.

2 Lise Owen and Sarah Smith, "Abuse of Faith: Missionaries Left Trail of Abuse, but Leaders Stayed Quiet," *Houston Chronicle*, May 31, 2019, https://www.houstonchronicle.com/news/investigations/article/Abuse-of-Faith-Missionaries-left-trail-of-abuse-13904418.php.

3 Chaves, *The Global Mission of the Jim Crow South*, 94.

4 T. C. Johnson, "Child Perpetrators—Children Who Molest Other Children: Preliminary Findings," *Child Abuse & Neglect* 12, no. 2 (1988): 219–229, doi:10.1016/0145-2134(88)90030-0, https://pubmed.ncbi.nlm.nih.gov/3395897/.

5 Chaves, *The Global Mission of the Jim Crow South*, 92–108.

6 Dee Ann Miller, *How Little We Knew: Confusion and Collusion with Sexual Misconduct* (Prescott, AZ: Prescott Publishers, 1993).

7 Dawn Araujo-Hawkins, "Surviving Hillcrest," *Christian Century*, February 2023, https://www.christiancentury.org/article/features/surviving-hillcrest; and my own interview with Letta Cartlidge, August 26, 2023.

Chapter 9: A Breeding Ground for Abuse

1 Zylstra, "Boarding Bust."

2 This account is taken from an interview Annie did with Lindsay Rodriguez, October 6, 2020, https://www.exposingreligiousabuse.com/post/part-1-interview-with-annie-abernethy-mk-abuse-survivor-from-faith-academy-philippines; as well as from my own interview with Annie, November 3, 2023.

3 "The Mango Jellies," *Life Unwasted*, December 28, 2022, https://podcasts.apple.com/us/podcast/life-unwasted/id1620087617?i=1000591538802.

4 I asked Faith Academy about Annie's case and received the following response from its Child Safety Team: "It would breach confidentiality to pass on any child safety records to you. Our records are only for Faith Academy leaders and statutory authorities." Email to the author, March 5, 2024.

5 Araujo-Hawkins, "Surviving Hillcrest"; and my own interview with Letta Cartlidge, August 28, 2023.

6 The advocacy group MK Safety Net has posted reports of investigations of abuse at Christian Academy in Japan, Hillcrest School in Nigeria, multiple boarding schools around the world run by New Tribes Mission (now Ethnos360), Congo Youth Hostel, and Mamou Alliance Academy in Guinea. Investigations were also done for Faith Academy in the Philippines and Rift Valley Academy in Kenya, but those findings have never been made public (according to correspondence with both institutions). In the course of my interviews and other research, I also heard or read accounts of abuse at Kent Academy in Nigeria, Ivory Coast Academy, Rethy Academy in what was then called Zaire, and other small mission boarding schools that are closer to an educational co-op. https://mksafetynet.org/?page_id=67.

7 The case of Mamou Alliance Academy in Guinea was particularly extreme, as documented in the 2012 documentary *All God's Children*, as well as in the concluding report on the the investigation, https://mksafetynet.org/wp-content/uploads/2022/05/1997-Mamou-Report.pdf.

Chapter 10: Sent Home

1 "I Am Purple: The Missionary Kid Experience with Michèle Phoenix," *Amplify,* April 1, 2022, https://michelephoenix.com/2022/04/01/an-interview-with-amplify/.
2 "Kevin," *Life Unwasted,* June 7, 2023, https://podcasts.apple.com/us/podcast/life-unwasted/id1620087617?i=1000616084682.
3 "Sarah," *Life Unwasted,* November 29, 2023, https://podcasts.apple.com/us/podcast/life-unwasted/id1620087617?i=1000636988942.
4 Interview with Tanya Crossman, December 29, 2023.
5 Kathryn Joyce, "The Silence of the Lambs," *The New Republic*, June 20, 2017, https://newrepublic.com/article/142999/silence-lambs-protestants-concealing-catholic-size-sexual-abuse-scandal.
6 João B. Chaves, Mikeal Parsons, and Bill Leonard, *Remembering Antonia Teixeira: A Story of Mission, Violence, and Institutional Hypocrisy* (Grand Rapids, MI: Eerdmans, 2023), loc 3157–3228 in the Kindle edition.
7 "Former IMB Missionary Sends Open Letter Confessing to Abuse," *Baptist Press*, June 18, 2002, https://www.baptistpress.com/resource-library/news/former-imb-missionary-sends-open-letter-confessing-to/.
8 Owen and Smith, "Abuse of Faith."
9 Interview with the author, October 23, 2023.
10 "Abuse Prevention and Response," International Mission Board, https://www.imb.org/abuse-response/.
11 Email to the author from Somer Nowak, June 28, 2024.
12 Cole, "Richmond, We Have a Problem."
13 Email to the author from the Faith Child Safety Team, March 5, 2024.
14 His definition of an independent investigation includes the institution having no control, fiduciary or any other kind, over the investigator; no control of the process; no control of the findings. The AIM investigation was done by one AIM employee and one external person; the findings were not released. AIM's CSO mentioned the cost of hiring

an external firm to conduct an investigation as being prohibitive for a small, non-profit organization like AIM in an email to me on November 11, 2011. Boz Tchividjian, "Liberty University: Now Is the Time for an Independent Investigation," *Religion News Service*, August 31, 2020, https://religionnews.com/2020/08/31/liberty-university-jerry-falwell-becki-independent-investigatio-board/.

15 Email correspondence, November 3, 2023. I tried unsuccessfully to verify the police report or to find any arrest records related to his case. He's also not on the sex offender registries of either that state or his current state of residence. I assume he was never charged.

16 Email correspondence, November 3, 2023.

17 GRACE, "Final Report for the Investigatory Review of Child Abuse at New Tribes Fanda Missionary School," August 23, 2010, http://fandaeagles.com/wp-content/uploads/2010/08/GRACE-Final-Report-on-NTM-Fanda.pdf.

18 Lindsay Rodriguez, "WASP Reformer—Boz Tchividjian," December 13, 2020, https://www.exposingreligiousabuse.com/post/wasp-reformer-boz-tchividjian.

19 Text of a speech by Richard Darr, provided to the author by him via email, November 6, 2023.

20 Tchividjian, "Liberty University."

21 Araujo-Hawkins, "Surviving Hillcrest"; and my own interview with Letta Cartlidge and Nathan Kruetter on August 28, 2023; email from Letta Cartlidge to the author on June 8, 2024.

22 Araujo-Hawkins, "Surviving Hillcrest"; interview with Letta Cartlidge and Nathan Kruetter, August 28, 2023; email from Letta Cartlidge to the author on June 8, 2024; email from Somer Nowak to the author June 28, 2024; and correspondence shared with the author by Letta Cartlidge between Nowak and Cartlidge. The IMB told me its "statement of support" was passed to the Steering Committee through C. Todd Willis, Chief Operational Officer and General Counsel to The United Methodist Church Global Ministries, on September 7, 2023. Mr. Willis communicated to the IMB on September

20, 2023, that he would be sharing that statement with the Survivors Committee. The Committee says they never received it.

23 Interview with the author, June 23, 2022.

24 Lindsay Rodriguez, interview with Annie Abernethy, October 6, 2020, https://www.exposingreligiousabuse.com/post/part-1-interview-with-annie-abernethy-mk-abuse-survivor-from-faith-academy-philippines.

Chapter 11: Fighting for Change

1 Unless otherwise noted, this account derives from an interview with the author, October 2, 2023, and Dianne's memoir, *Things Fell Apart, but the Center Held* (self-published, 2020).

2 Couts, *Things Fell Apart,* 104.

3 Couts, *Things Fell Apart,* 161.

4 David Briggs, "Mission Children Abused," *Cleveland Plain Dealer,* March 18, 2001, https://www.cleveland.com/pdextra/2010/04/mission_children_abused.html.

5 David Briggs, "At School in Africa, the Children of Missionaries Lived in a Secret Hell — Independent Inquiry Documents Decades of Physical, Sexual Abuse," *The Seattle Times,* November 10, 1998, https://archive.seattletimes.com/archive/?date=19981110&slug=2782703.

6 Briggs, "Mission Children Abused."

7 US Department of Justice press release, https://www.justice.gov/archive/opa/pr/2003/April/03_ag_266.htm.

8 For cases of missionaries being prosecuted: Associated Press, "US Ex-missionary Guilty of Sexually Assaulting Ugandan Girl," February 2, 2022, https://www.krqe.com/news/national/us-ex-missionary-guilty-of-sexually-assaulting-ugandan-girl/; Max Bearak and Rael Ombuor, "A Child Sex Abuser Evaded Justice in Kenya. Then an 'Ordinary Woman' Took Matters into Her Own Hands," *The Washington Post,* February 4, 2021, https://www.washingtonpost.com/world/2021/02/04/kenya-orphanage-child-abuse/; US Department

of Justice press releases: https://www.justice.gov/usao-wdnc/pr/federal-judge-sentences-former-minister-25-years-prison-engaging-illicit-sexual-contact;https://www.justice.gov/opa/pr/oregon-missionary-found-guilty-sexually-abusing-six-cambodian-children-orphanage; https://www.justice.gov/usao-wdva/pr/virginia-man-sentenced-23-years-prison-traveling-haiti-and-engaging-illicit-sexual; https://www.justice.gov/usao-mdfl/pr/sanford-missionary-pleads-guilty-producing-child-pornography;https://www.justice.gov/usao-mdfl/pr/sanford-missionary-pleads-guilty-producing-child-pornography; https://www.justice.gov/usao-edwi/pr/green-bay-pastor-arrested-online-crimes-targeting-venezuelan-child.

9 Araujo-Hawkins, "Surviving Hillcrest"; White House press release, https://www.whitehouse.gov/briefing-room/legislation/2022/09/16/bills-signed-h-r-5754-s-3103-s-4785/; Boz Tchividjian @bozlawpa on Twitter/X, September 16, 2022, https://twitter.com/bozlawpa/status/1570881093506826240.

10 Nurith Aizenman, "U.S. Missionary with No Medical Training Settles Suit over Child Deaths at Her Center," *National Public Radio*, July 31, 2020, https://www.npr.org/sections/goatsandsoda/2020/07/31/897773274/u-s-missionary-with-no-medical-training-settles-suit-over-child-deaths-at-her-ce; Lee Brown, "US Couple Facing Death Penalty in Uganda for Alleged Torture, Trafficking Foster Child," *New York Post,* December 22, 2022, https://nypost.com/2022/12/22/us-couple-facing-charges-in-uganda-for-trafficking-foster-child/; Tricia Neal, "Somerset Missionary Accused of Sexual Abuse in Belize," *Commonweatlh Journal*, October 19, 2021, https://www.somerset-kentucky.com/news/somerset-missionary-accused-of-sexual-abuse-in-belize/article_37eb0fde-0a62-5740-9764-b78983c79787.html; Bearak and Ombuor, "A Child Sex Abuser Evaded Justice in Kenya;" Amanda Garrett, "Ex-megachurch Pastor: I Did Nothing Wrong in Orphanage Sex-Abuse Scandal," *The Columbus Dispatch*, October 6, 2019, https://www.dispatch.com/story/lifestyle/faith/2019/10/06/ex-megachurch-pastor-i-did/2599081007/.

11 ECPAT, https://ecpat.org/countries/.

12 Bearak and Ombuor, "A Child Sex Abuser Evaded Justice in Kenya." The orphanage system around the world is notoriously awful, including the fact that many "orphans" aren't orphans at all, but voluntarily surrendered by parents who can't afford to care for them. Andreana Prichard, "Whether or Not a Man Convicted of Abusing African 'Orphans' Is Exonerated, the Missionary System That Brought Him to Kenya Was Always Deeply Flawed," *The Conversation*, May 1, 2023, https://www.yahoo.com/lifestyle/whether-not-man-convicted-abusing-120918338.html.

13 CSPN, "The 7 Key Elements of an Effective Child Safety Programme," https://cspn.org/elements/.

14 "IMB Statement on Child Abuse and Sexual Harassment," https://www.imb.org/for-churches/abuse-harassment/#:~:text=

15 Cole, "Richmond, We Have a Problem."

16 When asked about this, the IMB said, "It is our process and desire to be able to report the abuse to the appropriate agency and see said report be taken with the urgency and seriousness it deserves." Email from Somer Nowak to the author, June 28, 2024.

17 Interview with the author, April 2, 2024.

18 Email correspondence, November 3, 2023.

19 Rebecca Hopkins, "What Is a Missionary Kid Worth?", *Christianity Today,* November 21, 2022, https://www.christianitytoday.com/ct/2022/december/missionary-kid-abuse-statistics-safeguard-prevention.html; Joyce, "The Silence of the Lambs."

20 Interview with the author, August 25, 2023.

21 Statement by MK Safety Net about their meeting with CSPN, https://mksafetynet.org/wp-content/uploads/2023/10/Statement-re-MKSN-CSPN-meeting.pdf.

22 "What We Do," Child Safety and Protection Network, https://cspn.org/network/.

23 Castaneda and Heidelman LLP, "Mission Aviation Fellowship: Investigation Report: Sexual Misconduct by Jonathan Santhouse," June 2022, https://mksafetynet.org/wp-content/uploads/2023/03/2022-

Forge-Harbour-MAF.pdf; Interview by the author with Dianne Darr Couts, October 2, 2023.

Chapter 12: Theology Trumps Policy

1 Dr. David A. Wells, Executive Consultant and Principal, Global School Consulting Group, "Rift Valley Academy Culture Audit 2019 Follow-up Review," February 2022, 10–11. The report was released to RVA alumni.
2 Global School Consulting Group, "Rift Valley Academy—Culture Audit," January 2019, 6. The report was released to RVA alumni.
3 Interview with the author, August 25, 2023.
4 Interview with the author on September 19, 2023.
5 Brian Klaas, *Corruptible: Who Gets Power and How It Changes Us* (New York: Scribner, 2021), 64–79.
6 "Shame! Shame! Shame!," *The Cottage*, May 4, 2022, https://dianabutlerbass.substack.com/p/shame-shame-shame?utm_source=publication-search.
7 Verhaagen, *How White Evangelicals Think*, loc 1742 in the Kindle edition.
8 Verhaagen, *How White Evangelicals Think*, loc 932 in the Kindle edition.
9 Willis, *All According to God's Plan*, loc 2826 in the Kindle edition.
10 Curtis, *The Myth of Colorblind Christians*, loc 407 in the Kindle edition.
11 Interview with the author, October 2, 2023.
12 Interview with the author, October 2, 2023.
13 Diane Langberg, *Redeeming Power: Understanding Authority and Abuse in the Church* (Ada, MI: Brazos Press, 2021), loc 1194 in the Kindle edition.
14 Verhaagen, *How White Evangelicals Think*, loc 1816–1830 in the Kindle edition.
15 Interview with the author, November 27, 2022.
16 Interview with author, November 3, 2023.

Chapter 13: Getting Out of the Way

1 "Statement on the Wrongdoings of Past Leadership," Word Made Flesh International, June 12, 2020, https://wordmadeflesh.org/statement-on-the-wrongdoings-of-past-leadership/.

2 Robert, *Christian Mission*, loc 647 in the Kindle edition.

3 Case, *An Unpredictable Gospel*, loc 959 in the Kindle edition.

4 David R. Swartz, *Facing West: American Evangelicals in an Age of World Christianity* (Oxford: Oxford University Press, 2020), 35–62.

5 Lewis and Pierard, *Global Evangelicalism*, 225–232.

6 Quoted in Perbi et al., *Africa to the Rest*, 38.

7 This term encompasses two separate but related types, the first—usually called "foreign aid"—is money from foreign governments and multilateral institutions like the World Bank, and the second is private charity through NGOs, many of which receive significant funding from foreign aid.

8 This figure accounts for money from governments and multilateral institutions but is often distributed via NGOs.

9 See, for example, Dambisa Moyo, *Dead Aid: Why Aid Is Not Working and How There Is a Better Way for Africa* (New York: Farrar, Straus and Giroux, 2009 reprint edition). Meanwhile, larger structural reforms that could more meaningfully address poverty—such as ending American and European agriculture subsidies that distort markets and disadvantage farmers in developing nations—are left undone.

10 Again, to specify, this is talking about foreign aid. An interview with William Easterly, "The Vision of Jeffrey Sachs," July 6, 2007, https://bigthink.com/videos/the-vision-of-jeffrey-sachs/.

11 The Business Research Company, "NGOs and Charitable Organization Market 2022," January 2022, https://www.thebusinessresearchcompany.com/report/ngos-and-charitable-organizations-market; Peter Buffett, "The Charitable-Industrial Complex," *New York Times,* July 26, 2013, https://www.nytimes.com/2013/07/27/opinion/the-charitable-industrial-complex.html.

12 Shanrah Wakefield and Shyam Dodge, "It's 'The Office,' but for Aid Workers in Africa," *Vice*, April 14, 2014, https://www.vice.com/en/article/mbw5gb/its-the-office-but-for-aid-workers-in-africa.

13 Rasna Warah, "The Development Myth," in *Missionaries, Mercenaries, and Misfits,* 9. You see this same dynamic with government institutions as well.

14 According to African missiologists Perbi, Ngugi, and Bogunjoko, it's not uncommon for results to be exaggerated, and in my interviews, several MKs reported their parents' exaggerating the extent or impact of their work. A few reported financial crimes. *Africa to the Rest*, 124, 134.

15 Walls, *The Missionary Movement in Christian History*, 227, 230.

16 Interview with the author, May 20, 2022.

17 Lara Pawson, "A Charitable Apartheid," in *Missionaries, Mercenaries, and Misfits,* 109–118.

18 Walls, *The Missionary Movement in Christian History*, 238.

19 Haddis, *A Just Mission*, 95.

20 Post by @pastorbenmarsh on X, January 24, 2024, accessed January 26, 2024.

21 Haddis, *A Just Mission,* 103; Also see Perbi et al., *Africa to the Rest*, loc 2090 in the Kindle edition.

22 Gina A. Zurlo, Todd M. Johnson, and Peter F. Crossing, "World Christianity and Religions 2022: A Complicated Relationship," *International Bulletin of Mission Research* 46, no. 1, 71–80, https://doi.org/10.1177/23969393211046993.

23 The Return Mandate, "We Went, But Did We Make Disciples?" *Christianity Today Creative Studio,* June 13, 2022, https://www.christianitytoday.com/partners/return-mandate/we-went-but-did-we-make-disciples.html?fbclid=IwAR0wnAnW-ZpBGJXR_JyuzFB5N80F4AEPpGByaIMg_gYsHxlO0mVWM7PzHUg.

24 Zurlo et al., "World Christianity and Religions 2022."

25 For examples, see Ryan Shaw, *Rethinking Global Mobilization: Calling the Church to Her Core Identity* (IGNITE Media, 2022) and Craig

Greenfield, *Subversive Mission: Serving as Outsiders in a World of Need* (InterVarsity Press, 2022).

26 IMB, 2022 Annual Statistical Report, 4.

27 Interview with the author, October 6, 2023.

28 Case, *The Unpredictable Gospel*, loc 1771.

29 Barnes, *Power and Partnership,* 80. Barnes says there was much talk of partnership from the beginning of missions, but "always reasons not to turn over responsibility."

30 Haddis, *A Just Mission*, 184.

31 Diaa Hadid, "A World Vision Donor Sponsored a Boy. The Outcome Was a Mystery to Both," *New York Times,* August 2, 2016, https://www.nytimes.com/2016/08/03/world/middleeast/worldvision-palestinians-sponsor-a-child.html.

32 Hunter Farrell, "The Crushing Wheel: Shifting Missions Engagement from Transactional to Transformational," *The Better Samaritan,* December 9, 2022, https://www.christianitytoday.com/better-samaritan/2022/december/crushing-wheel-shifting-missions-engagement-from-transactio.html.

33 Haddis, *A Just Mission*, 97.

34 "Missionary Explorer," International Mission Board, https://www.imb.org/missionary-explorer/.

35 "Missionary Explorer."

36 Haddis, *A Just Mission*, 48.

37 Perbi et al., *Africa to the Rest*, 102, quote on 105.

38 Perbi et al., *Africa to the Rest*, 106.

39 See, for example, the case of Philip Watson, rescued by Navy SEALS in 2020 in northern Nigeria, a hotbed of Islamic terrorism and under a "do not travel" State Department travel advisory. Danielle Paquette, "U.S. Special Operations forces rescue American kidnapped in Niger," *Washington Post,* October 31, 2020, https://www.washingtonpost.com/world/africa/niger-us-rescue-kidnapped-seals/2020/10/31/2834f684-1b7a-11eb-8bda-814ca56e138b_story.html.

40 Perbi et al. also mention this point of view in *Africa to the Rest*, 50.

41 The Return Mandate, "We Went, but Did We Make Disciples?"

Chapter 14: Searching for Home

1 Kara asked that I not include the country's name for fear believers there would be persecuted.
2 Interview with the author, November 30, 2022.
3 The roots and wings of adult MKs have been discussed by numerous experts on the MK and TCK experience, including Michèle Phoenix, Tanya Crossman, and Dave Pollock.

Conclusion

1 Tim Alberta, *The Kingdom, the Power, and the Glory: American Evangelicals in an Age of Extremism* (New York: Harper, 2023), loc 2529 in the Kindle edition.
2 Alberta, *The Kingdom, the Power, and the Glory*, loc 5895.
3 Charles and Rah, *Unsettling Truths,* loc 2678 in the Kindle edition.
4 Alberta, *The Kingdom, the Power, and the Glory*, loc 4318.
5 Alberta, *The Kingdom, the Power, and the Glory*, loc 4287.
6 Alberta, *The Kingdom, the Power, and the Glory*, loc 2361.